Clean Architecture for Android

Creating scalable, maintainable and testable
native Android apps

2nd Edition

Eran Boudjnah

bpb

www.bpbonline.com

Second Revised and Updated Edition 2026

First Edition 2023

Copyright © BPB Publications, India

ISBN: 978-93-65891-676

LIMITS OF LIABILITY AND DISCLAIMER OF WARRANTY

To View Complete
BPB Publications Catalogue
Scan the QR Code:

Dedicated to

My endlessly supportive wife, Lea

Forewords

- There is a point in every Android developer's journey when the code starts to feel heavier than it should. The feature is simple, but the implementation drags. A small change in UI breaks something in the data. Business rules are scattered. No one is sure what touches what anymore.

At some point, the joy of building turns into the stress of maintaining.

That is usually when people start searching for better architecture. Some end up discovering Clean Architecture through blog posts or conference talks. Others try to piece it together through trial, error, and code reviews that go in circles. And many never get the time or clarity to understand what clean even means in the context of real-world Android apps.

This book is a gift to all of them.

It does not assume you already know Clean Architecture, but it also does not waste your time if you do. Instead, it offers something rare: a complete, opinionated, and practical walkthrough of Clean Architecture as it applies to modern Android development. It embraces tools we actually use—Hilt, Compose, Kotlin DSL—and gently reshapes Uncle Bob's core ideas to fit the messy, asynchronous, Google-evolving reality of our day-to-day work.

The author is not preaching from a pedestal. He is writing from the trenches. With over two decades of experience behind the keyboard, he has seen what bloats, what breaks, and what quietly survives release after release. His approach is shaped not just by principles, but by actual pain, and the relief of finding what works.

This is not a silver bullet. It is better than that.

It is a steady path out of chaos. It is a set of small, conscious decisions that add up to big clarity. It is architecture that lets you move fast—and keep moving.

Whether you are a developer trying to clean up your first app or a team lead looking for a sane structure to scale with, this book will not just show you how. It will help you think differently about what good code actually means.

Read it slowly. Rethink a few things, and maybe next time the code starts to feel heavy, it will not be because it is broken, but because it is solid.

- **Gaurav Thakkar**
Mobile applications specialist at BookMyShow

- In software engineering, we constantly navigate the tension between immediate delivery and long-term viability. The initial velocity of a project is often seductive, but without a solid architectural design, it inevitably gives way to the corrosive effects of software entropy. As the quote from Norman Foster in the introduction to this book reminds us, we must design for a future that is essentially unknown. This principle is the very soul of professional software development.

The journey of our industry in Android development has been a collective search for this architectural ideal. We evolved from monolithic UI components, where logic and display were dangerously intertwined, toward more disciplined approaches. We learned to separate concerns, first by creating orchestrating classes to direct our views, and later by adopting reactive models to create a seamless flow of data to the UI.

This is the critical problem that this second edition of Clean Architecture for Android solves with such clarity and conviction. It moves beyond transient patterns to advocate for a set of enduring principles. At its heart is the Dependency Rule, a non-negotiable mandate that all dependencies must point inward, toward the center of the application. This book provides the definitive blueprint for building a system around an inviolate Domain layer, where your pure business logic resides, entirely insulated from the outside world.

You will learn to treat the UI, the database, and the network as what they are: implementation details. The Data layer becomes a sophisticated adapter, negotiating with external systems and translating their chaos into the clean, stable language of your Domain. The Presentation layer becomes a thin servant to this core logic. By enforcing this separation, you build an application that is not just testable and maintainable, but truly resilient and adaptable.

This book is more than a technical manual; it is a guide to professional practice. It offers the disciplined framework required to build sophisticated, large-scale applications that are designed to last. For any developer who considers their work a craft, the principles within these pages are not just recommended; they are essential.

- **Jesus Rodriguez**
Senior Android Developer Manager

About the Author

Eran Boudjnah has been developing apps and leading mobile teams for a wide range of clients, from start-ups (JustEat, Plume Design) to large-scale companies (Sky, HSBC) and conglomerates since 1997. He has been working with Android since around 2013.

Eran is a developer with almost three decades of experience in developing mobile applications, websites, desktop applications, and interactive attractions. He is passionate about board games (with a modest collection of a few hundred games) and has a 90's Transformers collection on display, of which he's quite proud.

Eran lives in Brentwood, Essex, in the United Kingdom with Lea, his incredibly supportive wife.

Acknowledgement

On a personal note, writing a book about Clean Architecture proved to be quite an exciting journey. It was a great opportunity to challenge ideas and principles. None of it would have been possible if not for many people who challenged me, learned with me, helped me grow, and supported me along the way. While I cannot name all of them, I would like to name a few. If I have not mentioned you, I do apologize. I got help from so many people.

In no particular order, my gratitude goes to Jose Antonio Corbacho, Davide Cirillo, Sébastien Rouif, Amr Yousef, Tim Hepner, Manroop Singh, Muhamed Avdić, and Mahmoud Al-Kammar.

I am thankful to Igor Wojda for reviewing the first edition of this book so thoroughly. It would not have been as accurate or detailed if not for his invaluable feedback.

I would also like to thank my wife, Lea, who supported me throughout this process, which was quite demanding at times.

Lastly, thank you for taking the time to read this book. It is my hope that, having read it, you are now comfortable with Clean Architecture in the Android world. Maybe with your own ideas and experience, we can keep evolving it and make it ever better.

Preface

I asked him if he'd come to clean the windows, and he said no, he'd come to demolish the house. He didn't tell me straight away, of course. Oh no. First, he wiped a couple of windows and charged me a fiver. Then he told me.

- Douglas Adams

Clean Architecture is not new. It has been around since 2012. Applying it to Android is not a new idea either, and has been done by many teams over the years.

What is surprising is this: despite Clean Architecture being around for so long, there is still no definitive source if you want to figure out how to implement it in your project. At the time of writing, if you searched for one, you would find blog posts, articles, online courses, and a couple of books, published close to when the first edition of this book was published. Each one of those sources would suggest a somewhat different approach. All are valid, and I have seen them all implemented with varying degrees of success. None answered all the questions that I had when I got to the actual development of real-life projects.

This is a real shame because I could have used such a source. When a client of mine wanted to merge two of their Android apps into one, it sure would have helped us. Unfortunately, it was not there, and the merging process ended up dragging on for years. In hindsight, had the projects adopted Clean Architecture, the process would have been much smoother. We could have migrated it in parts, feature by feature, layer by layer, and plugged the common code in. I cannot begin to measure how much time and money could have been saved.

However, there was no definitive source of information for Clean Architecture back then, and we could not answer the questions that we had in a satisfactory way. We could not get a clear picture of how that solution would work for us.

We had many questions: what exactly is business logic? Where do I draw the line between business logic and presentation logic? Just how much responsibility should the UI have? How do models travel between the layers? How much logic should I have in my Data layer? What do I do if the backend work is still in progress? Having this book would have answered all our questions.

Another client of mine decided to go forward with Clean Architecture despite not having a clear understanding of the pattern. I cannot blame them for the reason mentioned previously. They made a good effort. Unfortunately, they also made quite a few mistakes. Unfortunately, this meant that the code was gradually becoming harder to maintain. Those mistakes alone were enough to lead them down a path of a full code rewrite. In retrospect, they are happy with their decision to rewrite the project. They are moving much faster now and scaling rapidly without having to slow down to onboard new developers. The architecture is self-explanatory, and all you need to implement a new feature is to look at one of the many other examples in the code. The test coverage and testing policy provide them with a high level of confidence.

As an Android consultant, I was fortunate enough to work with many skilled developers from all over the world over the course of over 12 years. Out of the 12 years, I spent six implementing Clean Architecture. Together with my colleagues, we have iterated, reiterated, polished, and rewritten our implementation. We had to answer all the questions mentioned above and many others.

It took four years for me to feel ready to share my understanding of architecture with you. It took another two to complete this second edition. I hope reading about my experience will help new developers as well as veterans. I aim for this book to be a resource you could come back to whenever you are not sure about any part of your architecture.

This book is divided into 15 chapters. We will cover the Clean Architecture principles as applied to Android and look at an end-to-end implementation. We will continue to explore testing as well as failures and exceptions. Then, we will demonstrate how to implement a new feature. Finally, we will discuss migrating existing projects and anything important that would not fit in any of the earlier sections.

Chapter 1: Introduction- Covers the motivation for writing the book, its key benefits for the reader, and sets the expectations in terms of how the book is going to be structured. It provides some background on Clean Architecture and Clean Code before we dive into greater detail. The first section will provide three real-life examples of where Clean Architecture could have saved (unnamed) clients from having to rewrite their app due to requirement changes.

Chapter 2: Clean Architecture Principles- This chapter will break down Clean Architecture into its individual layers as they are applied in the Android world. We will cover the responsibility of each layer and the components that live in each one.

Chapter 3: The Domain Layer- It is the first of five chapters in which we break down the key components of each Clean Architecture layer and how they all come together in a working app. In this chapter, we will discuss the Domain layer and cover usecases, repository interfaces, and domain models.

Chapter 4: The Presentation Layer- In this chapter, we continue our review of the Clean Architecture components. We cover viewmodels, presentation models, and bidirectional mapping between domain and presentation models.

Chapter 5: The UI Layer- This chapter follows up from the previous chapter and moves on to explain the UI layer. In it, we go over Activities, Fragments, Views, and composables, as well as UI models and bidirectional UI to presentation mappers.

Chapter 6: The DataSource and Data Layers- After exploring the architecture from the domain all the way to the UI, in this chapter, we go the other way and explore the data side of the app. We learn about repository implementations, datasources, and finally API and database dependencies. We will encounter the models that go in the datasource and data models, and the associated mapping for these models.

Chapter 7: Dependency Injection and Navigation- In this fifth and last chapter breaking down the Clean Architecture implementation, we cover the different options that we have for implementing navigation and dependency injection, bringing the different parts of the app together. We will also demonstrate how navigation can be done in this architecture.

Chapter 8: Unit Testing- We will demonstrate how Clean Architecture makes unit testing easier. We will start by briefly discussing the value of writing tests. We will then go layer by layer, discuss the components that can be tested, what needs to be covered by tests, and provide examples of how those tests look, using Junit 4 and Mockito.

Chapter 9: End-to-end Testing- We will discuss the parts that are harder to test: the UI and the integration of all the different parts. We will explain the robot pattern and provide examples for testing composables.

Chapter 10: Mocking the Server- We will continue covering integration tests and We will show the basics of mocking web server responses using MockWebServer.

Chapter 11: Failures and Exceptions- This chapter will cover the difference between failures and exceptions and how both can be handled in Clean Architecture. We will provide an example of an API timeout exception to demonstrate exceptions and a user not found error to demonstrate failures.

Chapter 12: Implementing a New Feature- We will demonstrate the implementation of a new feature in an existing app. We will focus on the best order in which to go about the task and explain why that order is important following an approach that was proven to work well for a single developer as well as large teams of developers.

Chapter 13: Dealing with Changes- This chapter is all about changing requirements. In it, we will see how Clean Architecture rewards us for our efforts by making changes easier. This chapter will provide two concrete examples: replacing a datasource and updating the user interface.

Chapter 14: Migrating an Existing Project- In this chapter, we will briefly touch on the common architectures out there. We will then discuss how a gradual migration can be performed. This will allow the reader to switch to Clean Architecture without it being a colossal endeavour. We will provide examples of migrating from MVVM and MVP to Clean Architecture (with MVVM or MVP) by introducing usecases for new requirements or while working on bug fixes. We will also show how logic can be moved out of poorly written usecases and into the Data layer. We will emphasise the importance of tests being in place to protect us from breaking the existing behaviour.

Chapter 15: Other Bits and Bobs- This is the final chapter. In it, we will mention that Clean Architecture is a tool. It is there to serve us and help us structure problems, not to tie our hands. We will remind ourselves that the other tools that we have acquired along our journey as developers are all still valuable and can still be applied. The SOLID principles, DRY and KISS are all still valid and should be considered when implementing Clean Architecture.

While this book is by no means gospel, I hope that you will find reading it helps all the pieces fall into place in your head. Ideally, when you later face a new feature request, you would easily visualize its implementation details in your mind.

Convention

This book follows a few conventions that are worth mentioning.

Many of the code snippets are incomplete. They highlight parts of the file that are worth discussing. The complete file as well as the whole project in the context of individual chapters can be found in the GitHub repository.

References to code are `highlighted`.

Important terms and library names are bold.

Emphasized words are in italics.

Tips and key takeaways are highlighted like this sentence.

The implementation of Clean Architecture presented in this book is an opinionated one. This means that in places it may be stricter than the official Clean Architecture model. This choice is based on accumulated experience from many past projects that I have been involved with over the years, in which different approaches were explored. You are welcome to stray off the path laid out in this book, but you will be doing so at your own peril.

Finally, I had to make some technical choices for this book:

- For dependency injection, I chose to use Hilt. This does not mean that you have to use Hilt, too.

- As an architectural pattern, I will mostly focus on **Model-View-ViewModel (MVVM)**.

- For Gradle scripts, I will I will be using the Kotlin **Domain Specific Language (DSL)** rather than the Groovy one. It was introduced in version 3.0 of the Gradle Build Tool as far back as August 2016 and has been the default for new builds since 2023.

Code Bundle and Coloured Images

Please follow the link to download the
Code Bundle and the *Coloured Images* of the book:

https://rebrand.ly/49cc1f

The code bundle for the book is also hosted on GitHub at

https://github.com/bpbpublications/Clean-Architecture-for-Android-2nd-Edition

In case there's an update to the code, it will be updated on the existing GitHub repository.

We have code bundles from our rich catalogue of books and videos available at https://github.com/bpbpublications. Check them out!

Errata

We take immense pride in our work at BPB Publications and follow best practices to ensure the accuracy of our content to provide an indulging reading experience to our subscribers. Our readers are our mirrors, and we use their inputs to reflect and improve upon human errors, if any, that may have occurred during the publishing processes involved. To let us maintain the quality and help us reach out to any readers who might be having difficulties due to any unforeseen errors, please write to us at: errata@bpbonline.com

Your support, suggestions and feedback are highly appreciated by the BPB Publications' Family.

At www.bpbonline.com, you can also read a collection of free technical articles, sign up for a range of free newsletters, and receive exclusive discounts and offers on BPB books and eBooks. You can check our social media handles below:

Instagram

Facebook

Linkedin

YouTube

Get in touch with us at: business@bpbonline.com for more details.

Piracy

If you come across any illegal copies of our works in any form on the internet, we would be grateful if you would provide us with the location address or website name. Please contact us at business@bpbonline.com with a link to the material.

If you are interested in becoming an author

If there is a topic that you have expertise in, and you are interested in either writing or contributing to a book, please visit www.bpbonline.com. We have worked with thousands of developers and tech professionals, just like you, to help them share their insights with the global tech community. You can make a general application, apply for a specific hot topic that we are recruiting an author for, or submit your own idea.

Reviews

Please leave a review. Once you have read and used this book, why not leave a review on the site that you purchased it from? Potential readers can then see and use your unbiased opinion to make purchase decisions. We at BPB can understand what you think about our products, and our authors can see your feedback on their book. Thank you!

For more information about BPB, please visit www.bpbonline.com.

Join our Discord space

Join our Discord workspace for latest updates, offers, tech happenings around the world, new releases, and sessions with the authors:

https://discord.bpbonline.com

Table of Contents

CHAPTER 1
Introduction

As an architect, you design for the present, with an awareness of the past for a future which is essentially unknown.

- Norman Foster

Introduction

Before we dive into concrete examples and code, we should have a bit of background. In this chapter, we will learn about the history of the Android operating system, have an overview of Clean Architecture, and compare it to **Model-View-ViewModel** (**MVVM**). Finally, we will discuss migrating existing projects to Clean Architecture and touch on the importance of Clean Code.

Structure

In this chapter, we will cover the following topics:

- History of Android
- Clean Architecture overview
- Clean Architecture vs. MVVM
- So now I must rewrite my project
- Clean Code

Objectives

By the end of this chapter, readers will have a general idea of what Clean Architecture is. Readers should also have a rough idea about how Clean Architecture could be introduced into existing projects. Lastly, I will share with you my view on code quality and how it affects the final product.

History of Android

Android is quite a mature platform and was unveiled in November 2007. The first device running on Android was the HTC Dream, shown in *Figure 1.1*, which was launched in September 2008. Ever since Android came out, there have been Android developers. In the early days, no architecture dominated the Android market. It was quite often that you would find massive **Activity** *god classes* holding the entire logic of the app.

Figure 1.1: The HTC Dream

It did not take long until we all started realizing that this would not work. As soon as apps had any complexity to them, it became impossible to maintain or scale the code. Writing tests was a nightmare.

The first architecture to take the Android world by storm was **Model-View-Presenter (MVP)**, illustrated in *Figure 1.2*. It gave us some structure. Code did not have to live inside the **Activity** anymore. We started having components with clear responsibilities. Our business logic would go in the **presenter**, along with the presentation logic. We could unit-test the presenter. Some implementations moved the business logic to the **model**. The **Activity**, **Fragment**, and custom **View** classes (Android **View**, not MVP View) would implement MVP-**view** interfaces, which the presenter used to drive our Android UI classes. The model used Retrofit services and database interfaces to access data. Only now, the presenter was getting bloated, and so were the view interfaces.

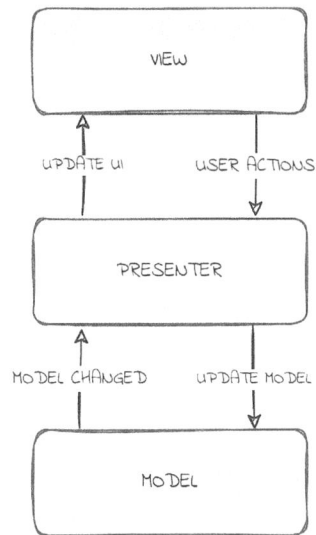

Figure 1.2: Model-View-Presenter

Along came Google's Architecture components, making our lives a bit easier. The great migration from MVP to **Model-View-ViewModel (MVVM)**, which is illustrated in *Figure 1.3*, began. Around mid-2017, if you were brave enough, you could have picked up the library, still in Alpha at the time. By November that year, you could have started using the first stable release. We got the lifecycle-aware **ViewModel** class (with its own host of issues). **LiveData** made observing the **viewmodel** reasonably straightforward. Unit-testing the viewmodel was also easy enough. However, viewmodels did not solve *all* our problems. They could still get incredibly bloated, carry way too much responsibility, and hold too much code.

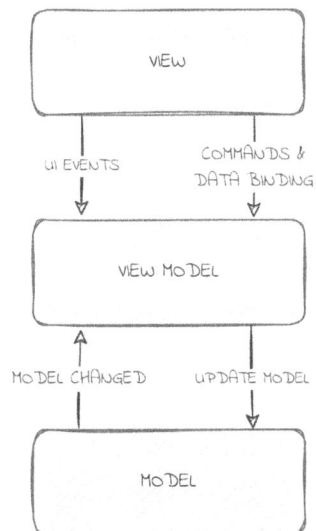

Figure 1.3: Model-View-ViewModel

It was not all bad. Not all architectures suffered from bloated presenters and viewmodels, some started adopting **Clean Architecture** to varying degrees. Some projects had **repositories** abstracting the different **datasources** for the presenters and viewmodels. Some even had **usecases**, connecting presenters and viewmodels to repositories.

This is not all that surprising, because Clean Architecture has been around since 2012, long before the great migration to MVVM, and only about three years after the earliest versions of Android were out.

Clean Architecture overview

Before going into what Clean Architecture is, let us first go over what a system architecture (the system being an application, in our case) is and why we need one.

An application, even the simplest one, has a few responsibilities. It needs to:

- Present the user with information.

- Collect input from the user, whether it is via taps, gestures, keyboard typing, or even voice commands.

- Process the input and perform actions based on that input.

- Quite frequently, it needs to send or retrieve data to or from a remote server or device.

Most applications have more responsibilities than that, and very few do not have all of them. Broadly speaking, it is possible to break down almost all applications into multiple responsibilities.

There are several reasons for us wanting to break down our application by responsibilities:

- **Testability**: We want to be able to test the different parts of the app in isolation.

- **UI independence**: We want to be able to change our UI without affecting the rest of the app.

- **Consistency**: When we or another developer approaches the code, having a consistent structure helps us understand the code and even predict it.

- **Maintainability**: This is tied to consistency. Consistent code is predictable and easier to work with. Generally, the fewer surprises you find in the code, the easier it is to maintain.

However, not all architectures are equal, and not all are fit for every purpose. This is crucial because it can be very hard to move away from many architectures once they are implemented.

This is where Clean Architecture shines. So, what is Clean Architecture, exactly?

On the surface, it is another system architecture. It is highly scalable and very easy to maintain. Since nothing comes for free, this comes at the cost of some initial writing overhead. However, that initial cost is easily paid back tenfold when you have maintainable and scalable code. It is an established understanding that the ratio between reading and writing code leans heavily in favor of reading.

While implementing Clean Architecture, I learned something new about it. It is more than just architecture. It is a philosophy. Once adopted, it changes your way of thinking about applications and feature implementation. While I know that the saying is *if all you have is a hammer, everything looks like a nail*, that situation does not describe a problem where your tool is a Swiss army knife. Clean Architecture really does solve a lot of problems quite intuitively.

Enough theory, though. Let us take a look at how Clean Architecture looks. I have borrowed the following diagram from *Robert C. Martin* (Uncle Bob)'s blog[1]. I modified it slightly to better reflect our use of it when developing Android apps. The same is illustrated in *Figure 1.4*:

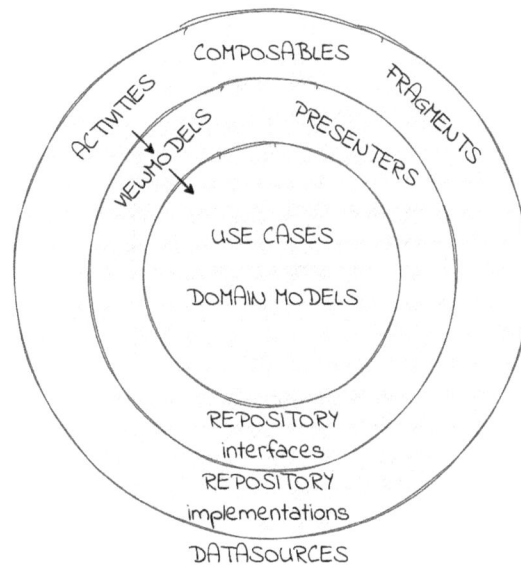

Figure 1.4: *Clean Architecture (Android)*

On the outermost circle, we can see the representation of two layers: the UI layer and the Data layer. This circle includes Activity and Fragment classes and composable functions, as well as concrete repositories. The next circle, holding viewmodels and presenters, is the Presentation layer. The repositories are in this circle too, representing the Data layer. The innermost circle represents our Domain layer, where usecases and Domain models reside.

Note that the arrows are pointing inwards. They represent what Uncle Bob refers to as *The Dependency Rule*. You can read these arrows as *knows about*. So, for example, **Activity** classes know about **viewmodel** ones. **Viewmodel** classes, in turn, know about **usecase** ones. The opposite is not true: **viewmodel** classes do *not* know about **Activity** ones, and **usecase** classes do *not* know about **viewmodels** ones.

---

1 You can find the original blog post here: **https://blog.cleancoder.com/uncle-bob/2012/08/13/the-clean-architecture.html**

You may have noticed that the datasource classes are placed outside of the circles. This is because they represent external dependencies, and in that sense are exceptional. They follow a reversed Dependency Rule, as we will see shortly.

Think of the circles as protective layers. Changes are most often driven by the outer layers: the API we rely on changes. Our design requirements change. Even the Android **software development kit (SDK)** changes. The layer separation makes our usecases very stable and less likely to change as a result. The circles also represent levels of abstraction. The outside circle is highly technical, while the innermost one represents intentions and ideas, the business logic.

Another way of looking at Clean Architecture is to take a vertical slice, see *Figure 1.5*:

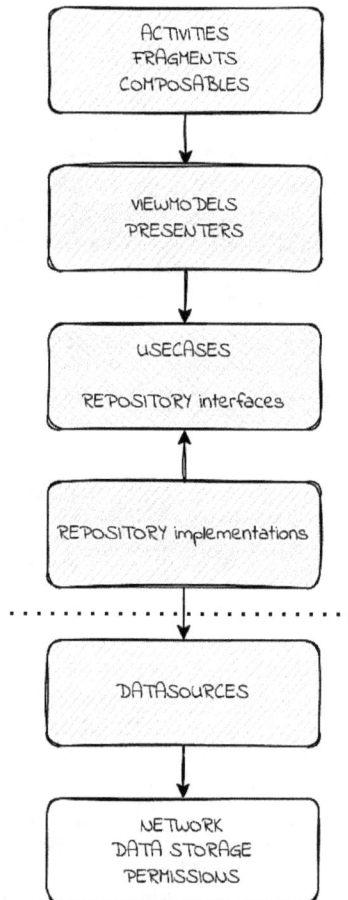

Figure 1.5: Clean Architecture vertical slice

Looking at a vertical slice, we can see how the different components come together. This would be a good representation of a common feature. Remember, the arrows represent dependencies. *They do not represent how data flows.* Data can flow in both directions.

Note the dashed line between the repository implementations and the datasources. It is there to emphasize the exception to the Dependency Rule. Since datasources are not tied to particular features, it makes no sense for them to know about concrete repositories. It is also reasonable for us to think about them as external to a feature, and thus to the architecture circles. In actual code, we will see that concrete repository classes depend on datasource ones.

A quick word about layers: layers can take different forms. A layer can be a package in your project. It can be a Gradle module. In fact, it can also be multiple Gradle modules, each representing a part of a layer for a particular feature. In this book, we will have all layers per feature, and they will be contained in a Gradle module per layer per feature.

Let us look at an example. Let us say that we have a composable function with a button (see *Figure 1.6*). Let us also assume that we are using MVVM, and so we have a viewmodel class. When the user taps the button, the composable communicates that tap to the viewmodel. The viewmodel calls the execute function of a usecase object that describes that event. Let us say that the usecase class is called **UpdateUserLastTapTimeUseCase**. That usecase object then calls a function on the repository object. We can call it **updateUserLastTapTime()**. In turn, that function can trigger the storage of the current time in local storage or the cloud via a datasource object.

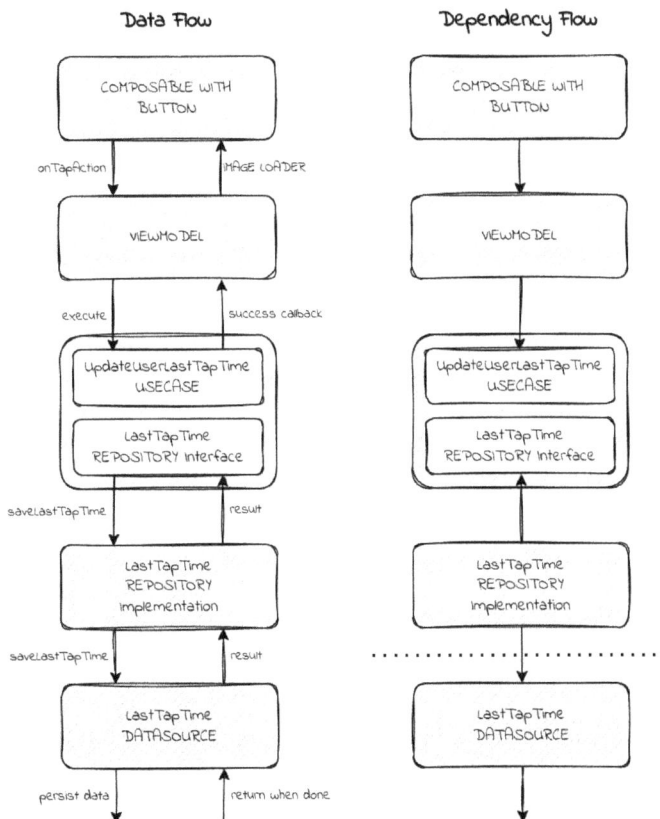

Figure 1.6: An example of Clean Architecture data and dependency flows

The repository can then inform the usecase that it was successful (or that it failed), and the usecase can report that result to the viewmodel. The viewmodel would update its ViewState field, triggering an update to the composable.

However, wait, I hear you say. You said that the usecase does not know about the repository. How can the usecase make that call to the repository? To respect the Dependency Rule, we apply dependency inversion. Dependency inversion is one of the SOLID principles[2]. Instead of having usecases depend on concrete repository classes, we introduce repository interfaces. The repository interface will reside alongside the usecase class. Its concrete implementation, however, will live elsewhere. Now, the usecase class no longer relies on the repository implementation. This allows us to cross boundaries without violating the Dependency Rule.

This, in short, is what Clean Architecture is all about. Slice your app into layers, protect the business logic, and embrace change in the outer layers. In the following chapters, we will explore how this is done and what the benefits are.

Clean Architecture vs. MVVM

So, you already have an app developed. You followed Google's advice and have implemented MVVM. You have viewmodels. Your composable functions and `Fragment` and `Activity` classes are your views. Your viewmodels are probably quite large and communicate with repository objects directly. Maybe you even have usecases (or interactors, which are an alternative name to usecases). Does adopting Clean Architecture, as suggested in this book, mean that you have to say goodbye to MVVM? The short answer is no.

The long answer is that the two do not contradict. You can adopt Clean Architecture with MVVM as well as with MVP. The reason that these architectures can co-exist is that they overlap. An exception to this is Google's architecture, which contradicts Clean Architecture when it comes to the Dependency Rule and considers usecases to be optional.

If we break down MVVM into its components, we can see how the overlap works. The model moves to the Data layer. The viewmodel stays in what becomes the Presentation layer. The view moves to the UI layer. The only change we need to make is to introduce usecases between the viewmodel classes and the model if we do not have those yet. The usecases become our Domain layer. This is demonstrated in *Figure 1.7* (refer to *Figure 1.3* earlier in the chapter to see how the architecture looked before the change):

2 See here: **https://en.wikipedia.org/wiki/SOLID**

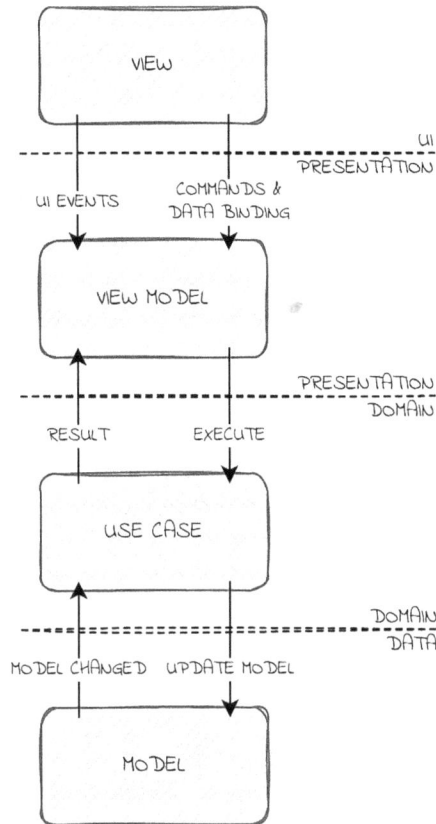

Figure 1.7: *Migrating MVVM to Clean Architecture, a linear view*

The change for MVP is very similar. Like with MVVM, the model moves to the Data layer. The presenter stays in what then becomes the Presentation layer. The view moves to the UI layer, just like with MVVM. Once again, the only change needed is the introduction of usecases to connect the presenter with the model, unless you already have those. Just as before, the layer holding the usecases becomes our Domain layer.

We will explore migration in detail in *Chapter 14, Migrating an Existing Project.*

So now I must rewrite my project

Quite often, when looking at a big change, rewriting the project comes to mind. This was the case with one of my clients. The requirement on the table was to completely overhaul the UI. Unfortunately, the codebase was a mess. Tens of developers worked on it over the course of many years. It had a mixture of architectures, tightly coupled classes, and models that were used by everything from the networking code to the UI. None of us had the confidence to change the UI without breaking the existing functionality. Clean Architecture would have given us that confidence.

Maybe you have an existing architecture in place. Maybe your project went through many developers over the course of a few years. Maybe you never got around to choosing an architecture, and you had to hack your project quickly and patch it over time. Changing the architecture of an existing project may seem daunting.

It sounds like you need to move a lot of code around to implement Clean Architecture. Is it worth the risk? What if the code breaks? Maybe this is such an expensive commitment that you would be better off rewriting your whole app? Once again, luckily, the short answer is no.

This longer answer is *probably not*. Depending on how tightly coupled your classes are and how well-defined your features are, in most cases, you could approach the change incrementally. You should be able to migrate your project one piece at a time, consciously and responsibly, with very little risk. There are, of course, extreme cases where the current implementation is such a mess that it is just not worth holding on to or maybe your project is mission-critical, and you simply cannot afford the risk.

Before giving up on your current project, try picking a candidate feature for migration. Here are a few scenarios that could be good choices:

- You have an isolated feature.

- You have a brand-new feature that you are about to introduce.

- A large change is coming to an existing feature.

These may be good opportunities to introduce Clean Architecture into the project. Taking this approach may set you on a path to migrating your project as a long-term commitment, without breaking your momentum.

Testing can boost your confidence that your code did not break. If you do not have test coverage, a good place to start would always be to write tests.

In most cases, migrating your existing project is doable and should not be too costly. We will go into details in *Chapter 12, Implementing a New Feature, Chapter 13, Dealing with Changes,* and *Chapter 14, Migrating an Existing Project*. Whatever the cost, it is likely to pay dividends.

Clean Code

This book is about Clean Architecture and applying it to Android projects. It looks at the big picture. However, there is no way of discussing the implementation details of Clean Architecture without discussing the code. As mentioned before, Clean Architecture is about more than architecture. It is a philosophy, a way of approaching coding projects with structure. The end goal is to develop projects that could easily be maintained by a large team, as well as by a single developer over the course of many years.

We cannot achieve this goal with architecture alone, no matter how solid the architecture is. Our code needs to be readable. It needs to be easy to follow. It needs to be as concise as it can be without hurting readability. It needs to be as verbose as it can be without overwhelming the reader. It needs to be clean.

As developers, we spend plenty of time naming things. We name packages and classes. We name functions and variables. We name constants and assets. This is a good thing. As mentioned earlier, a fact of coding life is that we write code once but end up reading it tens of times. The code should make sense to us. The initial cognitive effort pays back tenfold.

Clean Architecture relies heavily on well-named components and functions. The better the names that we come up with, the easier it will be to follow the implementation.

Clean Architecture is also about moving forward at a consistent pace. Without adequate architecture, this is impossible. We may start releasing features so fast that it would get heads spinning. However, as the complexity of requirements and features grows, we would lose control. Bugs would start popping up left, right, and center. Fixing a bug would lead to two new bugs popping up. We would be scared of touching the code, in fear of regressions. We would slow down to a crawl. Eventually, it would no longer make sense to keep the existing code. We would have to delete the code and start over.

To achieve consistent velocity, we must make a sacrifice. That sacrifice comes in the form of a bit of boilerplate fluff. It means that we will write more models. We will write a few mappers. We will write tests for our code.

If we work in a collaborative environment, we will pair-program. Or we will have code reviews[3]. Either way, we want our changes to be as small as possible. This is virtually impossible to achieve without adopting some principles.

One such principle is to keep our code clean. While there is no one universally accepted definition of what Clean Code is, a team-wide agreement can be reached.

I usually try to stick to consistent language conventions for code formatting and naming. This saves a lot of arguments about the placement of curly brackets or the introduction of new lines. I then try to reach meaningful names for every class, every function, and every variable. I challenge my naming by getting other developers to review it. If I struggle with naming, I consult with a colleague or with AI. I try to avoid magic numbers and other obscure values in favor of constants. I avoid comments to the extreme.

I highly recommend picking up a copy of Uncle Bob's Clean Code[4]. You do not have to agree with everything suggested in Clean Code. A lot of it is subjective, and I disagree with some of it myself. Approach it with an open mind, though, and you are guaranteed to improve as a developer.

Conclusion

In my many years as a consultant and software developer, I have come across many projects. Every single one of those could have tremendously benefited from having been implemented using Clean Architecture. It is important for me to say that Clean Architecture is not a silver bullet. It will not make all your software problems go away. It will make a lot of them go away.

---

3 This is a broad topic and I expand on it in another book, There is no I in IT.
4 **https://amzn.to/3qS3F5y**

For Clean Architecture to work for you, you need to adopt a philosophy. You need to set the bar high. Just like for every true professional in any other field, cutting corners should not be an option. Tests must be written. Boundaries must be maintained. The code must remain clean. If you keep following these key principles, Clean Architecture will work for you. It will save you considerable amounts of man-days.

I hope that after reading the introduction, you now have a clearer idea of what Clean Architecture is, in a broad sense. I tried to reassure you that adopting Clean Architecture for an existing project would not be too big a task and that it would be worth considering.

We have a lot of ground to cover on our journey to writing Clean Architecture and cleaner code. Our goal is to try to achieve a level of consistency with our delivery, both in terms of quality and velocity. I hope that this book will help you think in a structured way and write code that is modular, scalable, stable, and well-tested.

In the next chapter, we will explore the principles of Clean Architecture.

Points to remember

- Clean Architecture is an architecture of layered abstractions. It is meant to protect the code that should change the least from that which is likely to change the most.

- Clean Architecture does not replace MVVM or MVP.

- Clean Architecture can be applied to existing projects incrementally.

- Clean Architecture alone is not enough to deliver scalable and maintainable code. Clean Code and efficient testing are as important.

Join our Discord space

Join our Discord workspace for latest updates, offers, tech happenings around the world, new releases, and sessions with the authors:

https://discord.bpbonline.com

CHAPTER 2
Clean Architecture Principles

The objective of cleaning is not just to clean, but to feel happiness living within that environment.

- Marie Kondo

Introduction

Understanding Clean Architecture is key to implementing it correctly. Whenever Clean Architecture is discussed, there is consensus that it breaks a project into several components and follows a guiding Dependency Rule. We know that we have a main component of some form, and we know that we have several layers with a strict direction of dependency between them. That is as far as the theory gets us.

When it comes to concrete implementation, many of the resources presenting Clean Architecture are quite vague. They do not tell us how the components within each class work together, how each component looks, and how the layers communicate and transfer data between each other.

In this chapter and the following ones, we will discuss the ideas behind this architecture and how these ideas translate into real-life projects. We will see what role the application component plays in the architecture, what layers we aim to use, the responsibilities of each layer, and the rationale behind it, what components live in each layer, and how they all come together using dependency injection and navigation. We will cover popular components such as viewmodels and usecases, repositories and datasources, and other common classes such as mappers.

Structure

In this chapter, we will cover the following topics:

- The application and its role in the architecture
- The layers of Clean Architecture implementation
- Navigation

Objectives

This chapter should give you an understanding of how this book approaches the implementation of Clean Architecture in Android apps. It should give you a clear understanding of the responsibilities of the different layers and how they all come together as a working app. You will learn all about the UI, Presentation, Domain, Data, and DataSource layers. You will also know what responsibilities live in what layer. Knowing the different layers should give you a clear picture of how the Architecture is set to protect its innermost code from external changes, whether they come from a UI requirement change or an API getting updated. You will also have a clear grasp of the roles of the app module, viewmodels, usecases, repositories, datasources, and mapper in constructing a working Clean Architecture Android app. You will know how the different features of an app are bound together using navigation, and how navigation is abstracted away.

The application and its role in architecture

The **app** Gradle module has one very important characteristic that dictates its contents. This root module depends on every single module in the project[1]. This gives it two distinct advantages:

- For every interface, it has access to all concrete implementations, regardless of which Gradle module these implementations are in.
- It knows and has access to every destination in the app, regardless of which module it is defined in.

These advantages make it a perfect candidate for our **dependency injection (DI)** solution as well as our **navigation** solution. Refer to *Figure 2.1*:

---

1 This is true unless your project has dynamic feature modules. These require special treatment and is covered in *Chapter 15, Other Bits and Bobs*.

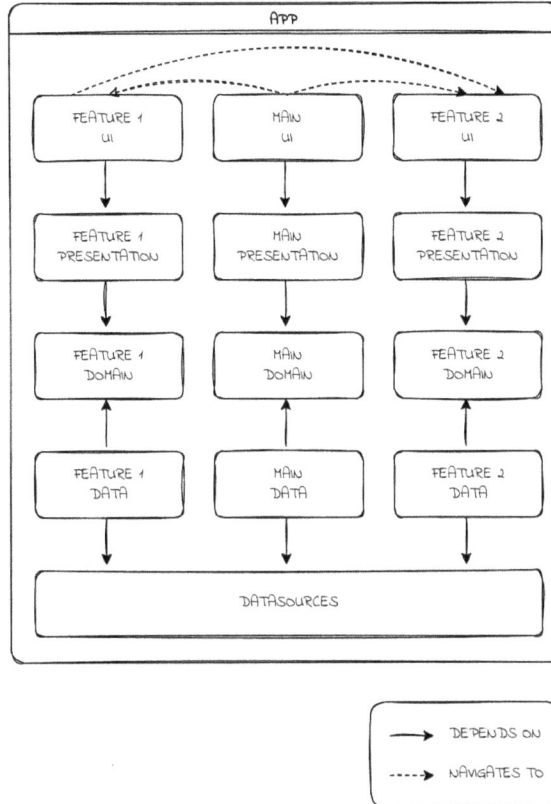

Figure 2.1: The App module depends on every module in the project, handles dependency injection, and controls navigation

We will start with DI. A proper implementation of Clean Architecture relies heavily on the dependency inversion principle. This principle is applied using DI. For the sake of our architecture, it does not matter which DI solution we choose, just that we have one[2].

The important thing is that Clean Architecture relies on a single place where all its different parts are bound together. We will call that place *The Dirty Main*. It is *dirty* because it is the messiest bit in our project (although we will try to keep it as tidy as we can). It has no notion of boundaries or layers. The *main* part of the name is there for historical reasons; in Java, just like in many C-family languages, *main* is the entry point function. While this is not the case in Android, the name stuck.

We said that the second important responsibility of the app module is navigation. We will discuss this at length later in the chapter. For now, it is enough for you to know that it does not matter what navigation solution you choose, whether it is Google's Navigation component, Fragment navigation, or even Activity navigation, they all work well with Clean Architecture. More importantly, you can painlessly change your navigation solution in one place at any time.

---

2 Popular dependency injection solutions at the time of writing are Hilt and Koin.

The layers of Clean Architecture implementation

Before we go into the different layers of Clean Architecture, I would like to share with you a thought exercise I will come back to frequently in this book, because it helps me visualize the problem space. I hope you will find it helpful too.

Imagine a cash machine. Now, imagine that our user needs to operate this cash machine. They could probably perform some simple actions. She can view her current balance. She can browse her recent transactions and, of course, she can withdraw cash. We will come back to this cash machine soon.

Another thought exercise that I find useful is to replace the user-facing part of an app with an entirely different interface in my mind. For example, try imagining that your app is controlled by voice commands or via a terminal. You can even imagine it controlled using a physical dashboard with knobs and levers. The same exercise works for the data side of your app. If your app relies on an API, imagine that there is no API and that you only have a local database instead. You can take this further and imagine that there is an actual person typing responses to your requests as they come[3].

These thought exercises help answer a lot of questions that arise when we approach designing our interfaces. They add clarity about the concerns and responsibilities of the different layers.

The Domain layer

The **Domain layer**, as seen in *Figure 2.2*, is the innermost layer in Clean Architecture. It contains our business logic.

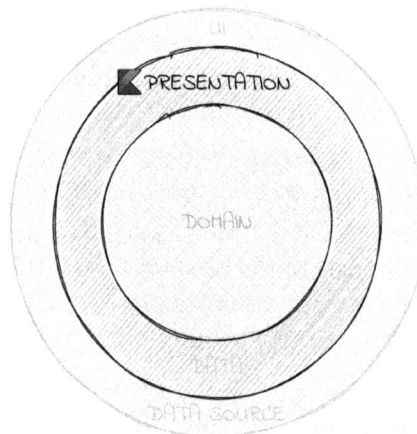

Figure 2.2: The Domain layer is platform-agnostic

---

3 This last idea is not so farfetched. An Amazon AI-powered solution turned out to be nothing but a large group of people reviewing video feeds. See here: **https://www.theguardian.com/commentisfree/2024/apr/10/amazon-ai-cashier-less-shops-humans-technology**.

In terms of code components, it contains usecase classes, Domain models, and repository interfaces (refer to *Figure 2.3*). To protect the Domain layer from changes that are not business logic specific, the Domain layer should rely on as few libraries as possible. It should not have any Android SDK references.

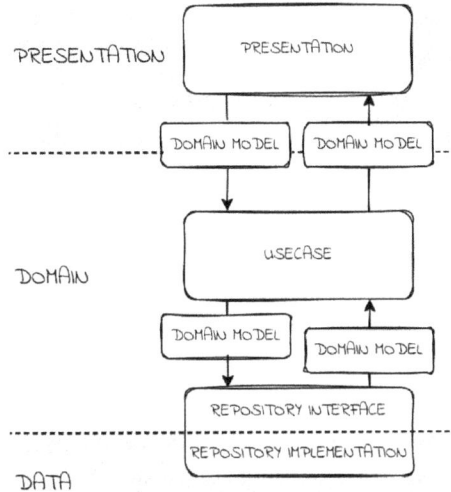

Figure 2.3: The Domain layer components in action

Business logic is the vaguest of the concepts introduced by Clean Architecture and requires clarification. The easiest way to think about business logic is by using usecases. Usecases should describe app requirements in the simplest form. Any action or event performed or triggered by the user that requires processing should be represented by a usecase. Usecases are also known as interactors, but I feel that this name is not as descriptive or clear. While it is hard to confirm, it seems that the industry has mostly adopted the usecase name[4].

Let us explore a few examples. Going back to our cash machine example that was presented in the previous section, we described a few usecases:

- The user requests their current balance.
- The user requests a list of recent transactions.
- The user withdraws cash.

The first usecase describes the user wanting to see their current balance. We do not need any information from the user to comply with their request, so this usecase would have no input. The output would be the current balance. As precision matters with currency, the returned type will likely be a Domain model.

The second usecase represents the user requesting a list of recent transactions. Depending on the detailed requirement, the input could be a starting date, an end date, a page number, or

---

4 Some treat interactors as special types of usecases that call other usecases. This was never intended and is not recommended.

any combination of these. As this input cannot easily be expressed using a primitive type (a Boolean, an Int, a String, and so forth), the input will be a Domain model. The output would be a list of transactions for the provided input in the form of a Domain model.

The third usecase reflects the user withdrawing cash from their account. The input would be the amount to withdraw. Again, because of precision concerns, this will likely be a Domain model. The output would likely indicate success or failure as a Domain model.

To support these usecases, we require repositories. Repositories are responsible for storing and fetching data as needed by each usecase. As the concrete details of *how* they perform their job are not the Domain layer's concern, repositories are implemented as interfaces. Each of the three usecases described previously would rely on a repository interface.

The first usecase will require a repository that returns the current balance. The second usecase will require a repository that returns a list of transactions given a date range and a page number. The third usecase will need a repository that performs cash withdrawals given an amount to withdraw.

If you ever wonder whether some logic belongs in your Domain layer, ask yourself whether changes to the Data layer, such as an API change, would require changes to the usecase. If so, the logic does not belong in the usecase, and *it is not business logic*. It is **Data logic**. Move it to the Data layer, protecting your Domain layer from those changes. Similarly, ask yourself whether changes to the way data is presented (not *what* data is presented, but *how* it is presented) to the user affect the usecase. If so, *it is not business logic*. It is either **Presentation logic** or **UI logic**, and it belongs in one of those two layers.

Let us go back to our cash machine example for a moment. When the user wants to check their current balance, this is what we consider a **feature**. The user enters the Current Balance screen (probably by tapping the appropriate button on the Main Menu screen). As soon as the Current Balance screen becomes active, we fire off a usecase. We do this by calling the execute function of the relevant usecase object. A good name for this usecase would be `GetCurrentBalanceUseCase`. We suffix the class name with `UseCase` to make its role clear. When the user wants to withdraw money, they rely on a `WithdrawCashUseCase` class instance.

In the following sections and chapters, we will use a concrete example to demonstrate Clean Architecture[5]. We will cover the different layers of an app that presents information about its users' current location to them based on their network connection. The app also allows the user to save their current connection details locally. The app uses two API services to obtain the connection information. It uses a hybrid of Fragments and Jetpack Compose, as well as several popular open-source libraries. Going forward, we will refer to this app as **WhoAmI**.

So, what about the Domain layer of **WhoAmI**? We would expect usecases classes such as `GetConnectionDetailsUseCase`, `SaveConnectionDetailsUseCase`, `GetHistoryUseCase`, and `DeleteHistoryRecordUseCase`. To follow the Interface Segregation SOLID principle,

---

5 The example can be found at **https://github.com/EranBoudjnah/CleanArchitectureForAndroid/**. I try to keep the project up to date with the latest capabilities and sensible trends regularly, so the source code may diverge slightly from the code presented in the book.

each class would rely on its own repository interface with a single appropriate function. The **GetConnectionDetailsUseCase** class would rely on a **GetConnectionDetailsRepository** interface with a **connectionDetails** function, the **SaveConnectionDetailsUseCase** class would rely on a **SaveConnectionDetailsRepository** interface with a **saveConnectionDetails** function, and so on.

Note: **When the Data layer is not yet implemented (more on this later in the chapter), we have no concrete repositories. This makes it impossible to use the usecases. It is therefore a good idea to implement stub repositories as soon as the repository interfaces are introduced. We can remove the stub repositories once we have concrete repository implementations in place.**

Having small, clear, single-responsibility usecase classes makes testing these usecase classes simple, too, as we will see later in the book. In fact, they become so simple that you can omit them from tests altogether at your own discretion.

We will look at the Presentation layer next.

The Presentation layer

The **Presentation layer** (see *Figure 2.4*) is an inner layer that exists between the **Domain layer** and the **UI layer**. Its role is to tell the UI *what* needs to be presented to the user. This layer is also responsible for binding **user interactions** to usecase execution and the results of usecase executions to view updates.

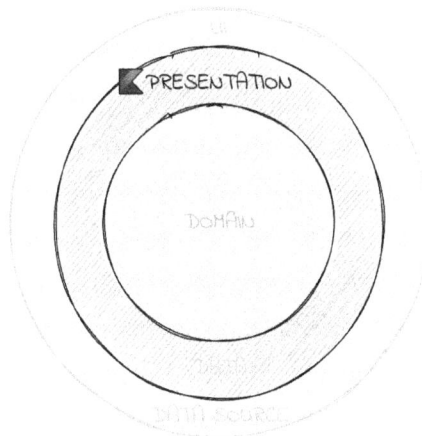

Figure 2.4: The Presentation layer is platform agnostic

In the Presentation layer, we expect to see:

- A controller of sorts (a **viewmodel** in the case of MVVM, a **presenter** for MVP).
- Domain to Presentation and Presentation to Domain **mappers**.
- Presentation **models**.

Take a look at *Figure 2.5* to see how these parts fit together.

As the Presentation layer is an inner layer, we want to keep it protected from external changes. It should therefore have as few library dependencies as possible. *This layer will not have access to any Android classes or resources.* No **Context**, no resources (string, color, or otherwise), these are all UI details. This point contrasts with Google's anti-pattern solution of holding the *UI state* (not to be confused with the *view state* in the MVVM sense) in the **ViewModel** class. It is best to avoid following this pattern that Google suggests.

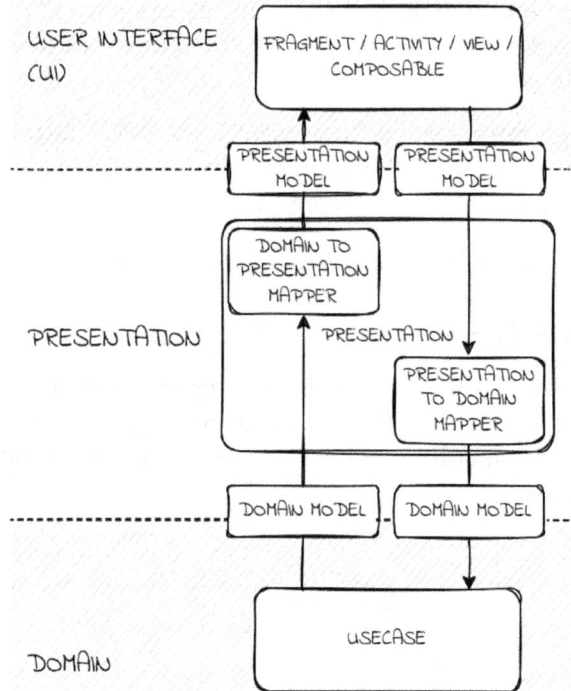

Figure 2.5: The components of the Presentation layer

Of high importance in the context of Clean Architecture is the principle that, following the Dependency Rule, the Presentation layer does not know anything about the UI layer[6]. Therefore, Google's approach of storing the view state in the **ViewModel** class violates the Dependency Rule of our Clean Architecture implementation. The Presentation layer does not know *how* data will be presented to the user. This is the responsibility of the UI layer, as we will see later.

In fact, it is hard to find value in Google's Architecture Components library. The **LiveData** class was useful for a time, but it is not necessary with the introduction of Kotlin **flows**[7]. The library's **ViewModel** class should have been named a **UiStatePersistor** to better reflect its use and avoid confusion. Even when named better, the **ViewModel** class adds little value when

---

6 This principle is fundamental to architectures such as MVP and MVVM, too.
7 Kotlin flows became stable in version 1.3.0 of the kotlinx.coroutines library back in 2019.

compared to the existing **savedInstanceState** and **rememberSaveable** solutions.

Here are a few rules of thumb to follow when implementing the Presentation layer:

- Tell the viewmodel what *happened,* not what to *do*:

  o **Do**: **fun onLoginAction(username: String, password: String)**

  o **Don't**: **fun login(username: String, password: String)**

- Avoid **UI terms** in your ViewModel:

  o **Do**: **fun onSearchAction(query: String)**

  o **Don't**: **fun onSearchButtonClick(query: String)**

- Your UI layer and your Data layer are your **sources of truth**. Your Presentation layer *is not*[8].

  o **Do**: **fun onSendEmailAction(emailAddress: String) { sendEmail(emailAd-dress) }**

  o **Don't**: **fun onSendEmailAction() { sendEmail(viewState.emailAddress) }**

It is worth remembering that the UI could be *absolutely anything,* as far as the Presentation layer is concerned. It can be a phone screen, an ancient black and green console, a microphone/speaker setup, or a dashboard with analog knobs, levers, and LEDs. See *Figure 2.6* for an example of how unexpected the UI can be:

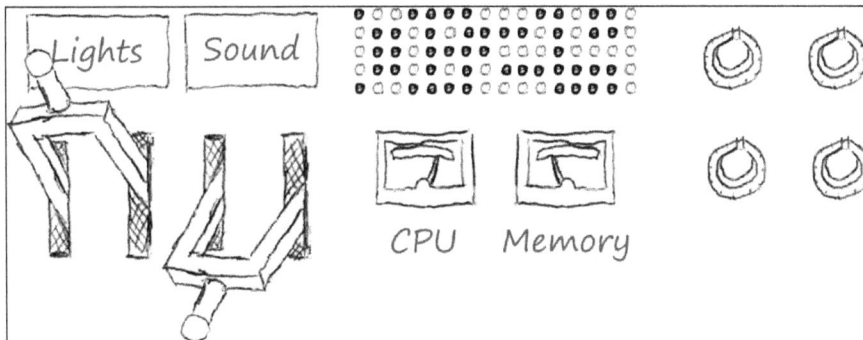

Figure 2.6: The UI could be quite unexpected

The UI could be implemented in any way imaginable and can be replaced entirely. Due to this, it should be replaceable without the Presentation knowing or caring about it. An everyday example of this is different layouts for phones and tablets (see *Figure 2.7*). Another, more recent example is the introduction of Jetpack Compose, replacing the Fragment, View, and XML approach.

---

8 Having a single source of truth is a good principle to follow. It helps prevent data inconsistencies, such as UI models holding data that differs from what the user sees.

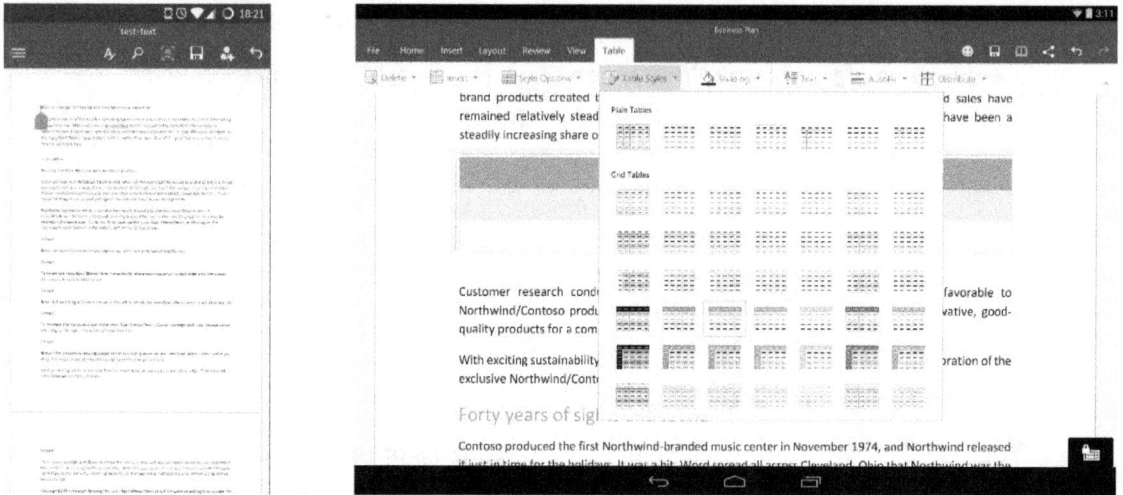

Figure 2.7: Microsoft Office on an Android phone (left) and tablet (right)

Let us go back to our cash machine example, and to our user wanting to check out their current balance. The user navigated to the Current Balance screen. At this point, we do not yet know their balance. However, we do not want to keep our users in the dark. We should provide them with some form of feedback to indicate that we are finding the balance in the background. To inform our user that we are working on their request, the viewmodel object updates the view state to an initial state of *loading*.

Note that we are not using terms such as *spinner* or *progress bar*. This is because these are **UI terms**. The Presentation is agnostic of UI implementation details. Whether we use a spinner, a progress bar, or a skeleton loading animation, the Presentation should remain unaffected. You will notice this motif throughout the book and across the layers. We are continuously conscious of the knowledge and visibility of each layer. This is related to the **Dependency Rule** and is a fundamental and crucial aspect of Clean Architecture.

When we discussed the Current Balance feature in the Domain layer section earlier, we mentioned that we executed the `GetCurrentBalanceUseCase` usecase as soon as the Current Balance screen was ready. This happens right after we set the initial view state. Once the usecase completes execution successfully, it returns the user's balance. We can then update the view state to tell the user that we are no longer in a loading state and that the user's current balance is the amount that was returned from the usecase.

What happens when the user wants to save their current connection details in our **WhoAmI** app? Let us explore the flow, assuming that the user is on the Home screen. First, here is the requirement:

- We have given the connection details on the screen.

- When the user taps the Save button, we want to persist these details in the connection history persistence.

- Once the connection details have been persisted, we want to take the user to the Connection History screen.

- The newly saved record should be highlighted.

Figure 2.8 provides a visual representation of the requirement:

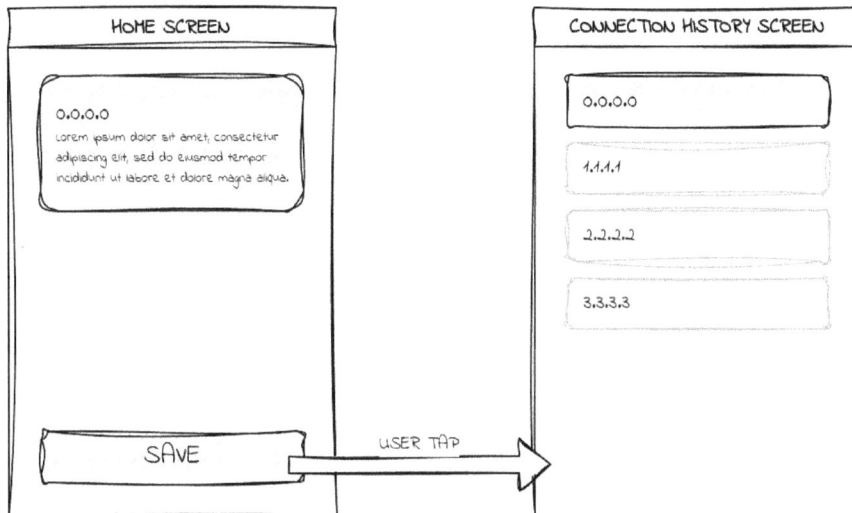

Figure 2.8: *Navigation flow from the Home screen to the Connection History screen in WhoAmI*

We will explore the flow starting from the Home screen. On the Home screen, the user is presented with their current connection details[9]. It is safe to assume that a **HomeViewModel** object is driving the Home screen.

The viewmodel instance will have an **onSaveDetailsAction(HomeViewState.Connected)** function. This is an interface for the view to inform us that the user has, you guessed it, requested to save the connection details. As it describes an event, the function name is prefixed with **on**, followed by the description of the user's action (**SaveDetails**), and finally suffixed with **Action**. The View will also provide us with the connection details that are currently presented to the user.

Once again, it is important to note that we do not use terms such as *Click* or *Tap*. These are *UI terms*. Our presentation is agnostic of such implementation details. Whether you tap, swipe, or use a voice command to trigger a save request is irrelevant to the Presentation layer. At this layer, we only care about the intention, which was to save the current connection details. The UI is responsible for providing the user with a mechanism with which to express their intentions, as we will see in the next section, which covers the UI layer.

Once the UI informs the Presentation that the user wants to save the connection details, the viewmodel instance determines the next course of action. In this case, this is what it does:

---

9 Note that in this case what the user sees is the source of truth. If the connection has changed without the user knowing, we would not want to save details which the user does not know about.

1. It calls the **execute** function of the **SaveConnectionDetailsUseCase** object. The viewmodel provides the function with the connection details, mapped from a Presentation model to a Domain model using a mapper.

2. When the usecase completes, it updates the view:

    a. If the execution was successful, it directs the view to inform the user of the success (by emitting a **ConnectionSaved** object) and navigate onwards (by emitting an **OnSavedDetails** object). As features are decoupled, *the Home feature does not know where we would be navigating to*. It only knows that we would be navigating away and that the trigger for the navigation is the successful saving of the connection details. We will discuss this in greater detail when we discuss navigation later in this chapter.

    b. If the execution fails, it sets the view state to the error state, mapped from a **DomainException** instance to a **PresentationError** one using a mapper.

Let us get back to where we left **WhoAmI**. We just navigated from the Home screen and landed on the Connection History screen. The Connection History screen is controlled by a **HistoryViewModel** object, which, as expected, presents the history of saved records to the user.

Viewmodel classes often depend on usecases and mappers. Specifically, they depend on Presentation to Domain and Domain to Presentation mappers. Our connection history viewmodel will hold instances of **GetHistoryUseCase** and **SavedIpAddressRecordToPresentationMapper**. It has another usecase and mapper for deleting records, but let us ignore these for now.

We covered usecases before, but mappers are a new concept we are touching on, so let me explain. As our implementation of Clean Architecture relies on strict layer separation, our UI has no access to Domain models, because the Presentation layer is in the middle. For this reason, it is the responsibility of the Presentation to convert (or map) the Domain model to a Presentation model, which the UI could access. This conversion is done using **mappers**. Mappers encapsulate the conversion logic between layers. We will encounter mappers again when converting Presentation models to UI ones, when converting Domain models to Data models, and when converting Data models to API or Storage models.

Models can be mapped in both directions. When the UI provides the viewmodel with data, it will be in the form of primitive types or Presentation models. In the case of Presentation models, to pass one to a **usecase** object's execute function in the Domain layer, we would first map the model to a Domain one.

Each mapper encapsulates a single responsibility and should be straightforward to unit test. When a model contains fields of a complex type, nested mappers can be used. This prevents our mappers from growing exponentially in complexity. The time to introduce nested mappers is when you identify that the number of test cases that you need to cover becomes unreasonably large. A good rule of thumb is that a mapper should be testable by validating no more than ten cases.

With mapper classes taking care of data conversion and usecase classes encapsulating the business logic, the viewmodel class should usually be reasonably slim. This makes unit-testing the viewmodel class quite simple.

With the Presentation layer covered, we can proceed to explore the UI layer.

The UI layer

While it is possible to develop an Android app without a user-facing interface, it is seldom that we see an Android app with no **user interface** (**UI**) at all. As you must have guessed by now, this is what the UI layer (*Figure 2.9*) is all about:

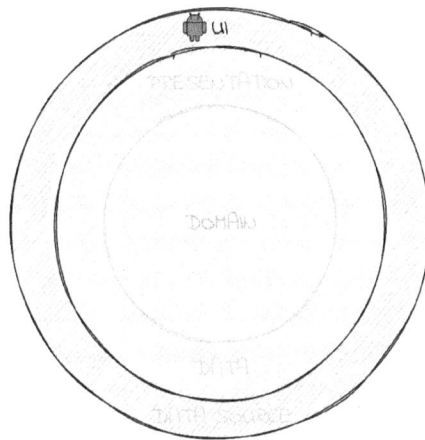

Figure 2.9: The UI layer is Android-aware

The UI layer is an **outer layer**. This means that it is exposed to the outside world. Being exposed to external dependencies makes the UI layer relatively volatile. The UI layer needs to be updated frequently (because of library changes as well as UI requirement changes). For this reason, no other layers rely on the UI. In our implementation, the UI layer relies on the Presentation layer (but not the Domain or Data layers, more on this later).

It is in this layer that the app exposes information to the user. It is also the layer that captures user input: if your user can interact with the app in any way, be it via a button tap, typing in some text, using a swipe gesture, or even by using their voice, the UI layer is responsible for capturing that input.

Your UI could be using XML layout inflation. It could be constructed in code from View classes. It could even be using Jetpack Compose[10]. These methods all work with Clean Architecture. What is more important is that *you can easily swap your UI layer implementation without affecting any of the other layers.*

---

10 **https://developer.android.com/jetpack/compose**

You will commonly find **Activity**, **Fragment**, and custom **View** classes (widgets) in this layer. **Composable** functions also belong in this layer. Our Android resources (layouts, drawables, colors, strings, dimensions, and so on) also belong in this layer, despite them residing in a different folder than our code. In addition, you will find UI **models** here. These are models that represent data in a way that is meaningful to the UI. It makes sense to hold references to string, color, or drawable resources in the UI models. UI models are usually constructed by Presentation-to-UI **mappers**. They can also be mapped back to Presentation models via UI-to-Presentation mappers. *Figure 2.10* shows how all these different components work together:

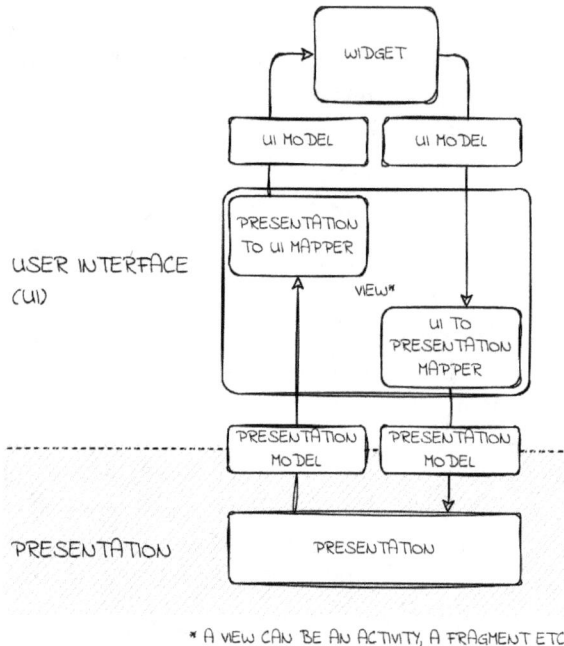

Figure 2.10: The components of the UI layer

Modules in the UI layer will almost certainly depend on the Android SDK. They may rely on image-loading libraries, custom widgets, or effect libraries, and other UI-specific libraries. Somewhat surprisingly, you will also find your *analytics dependencies* here. As analytics events are commonly coupled with user actions, analytics fit well in the UI layer. UI layer modules may rely on other UI layer modules (if your project has standalone feature modules split by layers). Lastly, remember that the UI layer *knows about* the Presentation layer. This means that you may find dependencies on Presentation layer modules here, too.

You should *never* see a UI module depending on a Domain or a Data module. While Clean Architecture allows for this, ignoring this advice would lead to a direct violation of the proposed Clean Architecture implementation presented in this book. I strongly advise you not to have the UI layer depend directly on Domain or Data code, as doing so would lead to tightly coupled code and would have a negative impact on the stability and maintainability of the system.

This advice is contrary to that given by Google in their proposed Android Architecture (not to be confused with Clean Architecture). According to *Google*, the UI layer should depend on an (optional) Domain layer and may depend directly on the Data layer. This introduces a significant risk of tightly coupled code: a change to an API can easily ripple to the code on the UI, which is often unintended. The Android Architecture has similar issues when other layers are concerned, too, but we will get back to that when we discuss the Data layer.

For now, let us think back to our cash machine. The UI layer would be where we actually take care of informing the user of their current balance. This could be via a terminal or even a printer with a few switches and sliders attached.

We mentioned that the UI layer holds UI models. UI models are a convenient way to communicate state to adapter and custom **View** classes, **composable** functions, and other UI components. They prevent tight coupling between the Presentation layer and the UI layer. A Presentation-to-UI mapper (and a UI-to-Presentation mapper, when the need arises) handles the conversion between the Presentation and UI models.

In the following section, we will focus on making sure that the data that the feature is working with is real.

The Data layer

The Data layer, illustrated in *Figure 2.11*, is responsible for protecting our business logic, which lives in our Domain layer, from external details. External details include web APIs, data storage solutions (databases, **SharedPreferences**, and memory storage, to name a few), Bluetooth devices, and third-party SDKs that do not face the user. It is common to see implementations in which the Data layer tends to group two layers into one: the Data layer and the DataSource layer. We keep the two separated because they have clear responsibilities and critical differences. We will discuss the DataSource layer right after the Data one, and it will all make sense.

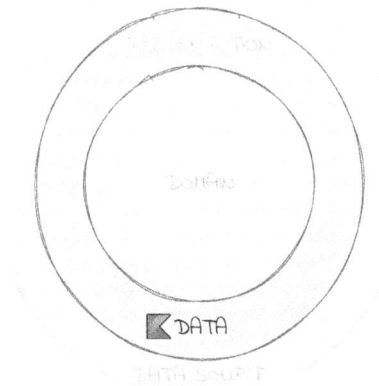

Figure 2.11: The Data layer is platform-agnostic

The Data layer is an **inner layer**. It contains **repository implementations**. The interfaces that these repositories implement are the ones that we defined in the Domain layer. This is how we enforce the Dependency Rule: the Data layer depends on the Domain layer, but the Domain layer knows nothing about the Data layer. The fact that the repository classes implement an interface declared in the Domain layer tells us that these layers are feature-aware.

Before we continue, I promised you that I would get back to Google's Android Architecture. While many developers mistake this architecture for Clean Architecture, the two share little more than the names of the layers. In Android Architecture, the Domain layer and sometimes even the UI layer depend directly on the Data layer. This means that the Data layer offers no protection against external changes other than by abstraction. Changes to the code in the Data layer may require changes to the Domain layer (or even the UI layer!) for the code to compile. It is important that you understand the distinction between decoupling by abstraction and decoupling by inversion of controls. The first still couples the Domain code to the Data code by interface, while the latter does not.

With this out of the way, we can get back to the Data layer. This layer is platform agnostic. We should keep our library dependencies in it to a minimum. This layer depends on the Domain layer. In the Data layer, we expect to find **repository implementations**, as we just discussed. In addition, we expect Domain-to-Data model mappers and Data-to-Domain model mappers, see *Figure 2.12*:

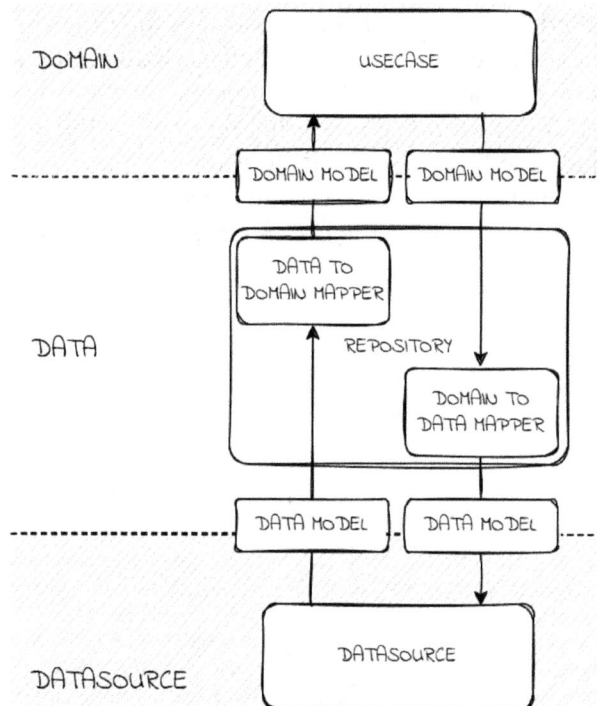

Figure 2.12: The components of the Data layer

With the Data layer covered, let us proceed to discuss the DataSource layer.

The DataSource layer

Moving on to the DataSource layer. Like the UI layer, the DataSource layer is an outer layer, as shown in *Figure 2.13*. This means that it is connected to the outside world and external dependencies. It is worth noting that there is an anomaly here: while the DataSource layer is an outer layer, the Data layer depends on it. This goes against the Dependency Rule but allows for better code reuse while also mirroring the UI's dependency on external libraries. It may help you to think of the DataSource layer as an external library that your app happens to own.

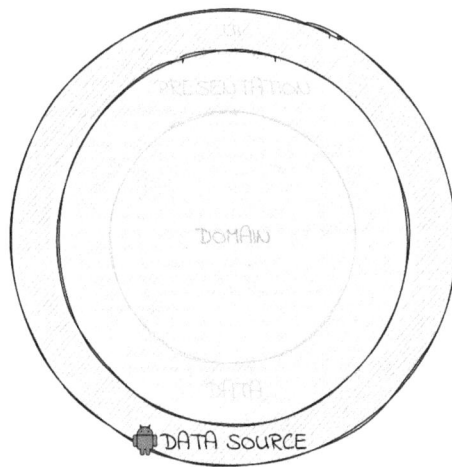

Figure 2.13: *The DataSource layer is Android-aware*

This layer contains **datasource** classes, Data and DataSource **models** (API, memory, and database models fall under this category), and Data-to-DataSource **mappers** (and vice-versa), see *Figure 2.14*:

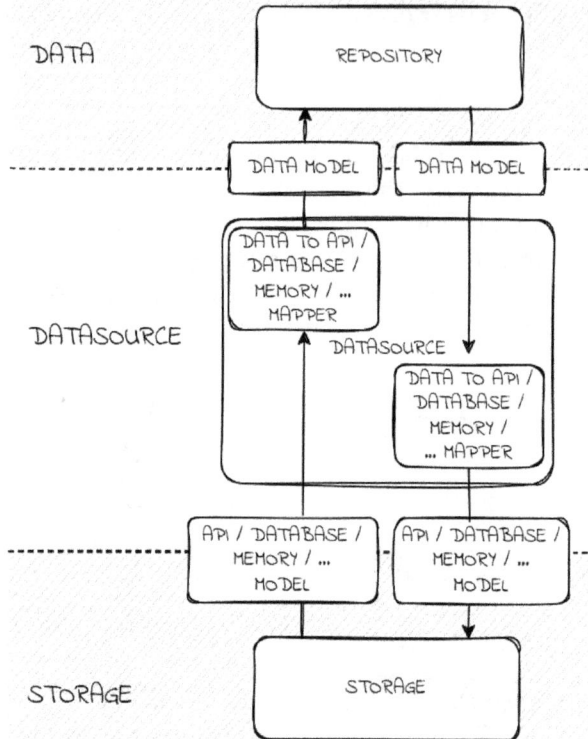

Figure 2.14: *The components of the DataSource layer*

Datasource are classes that communicate with storage, or the *outside world*, whether it is a Retrofit Service, Ktor network calls, a Bluetooth device, or a **SharedPreferences** store. As datasource classes are tightly coupled to external components[11], their direct correlation to features is loose. It is convenient to think of them as feature-agnostic. They represent, as the name suggests, sources in which our Data models are stored.

This means that the repository implementations in the Data layer serve as a bridge between the feature-specific Domain layer and a feature-agnostic DataSource layer.

For datasource classes to communicate with repository implementations, a bridging model is required. The Data models fulfill this purpose. They are suffixed with **DataModel** and belong in the DataSource layer.

Let us focus on the DataSource models (excluding the Data models) for a minute. We intentionally distinguish between API and database models, despite them co-existing in the same layer. We make that distinction so that there is no dependency between our API and our storage solutions. We want to be able to change our storage solution without API models being affected. We also want to be able to comply with a new API contract without having to update our database models.

---

11 With the exception of memory stores, which are probably the only store that is not truly external.

Let us look at an example. Imagine that your local persistence and network persistence shared models. One day, you want to switch your JSON serialization in your API models that are used by Ktor from Gson to `kotlinx.serialization`. Gson uses the **@SerializedName** annotation for mapping JSON keys to field names, while `kotlinx.serialization` uses the **@SerialName** annotation. So, you go ahead and migrate all your models from using the **@SerializedName** annotation to using the **@SerialName** one. What would happen to your local persistence code? That is right, it will break.

In our cash machine example, the datasource object will likely communicate with the banking API, and the repository classes would serve as a bridge between the usecase objects and the datasource one. So, when the user requests their current balance, the **execute** function of a usecase object (**GetCurrentBalanceUseCase** would be a likely name, as was mentioned earlier) will be executed. The usecase function will call a function on a **CurrentBalanceRepository** implementation. This function will probably be called **currentBalance**. The repository function, in turn, would call a **currentBalance** function on the **CurrentBalanceDataSource** implementation, and the datasource function would perform a GET operation on an HTTP endpoint. The datasource function would then return the data to the repository function, which will in turn return it to the usecase one.

When we discussed the Domain layer, I suggested stubbing our repository implementation. Looking back at **WhoAmI**, having stubs allowed us to move forward with the implementation of the Presentation and eventually the UI without waiting for the Data layer implementation to be complete. Depending on our team size, we may want to tackle the Presentation and Data layers in parallel, or we may choose to implement them sequentially. Either way works. That is one of the benefits of implementing Clean Architecture in our app.

When the repository and datasource classes are implemented, our usecase objects can start returning real values. With the Presentation and the UI layers implemented, our feature is completed.

In the following section, we will see how to connect features using navigation.

Navigation

Most apps span more than one screen. An app screen does not have to cover the entire screen of the device. It could be a fragment, a dialog, a card, or a composable, too. A screen is any user-facing interface that either conveys information to the user, provides the user with a mechanism to input data, or both.

For an app to work, these screens need to be connected somehow, and the user needs to be able to switch from one to another. This is what we refer to as *navigation*. In the Android world, we currently have a few common mechanisms of navigation:

- **Native navigation**: Launching **Activity** classes using **Intent** objects, using **FragmentManager** objects to present **Fragment** objects, and launching dialogs directly (commonly using an **AlertDialog.Builder** object).

- **Using the Navigation component**: Google offers this framework for navigation that relies heavily on XML navigation graphs.

- If we are using Compose, we have a navigation library.

In Clean Architecture, we consider these different options *details*. This means that using one over the other or swapping one for another should have minimal impact on other code. This is very similar to our DataSource layer, where one data storage solution can be swapped for another with limited impact.

To achieve this level of freedom, we need to abstract our navigation. In its simplest form, a navigation system is a collection of actions having an origin and a destination. Each such action can hold some metadata that provides context for the destination.

For example, in a cash machine, when navigating from a screen with a list of transactions to a particular transaction details screen, our origin is the list of transactions screen. Our destination is the transaction details screen (**TransactionListNavigationEvent** could be an appropriate name for a **sealed interface** containing all the navigation events, and the specific event could be **OnViewTransactionDetails**). Our payload is likely to be the unique identifier of the transaction in question.

From a Presentation perspective, each feature has one or more entry points. These are characterized by their associated payload.

Each feature can also have one or more exit points (it can have none, too). As we want to keep our features independent, it is important to perceive these exit points by the action or *event* that triggered them, rather than by their expected destination. For example, **OnSavedDetails** has a better destination description than **GoToHistoryScreen**. This distinction gives us the freedom to later reuse features in different contexts or change our minds about where to take the user when the event occurs.

In his book *Clean Architecture, Robert C. Martin* suggests having a *dirty main* function. It is this function that *glues* all the different classes together. This is replaced in Android with **dependency injection** (**DI**) solutions such as **Hilt** or **Koin**. There is another aspect to *gluing* everything together. Indeed, I am referring to the navigation. The only component that should know how the features come together is the app itself.

Let us look at a concrete example from our **WhoAmI** app.

Navigation is triggered by the Presentation layer. More specifically, it is launched from a viewmodel object. Assuming that we have a **BaseViewModel** class that all viewmodel classes extend, we start by implementing a **navigationEvent** field on that **BaseViewModel**, which is of type **Flow<PresentationNavigationEvent>**. An **emitNavigationEvent(PresentationNavigationEvent)** function that is only exposed to concrete viewmodel classes emits navigation events via the **navigationEvent** field.

So, let us say that the user tapped the View History button. Our view would inform our **HomeViewModel** object of the event by calling **onViewHistoryAction()**. The viewmodel object would then inform the view that the user should be taken to wherever *View History* should take them by calling the **emitNavigationEvent** function, passing in **OnViewHistory** (an implementation of **PresentationNavigationEvent**), to indicate the navigation intent.

Once a navigation event is emitted via the **navigationEvent** field of the viewmodel object, the observing view can proceed with navigation.

In a Jetpack Compose world, we have a **collectAsState** call in our composable function that would collect the emitted **PresentationNavigationEvent** object from the viewmodel object. In turn, a **LaunchedEffect** composable would use a **NavigationEventDestinationMapper** object to map the **OnViewHistory** Presentation navigation event to a UI destination.

The **NavigationEventDestinationMapper** class has a generic type, which is either the **PresentationNavigationEvent** interface or an extension of it. This generic type is there to enforce the contract between the feature and the app. It exposes any presentation navigation events to the app. The feature expects the app to translate these events to navigation destinations.

The output of the mapper is a **UiDestination** implementation. **UiDestination** is a fun interface with a single function: **navigate**. This allows us to encapsulate navigation details for every individual destination. When using Google's Navigation component, it makes sense to pass a **NavController** instance to this function, as it may be necessary for actual navigation. The **navigate** function is called immediately after the **UiDestination** object is returned from the mapper. Depending on your individual navigation solution choices, you may have to provide other dependencies to your mapper and the concrete destinations. The pattern will remain the same whether you use Google's Navigation components or any other navigation approach.

From a feature perspective, Presentation navigation events are named by exit points, not entry points. In our example, the Home feature knows that the user wants to view the saved connection details history, so **OnViewHistory** is an appropriate name. Suppose we decided to change the connection history feature name (let us say we decided to name the feature *past connections*). This should not affect the destination name in the Home feature. Presentation navigation events are grouped using a sealed interface. This sealed interface implements **PresentationNavigationEvent** and is the generic type that we use in the **NavigationEventToDestinationMapper**. This gives us compile-time safety, *as long as we avoid using the else branch* in our **when** statement, which checks the event type.

The code for every UI destination is implemented within the mapper because these destinations are inherently tightly coupled with the mapper. The mapper knows every UI destination for a specific feature. The navigation mapper itself is implemented in the app. This makes sense because only the app knows all the different destinations that it supports.

To test our Presentation to UI destination mappers, we can use a parameterized test. The input would be the Presentation destination model. Since the UI destination models are private, we would instead execute the **navigate** function of the mapper output and verify that the expected destination was navigated to.

Conclusion

You should now have a clear understanding of how our Clean Architecture implementation is built. We have covered every layer, from the Domain to the Presentation, the UI, and the Data. We discussed how we could introduce a DataSource layer as well, and how it should be kept decoupled from individual features. We covered how the different classes play essential roles within their corresponding layers to make our app work while keeping the innermost layers protected from external changes. We also saw how each part of the app that holds logic can be isolated for easier testing.

In the next chapter, we will start looking at concrete code. We will see how the different components, from composable functions to viewmodel, usecase, repository, and datasource classes, fit together.

Points to remember

There are a few important points worth remembering when it comes to our Clean Architecture implementation:

- Keep your interfaces and components small. Remember to follow the Single Responsibility principle (each component should have one reason to change) and the Interface Segregation principle (a client should not be exposed to methods it does not need). This will make testing easier and help keep your components decoupled.

- A primary goal of having layers is to protect the business logic from external changes. Keep external dependencies isolated and do not let their code leak into your Presentation or Data layers.

- Naming is critical. Being pedantic about names helps everyone get used to the architecture until it becomes second nature.

Join our Discord space

Join our Discord workspace for latest updates, offers, tech happenings around the world, new releases, and sessions with the authors:

https://discord.bpbonline.com

CHAPTER 3
The Domain Layer

The only way to go fast, is to go well.

- Robert C. Martin

Introduction

In the upcoming five chapters, we will get technical and explore the full implementation of a Clean Architecture project. In these chapters, we will explore key files of every layer of our Clean Architecture implementation. We will also dissect every base class along with a concrete feature example. Please bear in mind that this is an opinionated implementation of Clean Architecture. It is based on experience and solves many problems that you might encounter if you were to take a different route. This does not mean that you should not explore other paths.

The implementation presented in the following chapters is a multi-module one and thus breaks the app down into Gradle modules. I will mention the relevant module for the code that we will be discussing as we progress.

We will go layer by layer, starting with the Domain layer, going through the Presentation, UI, DataSource, and Data layers. After we covered all layers, we will discuss the app itself, along with dependency injection and navigation.

The current chapter covers the layer that is at the heart of any Clean Architecture project, the Domain layer. When working on a new feature, this is the layer that I recommend starting with.

Structure

In this chapter, we will cover the following topics:

- A brief introduction to the Domain layer
- The Domain architecture code
- The Domain feature code

Objectives

This chapter should give you a clear idea of what the Domain layer in a Clean Architecture app looks like. It will cover every important file in this layer in detail. By the end of this chapter, you should be familiar with the classes that exist in the Domain layer and the role that each class plays. You should also have an understanding of how the different classes fit together.

A brief introduction to the Domain layer

We should start the implementation of any new feature with the Domain layer. This serves several purposes:

- No other layers will influence our design of the Domain layer.
- There would be no dangling code at any point in time since the Domain layer relies on no other layer.
- It is quick and easy to implement, so we make initial progress very quickly.

The Domain layer is the simplest of all layers. This is intentional. The less complex the logic in this layer is, the less often its code will have to change. This is a good thing. We want our Domain layer to be the most stable of them all. For that reason, we also try to keep it free of any frameworks or third-party libraries. This is not always possible, and we do often rely on a few select ones, such as the Kotlin standard library. An important library to note is the Android SDK, which should notably be absent from the Domain layer.

Let us see what the code in the **domain** subpackage of the **architecture** package looks like.

The Domain architecture code

In *Figure 3.1*, you can see the structure of our architecture Domain Gradle module:

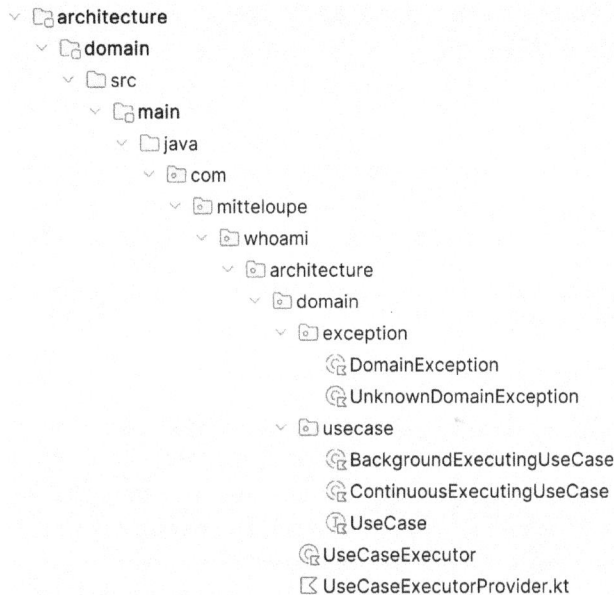

> ∨ ▢ architecture
>   ∨ ▢ domain
>   ∨ ▢ src
>   ∨ ▢ main
>   ∨ ▢ java
>   ∨ ▢ com
>   ∨ ▢ mitteloupe
>   ∨ ▢ whoami
>   ∨ ▢ architecture
>   ∨ ▢ domain
>   ∨ ▢ exception
>   ▢ DomainException
>   ▢ UnknownDomainException
>   ∨ ▢ usecase
>   ▢ BackgroundExecutingUseCase
>   ▢ ContinuousExecutingUseCase
>   ▢ UseCase
>   ▢ UseCaseExecutor
>   ▢ UseCaseExecutorProvider.kt

Figure 3.1: The structure of the architecture Domain module

Going forward, we will distinguish between *architecture* code and code specific to *features*. We will treat the architecture code as a special feature that holds the building blocks for the rest of our app. The architecture modules of our project will be grouped under an **architecture** directory at the root of our project. The Domain architecture files will live in the **architecture:domain** module. The first file that we will be exploring is **UseCase.kt**.

The most important component in the Domain layer is the usecase. A usecase class describes a single event that is triggered by the user. These are also known as interactors, but as I mentioned earlier, we will stick with the usecase name. Let us take a look at what the **UseCase** interface looks like:

UseCase.kt
```
1.    package com.whoami.architecture.domain.usecase
2.
3.    interface UseCase<REQUEST, RESULT> {
4.        suspend fun execute(input: REQUEST, onResult: (RESULT) -> Unit)
5.    }
```

The **UseCase** interface is used to declare a contract for executing usecases. If it looks very simple to you, that is because it is. A single **UseCase** has a single responsibility, and it is to perform a single action. Nothing more. Our basic **UseCase** interface does not concern itself with any technical details, it does not care about threading, for example. That would be an implementation detail. Well, almost. The only trace of an implementation detail is the suspend keyword. Unfortunately, this is the least boilerplate we have to introduce if we want to rely on Coroutines.

Note the **architecture** part of the **UseCase.kt** file's package name. This is our feature name for the Clean Architecture building blocks, as we mentioned earlier. The **usecase** subpackage is used for consistency with concrete usecases, as we will see when we explore a concrete usecase later in this chapter.

Usecase classes are executed from viewmodel classes. We will discuss viewmodels in detail when we cover the Presentation layer in *Chapter 4, The Presentation Layer*. For now, know that for at least two reasons, using a **UseCaseExecutor** class to execute usecases is a good idea:

- To avoid exposing every viewmodel class to the coroutine dependency, or to any other mechanism usecases use for execution.

- To provide a common cancellation mechanism.

As the name suggests, a **UseCaseExecutor** class executes usecase classes for us. It encapsulates the execution details of usecases and can provide us with a mechanism to track and cancel the execution of any usecase (we will explore this possibility at the end of the book in *Appendix, Legacy Code and Advanced Topics*). The **UseCaseExecutor** instance is injected into our **BaseViewModel** class via the **BaseViewModel**'s constructor. Here is the code for the **UseCaseExecutor** class:

UseCaseExecutor.kt

```
1.    package com.mitteloupe.whoami.architecture.domain
2.
3.    [imports...]
4.
5.    class UseCaseExecutor {
6.        fun <INPUT, OUTPUT> execute(
7.            useCase: UseCase<INPUT, OUTPUT>,
8.            value: INPUT,
9.            onResult: (OUTPUT) -> Unit = {},
10.           onException: (DomainException) -> Unit = {}
11.       ) {
12.           try {
13.               useCase.execute(value, onResult)
14.           } catch (throwable: Throwable) {
15.               val domainException = ((throwable as? DomainException) ?:
16.                   UnknownDomainException(throwable))
17.               onException(domainException)
18.           }
19.       }
20.   }
```

This is a minimalistic implementation. Starting at the first line, we can see that the **UseCaseExecutor** file is stored in the same base **domain** subpackage as our **UseCase** interface.

The **execute** function takes a **UseCase** implementation, an input value, and two callback lambdas: **onResult** and **onException** (see these parameters on *lines 7 to 10*).

The **UseCaseExecutor**'s **execute** function executes the **UseCase**. The execution part is straightforward—we call the **execute** function of the provided **UseCase** instance with the **input** value and the **onResult** callback (*line 13*). We wrap the execution in a **try/catch** block (*lines 12 to 18*). Any exception occurring during the execution of our **domain/data/datasource** code would be captured and returned via the **onException** callback (*line 17*) as a concrete **DomainExceptions** implementation. On *line 15*, we first check for meaningful **DomainExceptions** (likely thrown by a repository or a **UseCase** object). We fall back to an **UnknownDomainException** wrapper object (*line 16*) for all other **Throwable** instances.

For completion, this is our **DomainException** class:

DomainException.kt

```
1.  package com.mitteloupe.whoami.architecture.domain.exception
2.
3.  abstract class DomainException(
4.      open val throwable: Throwable
5.  ) : Exception(throwable) {
6.      constructor(message: String) : this(Exception(message))
7.  }
```

The following is the **UnknownDomainException** class:

UnknownDomainException.kt

```
1.  package com.mitteloupe.whoami.architecture.domain.exception
2.
3.  class UnknownDomainException(throwable: Throwable) :
4.      DomainException(throwable) {
5.      constructor(errorMessage: String) : this(Throwable(errorMessage))
6.  }
```

When working with Clean Architecture, you may find that you have other requirements for your Domain layer. You may want to implement long-running usecase instances that emit multiple values. You may want to make your usecase objects cancellable. This is all possible with small modifications to the implementation presented here.

Did you notice how the execute function takes a lambda as its second parameter? This is because usecase classes can have asynchronous execution. The result of the execution of a usecase may also be multiple values. A lambda can be executed when the results are ready and may be executed multiple times. While there are many mechanisms for achieving asynchronous and flow-like behavior, most rely on an external library (**RxJava** and **Coroutines** are such libraries). A lambda relies solely on the features of Kotlin itself. It may be tempting to use a coroutine flow, but remember that not all **UseCase** implementations return multiple values or any values at all.

Going back to threading, here is our **BackgroundExecutingUseCase** implementation, which executes a usecase in a background thread using coroutines:

BackgroundExecutingUseCase.kt

```
1.   package com.mitteloupe.whoami.architecture.domain.usecase
2.
3.   [imports...]
4.
5.   abstract class BackgroundExecutingUseCase<REQUEST, RESULT>(
6.       private val coroutineContextProvider: CoroutineContextProvider,
7.       private val coroutineScope: CoroutineScope =
8.           CoroutineScope(Dispatchers.Main)
9.   ) : UseCase<REQUEST, RESULT> {
10.      final override fun execute(
11.          input: REQUEST, onResult: (RESULT) -> Unit
12.      ) {
13.          coroutineScope.launch {
14.              val result = withContext(coroutineContextProvider.io) {
15.                  executeInBackground(input)
16.              }
17.              onResult(result)
18.          }
19.      }
20.
21.      abstract fun executeInBackground(request: REQUEST): RESULT
22.  }
```

BackgroundExecutingUseCase is a coroutine-specific **abstract** class. You can use whatever mechanism you want to handle your threading; this is just one way. In fact, you *can* have different mechanisms in the same project if you have a good reason to. I never found a justification for having more than one mechanism in the projects I have worked on. **BackgroundExecutingUseCase** happens to use coroutines, because this is the most common mechanism at the time of writing.

The responsibility of **BackgroundExecutingUseCase** is twofold:

- It abstracts all the coroutine boilerplate code away for us; it lets us keep our concrete usecase implementations clean and focused on their own unique functionality.

- It hides its coroutine nature from the consumers of the usecase.

Note that because **BackgroundExecutingUseCase** is coroutine-specific, our usecase requires two objects: a coroutine *scope* and a coroutine *context*. These are provided to it by passing in instances of **CoroutineContextProvider** and **CoroutineScope** via its constructor (*lines 6 to 8*). **CoroutineContextProvider** can be as simple as:

CoroutineContextProvider.kt

```
1.    package com. mitteloupe.whoami.coroutine
2.
3.    interface CoroutineContextProvider {
4.        val main: CoroutineContext
5.        val io: CoroutineContext
6.    }
```

This abstracts the provision of coroutine contexts away. The **coroutineScope** parameter defaults to **CoroutineScope(Dispatchers.Main)**.

Let us get back to **BackgroundExecutingUseCase**. The **execute** function implementation is made **final** (*line 10*) to prevent child usecase classes from overriding it. Its body is wrapped in a coroutine by calling **launch** on the provided **CoroutineScope** object.

Note the abstract **executeInBackground** function on *line 21*; the **execute** function wraps the call to this abstract function in an **input/output** (**I/O**) context block and stores its result (*lines 14 to 16*). This sorts out the asynchronous nature of the call for us. On *line 17*, the usecase execution is wrapped up by executing the **onResult** lambda with the result saved in the **result** variable. Note that the call is made outside of the IO context block.

Looking at the **UseCase** interface presented earlier, it requires specifying two generic types: an *input* type and an *output* one. Both input and output usecase arguments should be either primitive types, models, or **Unit**. If they are models, remember that the only model type that the Domain knows about is the Domain model. Domain models are the models that are declared in the Domain layer. We will see an example of such models when we explore the Domain feature code.

To see how all the preceding code comes together, have a look at *Figure 3.1*.

This wraps up the architecture aspect of the Domain layer of **WhoAmI**. What about the feature Domain modules? We will explore this next.

The Domain feature code

Now that we have the base classes for our Domain layer, we can look at a feature. The structure of a feature's Domain layer can be seen in *Figure 3.2*:

```
∨ 🗁 home
  > 🗁 data
  ∨ 🗁 domain
    ∨ 🗁 src
      ∨ 🗁 main
        ∨ 🗁 java
          ∨ 🗁 com
            ∨ 🗁 mitteloupe
              ∨ 🗁 whoami
                ∨ 🗁 home
                  ∨ 🗁 domain
                    ∨ 🗁 exception
                         🅰 NoIpAddressDomainException
                         🅰 NoIpAddressInformationDomainException
                         🅰 ReadFailedDomainException
                    ∨ 🗁 model
                         🅰 ConnectionDetailsDomainModel
                    ∨ 🗁 repository
                         🅰 GetConnectionDetailsRepository
                         🅰 SaveConnectionDetailsRepository
                    ∨ 🗁 usecase
                         🅰 GetConnectionDetailsUseCase
                         🅰 SaveConnectionDetailsUseCase
```

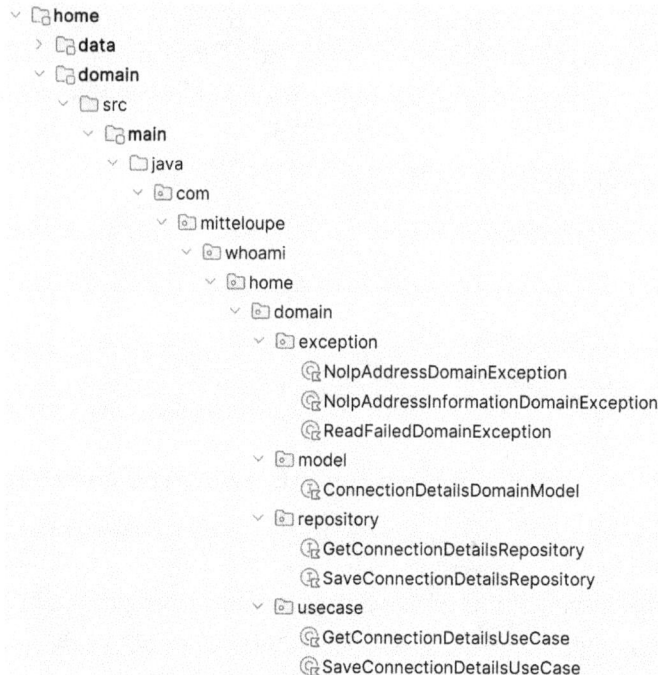

Figure 3.2: The structure of the Home feature Domain module

The feature code of our app lives under a directory at the root of the project that is named after the feature. The code is broken down by layers, and the Domain code lives under the **featurename:domain** module. In this and the following chapters, we will explore the *home* feature, and its Domain code is saved under **home:domain**.

In an app's feature Domain module, we would expect to find concrete usecase classes such as **GetConnectionDetailsUseCase** and **SaveConnectionDetailsUseCase**.

The following is an example of how the **GetConnectionDetailsUseCase** class would look:

GetConnectionDetailsUseCase.kt

```
1.    package com.mitteloupe.whoami.home.domain.usecase
2.
3.    [imports...]
4.
5.    class GetConnectionDetailsUseCase(
6.        private val repository: GetConnectionDetailsRepository,
7.        coroutineContextProvider: CoroutineContextProvider
8.    ) : ContinuousExecutingUseCase<Unit, ConnectionDetailsDomainModel>(
9.        coroutineContextProvider
10.   ) {
```

```
11.        override fun executeInBackground(request: Unit) =
12.            repository.connectionDetails()
13.    }
```

Starting with the first line, we get a first glimpse of the package structure in a Clean Architecture implementation. The package name starts with the app package prefix (**com.mitteloupe. whoami**) followed by the feature name (**home**), the layer (**domain**), and finally **usecase**. This is the package in which we save every usecase belonging to this feature.

On line 6, we see the first constructor parameter for our usecase: a repository instance that fits the requirements of the usecase. In this case, the requirement is to provide us with the connection details. This is an important point. Remember that our Domain layer knows nothing about any other layer. This means that we can write our code in the purest possible way, devoid of any external constraints. We have absolute freedom. Do we need to make multiple API network requests to obtain all the connection details? We do not care. Does the name or type of returned fields from the API differ from our model? Again, we do not care. We know what we need, and that is all we are going to base our design on. This means that our **GetConnectionDetailsRepository** interface will have a single function, returning precisely what we need: a single connection details Domain object.

The second constructor parameter (*line 7*) is a **CoroutineContextProvider** instance, which we pass as-is to our **ContinuousExecutingUseCase** superclass (*lines 8 to 10*). You may have noticed the use of **ContinuousExecutingUseCase**, it is a subclass of the **UseCase** interface, and we will expand on it shortly. For now, know that as its name implies, it executes continuously, emitting values as they are returned from the repository. In our case, this is achieved using coroutines and a flow. **ContinuousExecutingUseCase** is an abstract class with two generic types, just like the **UseCase** interface: an input type and an output one. This usecase has no input, and it outputs the current connection details, and thus the generic types are set to **Unit** and **ConnectionDetailsDomainModel** correspondingly (*line 8*).

Lines 11 to *12* are where we define the concrete usecase behavior. Since we extended **ContinuousExecutingUseCase**, we override its abstract **executeInBackground** function (this function serves a similar role to the function of the same name discussed earlier when we looked at **BackgroundExecutingUseCase**). It has one parameter of the type that we defined earlier as the first generic type (set to **Unit**). The function returns a single value of a type that we also defined earlier as the second generic type, set to **ConnectionDetailsDomainModel**. The value to be returned is obtained by calling **connectionDetails()** on an object stored in the **repository** variable.

You will notice that our usecase is *extremely* simple. I encourage you to either use **test-driven development** (**TDD**) to write it or, at the very least, to cover it with a unit test. Tests not only validate the implementation, but they also document the requirement.

To help us understand what the **GetConnectionDetailsUseCase** class does under the hood, here is the source for the **ContinuousExecutingUseCase** abstract class:

ContinuousExecutingUseCase.kt

```
1.    package com.mitteloupe.whoami.architecture.domain.usecase
2.
3.    [imports...]
4.
5.    abstract class ContinuousExecutingUseCase<REQUEST, RESULT>(
6.        private val coroutineContextProvider: CoroutineContextProvider
7.    ) : UseCase<REQUEST, RESULT> {
8.        final override suspend fun execute(
9.            input: REQUEST,
10.           onResult: (RESULT) -> Unit
11.       ) {
12.           withContext(coroutineContextProvider.io) {
13.               executeInBackground(input).collect { result ->
14.                   withContext(coroutineContextProvider.main) {
15.                       onResult(result)
16.                   }
17.               }
18.           }
19.       }
20.
21.       abstract fun executeInBackground(request: REQUEST): Flow<RESULT>
22.   }
```

Note that the **ContinuousExecutingUseCase** class is part of the *architecture* feature, not the *home* one. As you can see, the **ContinuousExecutingUseCase** class is similar to the **BackgroundExecutingUseCase** one. The primary difference between the two is that the continuous implementation relies on a *flow* implementation (*line 21*) and executes the **onResult** lambda for every emitted value (*lines 13 to 17*).

Next, for completeness, let us take a look at what the **GetConnectionDetailsRepository** interface looks like:

GetConnectionDetailsRepository.kt

```
1.    package com.mitteloupe.whoami.home.domain.repository
2.
3.    [imports...]
4.
5.    interface GetConnectionDetailsRepository {
6.        fun connectionDetails(): Flow<ConnectionDetailsDomainModel>
7.    }
```

As you can see, the repository interface is as straightforward as they come. It defines the usecase requirements accurately: the usecase needs the connection details, and no input is required. Note that the package name is much like that of the usecase. Instead of **usecase** in the package name, we have **repository**. The rest of the package path is identical.

To make your domain usable straight out of the box, it is a good idea to introduce a dummy implementation of the repository at this stage. Just mark your implementation by including a suitable word in its name. The terms **Fake**, **Dummy**, or **Stub** all work. So, for example, a dummy **GetConnectionDetailsRepository** class could look like this:

GetConnectionDetailsDummyRepository.kt

```
1.   package com.mitteloupe.whoami.home.domain.repository
2.
3.   [imports...]
4.
5.   class GetConnectionDetailsDummyRepository :
6.       GetConnectionDetailsRepository {
7.       override fun connectionDetails() =
8.           flowOf(ConnectionDetailsDomainModel(...))
9.   }
```

Note that we implement our **GetConnectionDetailsDummyRepository** class in the same package as our interface, in the Domain layer of the home feature. We can safely remove it once we have a concrete implementation in the Data layer. Also, note that it does not matter much which values we assign to the response. If you feel that a certain initial value would make your life easier later, go with that value. Otherwise, any value will do.

We can now provide this dummy repository to the usecase class and use the usecase straight away. We will swap this implementation for a real one when we get to the Data layer.

When we looked at the output of the **executeInBackground** function of our usecase implementation, we noted that it returned a flow of **ConnectionDetailsDomainModel** objects. In case you were wondering what the **ConnectionDetailsDomainModel** entity looked like, here it is:

ConnectionDetailsDomainModel.kt

```
1.   package com.mitteloupe.whoami.home.domain.model
2.
3.   [imports...]
4.
5.   sealed interface ConnectionDetailsDomainModel {
6.       data class Connected(
7.           val ipAddress: String,
```

```
8.              val city: String?,
9.              ...,
10.         ) : ConnectionDetailsDomainModel
11.
12.         data object Disconnected : ConnectionDetailsDomainModel
13.
14.         data class Error(val exception: DomainException) :
15.             ConnectionDetailsDomainModel
16.
17.         data object Unset : ConnectionDetailsDomainModel
18.     }
```

The **model** package resides next to the **usecase** and **repository** packages of the same feature. You may be asking yourself if this means that different features would have different models, even when representing the same underlying entity. *My advice to you is to do just that.* Keep the models separate. The duplication is coincidental. Different features may end up requiring different fields or a different structure altogether. You do not want to increase the complexity of your model beyond the scope of your current feature's needs. Imagine another feature where a list of connections is needed. Each connection in that list may not care about the `city` field (*line 8*). Having that field in a cross-feature **ConnectionDetailsDomainModel** would mean that you would have to figure out the city value for a connection, *even if you do not need it*. You may also have to worry about handling the data that you do not need in the first place. Furthermore, you want to limit the scope of changes to a feature. You do not want to have to update every feature when a single feature no longer needs a field or when a feature requires data in a different format.

I suffix my Domain model names with **DomainModel**. This makes it easy for me to identify the layer that the model originated from when reading the code. It makes it easier to distinguish between Domain and Presentation models or Domain and Data models in the same code.

Domain model fields will always be of a primitive type or a Domain model type. They will never be of any other type. This guarantees that our Domain layer is not coupled with any external dependency.

This wraps up the contents of the feature's Domain implementation. We have covered every component in detail. Next, let us consider testing this code.

What should we test? As mentioned earlier, our usecases could have unit test coverage. Using TDD here would be trivial. We will take a look at how a usecase test would look in *Chapter 8, Unit Testing*.

The easiest order in which to implement the Domain layer of a feature is as follows:

1. Domain models

2. Repository interfaces (and their dummy implementations)

3. Usecases

This way, you avoid having dangling code at any point. You could compile your code throughout the implementation.

Domain exceptions can be added at any point. These exceptions can be thrown by repository implementations in the Data layer to communicate any known exceptional events.

This concludes our Domain implementation for a feature. We will look at the Presentation layer next.

Conclusion

You should now have a clear understanding of how our Clean Architecture Domain layer is built. We have covered all the key files, including the UseCase interface, the UseCaseExecutor class, different types of usecases, Domain models, and repository interfaces. We discussed how the Domain layer, as the innermost one, is protected from external constraints and changes.

In the next chapter, we will venture into the realm of Presentation. We will explore this layer, its components, and how it interacts with the Domain layer.

Points to remember

There are a few important rules that I suggest you keep in mind when implementing your Domain layer:

- **Start with the Domain**: When implementing a feature, always start by implementing the Domain layer.

- **The Domain layer is simple**: Keeping this layer as simple as possible helps us protect it from changing frequently.

- **Isolate the domain**: The Domain layer is our innermost layer. Protect it from external constraints such as API details or UI changes.

- **Each usecase has a dedicated repository interface**: Make sure that the repository caters to the specific usecase.

- **Remember testing**: always write your code with tests in mind. Remember that you would likely want to unit test your usecases.

Join our Discord space

Join our Discord workspace for latest updates, offers, tech happenings around the world, new releases, and sessions with the authors:

https://discord.bpbonline.com

CHAPTER 4

The Presentation Layer

The job of the presenter is to orchestrate, not to calculate.

- Michael Feathers

Introduction

In the previous chapter, we learned about the Domain layer and its responsibility as the core of our app. In this chapter, we will explore the code that lives in the Presentation layer of our Clean Architecture project. The Presentation layer depends solely on the Domain layer. We will dissect every file in this layer, discuss its role, and see how it fits into the grand design.

Structure

In this chapter, we will cover the following topics:

- The Presentation layer
- The Presentation architecture code
- The Presentation feature code

Objectives

This chapter aims to give you an understanding of how to implement the layer between the Domain layer and the **user interface (UI)** layer. The responsibility for bridging the gap between these layers is covered by the Presentation layer. We will go over its implementation details, going over every key class in this layer and its responsibilities. By the end of this chapter, you should know how to implement the Presentation layer in a Clean Architecture app.

The Presentation layer

With the Domain layer implemented, we can proceed to work on our Presentation layer. The Presentation layer is responsible for orchestrating the interaction between the UI layer and the Domain layer. It translates user intents to Domain usecases and conveys the output of these usecases back to the user interface for presentation to the user.

It is important to distinguish between the Presentation layer and the UI layer. The Presentation layer of our implementation is not user-facing. We will cover the UI layer, which is exposed to the user, in the next chapter.

To understand the implementation details of the Presentation layer, let us start with the Presentation architecture code. We will then continue to explore the Presentation code of a feature as a practical example.

The Presentation architecture code

In *Figure 4.1*, we can see the structure of the architecture part of the Presentation layer. The code for the architecture Presentation goes into the **architecture:presentation** Gradle module.

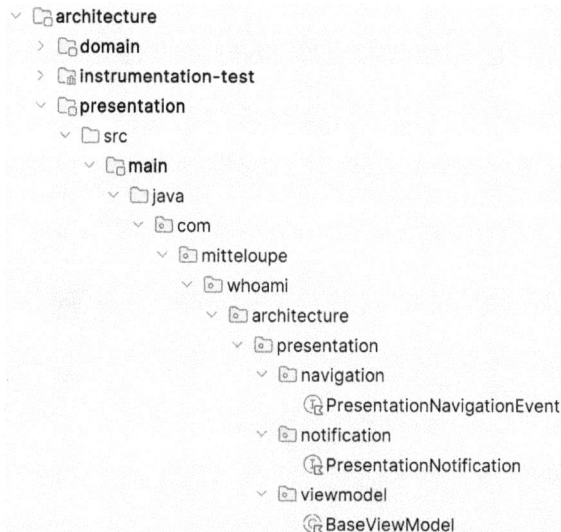

Figure 4.1: The structure of the architecture Presentation module

As mentioned in *Chapter 2, Clean Architecture Principles*, our Presentation layer, much like the Domain layer, should not depend on the Android SDK. Unfortunately, this is not possible if we want to use Google's Architecture Components or Hilt. It is for that reason that in this edition of the book, I propose that you *use neither the Architecture Components nor Hilt in your Presentation layer*. As you will see, this layer is reasonably simple and does not require additional libraries. It is important to remember that the Presentation layer should be stable enough not to require updating when the UI requirements (or the Android SDK that is used by it) change.

The Presentation layer informs the UI layer of state changes via state updates. Depending on the architectural pattern that we choose (MVP or MVVM, for example), the actual way in which this is achieved will vary. Throughout this book, we will default to MVVM and rely on the **Flow** interface and implementations from the Kotlin Coroutines library. To be more specific, we will communicate view changes via three channels: the **view state**, the **notifications**, and the **navigation events**.

All three channels are instances of the **MutableStateFlow** class. The **view state** emits information such as whether we are currently loading data and what data to present to the user.

Note: **Remember that the viewmodel is not responsible for maintaining or storing the current view state. Once the viewmodel reports the state to the View, its job is complete. This is important because data should have a single source of truth, and the only real sources of truth are the UI as presented to the user and the data that was obtained from the Data layer.**

Figure 4.2 demonstrates how the view state ends up getting presented to the user:

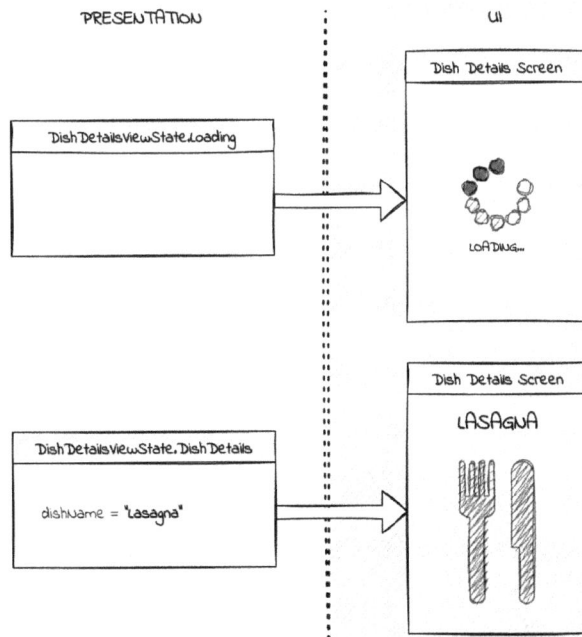

Figure 4.2: *The view state model as interpreted by the UI*

Next, we have the **notifications** and **navigation events** channels. Both channels represent events that must only be consumed once. This is important, and we can see why by imagining their usage:

1. We are on Screen 1.

2. We tap a button to navigate to the next screen, which we will call Screen 2.

3. The viewmodel updates the **navigationEvent** to take us to Screen 2.

4. From Screen 2, we navigate back to Screen 1.

5. Upon loading Screen 1, we observe the navigation state for the screen.

If, in *step 5*, the navigation event contained the same value that it contained in *step 3*, we would immediately navigate back to Screen 2. Therefore, the navigation event and notification states must reset once consumed.

The **MutableSharedFlow** implementation of the **Flow** interface that we chose for our channels has an implicit default replay value of 0 and achieves precisely what we need.

Let us see how it all translates into the **BaseViewModel** abstract class:

BaseViewModel.kt

```
1.    package com.mitteloupe.whoami.architecture.presentation.viewmodel
2.
3.    [imports...]
4.
5.    abstract class BaseViewModel<VIEW_STATE : Any,
6.        NOTIFICATION : PresentationNotification>(
7.        private val useCaseExecutor: UseCaseExecutor
8.    ) {
```

While the **BaseViewModel** implementation presented in this book is minimalistic, there is not really any need to extend it considerably. I have successfully used very similar variations to this one in projects that were quite feature-rich and complex.

On *lines 5* and *6*, we define our generic type parameters. First is the **VIEW_STATE**. Its only constraint is that it cannot be **null**. This is expressed using the **Any** class. Implementations of **BaseViewModel** will set this to be the view state data type for the view that they drive.

The second generic parameter is the **NOTIFICATION** one. It, too, has only one constraint: it must be an extension of **PresentationNotification**. **PresentationNotification** is an empty interface. **BaseViewModel** implementations will usually set **NOTIFICATION** to a sealed class (or a sealed interface) containing all the possible notification types for their corresponding views.

On *line 7* of our **BaseViewModel** we pass in a **UseCaseExecutor** instance. We discussed this class when we covered the Domain layer in *Chapter 3, The Domain Layer*.

Let us continue with our **BaseViewModel**:

BaseViewModel.kt (continued)

```
 9.    val viewState: Flow<VIEW_STATE>
10.        field = MutableSharedFlow()
11.
12.    val notification: Flow<NOTIFICATION>
13.        field = MutableSharedFlow()
14.
15.    val navigationEvent: Flow<PresentationNavigationEvent>
16.        field = MutableSharedFlow()
```

As discussed earlier, the view can observe the **viewState** (*line 9*), the **notification** (*line 12*), and the **navigationEvent** (*line 15*) states. Now that we know what view states we support (i.e., those declared in the **VIEW_STATE** implementation), it is time to expose those states to the UI layer for observation (*lines 9* and *10*). On *line 10*, you will note that our **viewState** holds a **MutableSharedFlow** object and does not retain any state. This is important and intentional. We do not want our viewmodel to become a secondary source of truth.

Our **viewState**, **notification**, and **navigationEvent** fields need to be mutable for us to be able to update them. However, we do not want this mutability to be exposed outside of our viewmodel class because that would allow the view (and other classes) to manipulate the state. We therefore use explicit backing fields (**field = ...** on *lines 10, 13,* and *16*). By using explicit backing fields, we ensure that subclasses can only use the provided internal functions, which we will explore as follows, to update the state.

The **navigationEvent** (*line 15*) is worth a quick overview. Navigation events will usually be sealed interfaces and will implement the **PresentationNavigationEvent** interface:

PresentationNavigationEvent.kt

```
1.    package com.mitteloupe.whoami.architecture.presentation.navigation
2.
3.    interface PresentationNavigationEvent {
4.        object Back : PresentationNavigationEvent
5.    }
```

The **PresentationNavigationEvent** interface is useful for cases where we want to support app-wide, or global events, such as the user navigating back. Other similar events could be the user navigating to the help interface, the home screen, or even exiting the app. Having said that, be very, *very* cautious about adding destinations here. Only add destinations that you *know* that *every* screen in your app will support. Do not let it grow out of control. You can always compose several interfaces to achieve a similar solution that will be less bloated. It is perfectly okay to leave **PresentationNavigationEvent** as an empty interface.

Let us get back to the **BaseViewModel** class and see the internal functions that I mentioned earlier for updating state:

BaseViewModel.kt (continued)

```
17.    protected fun updateViewState(newState: VIEW_STATE) {
18.        MainScope().launch {
19.            viewState.emit(newState)
20.        }
21.    }
22.
23.    protected fun notify(notification: NOTIFICATION) {
24.        MainScope().launch {
25.            this@BaseViewModel.notification.emit(notification)
26.        }
27.    }
28.
29.    protected fun emitNavigationEvent(
30.        navigationEvent: PresentationNavigationEvent
31.    ) {
32.        MainScope().launch {
33.            this@BaseViewModel.navigationEvent.emit(navigationEvent)
34.        }
35.    }
```

Here, you can see all the internal functions that the **BaseViewModel** class exposes to its subclasses. To update the view state, subclasses would call **updateViewState** with a brand-new state (*lines 17* to *21*). To present a notification, we would call **notify** (*lines 23* to *27*). Lastly, to report a navigation intent, we would call **emitNavigationEvent** (*lines 29* to *35*), providing a **PresentationNavigationEvent** instance.

The last two functions in our **BaseViewModel** are protected operator extension functions. They expose a mechanism for subclasses of **BaseViewModel** to execute **UseCase** instances using the **useCaseExecutor** instance. Refer to the following code:

BaseViewModel.kt (continued)

```
36.    protected operator fun <OUTPUT> UseCase<Unit, OUTPUT>.invoke(
37.            onResult: (OUTPUT) -> Unit = {},
38.            onException: (DomainException) -> Unit = {}
39.        ) {
40.            useCaseExecutor.execute(this, onResult, onException)
41.        }
42.
```

```
43.       protected operator fun <INPUT, OUTPUT> UseCase<INPUT, OUTPUT>
44.           .invoke(
45.               value: INPUT,
46.               onResult: (OUTPUT) -> Unit = {},
47.               onException: (DomainException) -> Unit = {}
48.           ) {
49.               useCaseExecutor.execute(this, value, onResult, onException)
50.           }
51.   }
```

With the **BaseViewModel** done, we have completed the overview of the Presentation architecture implementation. Next, we will see how a feature leverages the code that was introduced so far to provide its Presentation layer.

The Presentation feature code

Figure 4.3 shows the structure of the Presentation layer of the home feature. The code for the home feature Presentation implementation goes into the **home:presentation** module.

```
home
  data
  domain
  presentation
    src
      main
        java
          com
            mitteloupe
              whoami
                home
                  presentation
                    mapper
                      ConnectionDetailsDomainMapper
                      ConnectionDetailsPresentationMapper
                      ExceptionPresentationMapper
                    model
                      ErrorPresentationModel
                      HomePresentationNotification
                      HomeViewState
                    navigation
                      HomePresentationNavigationEvent
                    viewmodel
                      HomeViewModel
```

Figure 4.3: *The structure of the home feature's Presentation module*

When we focused on the Domain layer, we implemented a usecase for the home screen. In this section, we will continue with the same screen. Given the home screen, it is safe to assume that we have a **HomeViewModel** driving that screen. The viewmodel is the main class in the Presentation layer, and a snippet of the **HomeViewModel** may look like:

HomeViewModel.kt (snippet)

```
1.    package com.mitteloupe.whoami.home.presentation.viewmodel
2.
3.    [imports...]
4.
5.    class HomeViewModel(...) :
6.        BaseViewModel<HomeViewState, HomePresentationNotification>(
7.            useCaseExecutor
8.        ) {
9.        ...
39.        fun onViewHistoryAction() {
40.            emitNavigationEvent(OnViewHistory)
41.        }
```

If we start by breaking down the package name of the **HomeViewModel.kt** file (*line 1*), we will note that right after the app package prefix, we have the feature name (**home**) followed by the layer name (**presentation**). Finally, viewmodel files go into the **viewmodel** package.

On *line 5*, we see the name of our viewmodel class. **ViewModel** classes are named after the screen that they control (**Home**, in our case), suffixed by **ViewModel**. Note that despite sharing its name with the feature, **Home** in this context is a *screen* name, not a *feature* name. This distinction is important because a feature may have more than one screen.

Note: **An important thing to notice in this edition of the book is the omission of the Hilt @ViewModel annotation. As mentioned earlier, we are not using Hilt to avoid coupling the Presentation layer with Android dependencies. There is a second reason: to reduce the dependency on Hilt (or Dagger, for that matter), I advise you to avoid constructor injection where possible. This would make migration to an alternative dependency injection solution less painful if you ever wanted to consider it.**

To understand the generic types that are specified in our implementation of the **BaseViewModel** (*line 6*), we need to recall **BaseViewModel**. Note that the two generic types, in order, are the view state sealed interface (**HomeViewState**) and the notifications sealed interface (**HomePresentationNotification**). Both have names that are prefixed with the screen name (**Home**) and suffixed with their type, **ViewState** and **Notification**, respectively.

On *line 7*, we pass the **UseCaseExecutor** instance to the **BaseViewModel** superclass.

Lines 10 to *38* were omitted, but do not worry, we will get back to them shortly.

On *lines 39* to *41*, we have the **onViewHistoryAction()** function. This is an interface for the view to inform us that the user has requested to see the location history, probably by tapping a button (although the actual mechanism is entirely up to the UI). As it describes an event, the function name is prefixed with **on**, followed by the description of the event using the infinitive form of the verb *view* and relevant subject nouns (**ViewHistory**), and suffixed with **Action**.

Note: Once again, it is important to note that we do not use terms such as click or tap. These are UI terms. Our presentation is agnostic of such implementation details. Whether you tap, swipe, or use a voice command to indicate that you want to see the location history is irrelevant for the Presentation layer. At this layer, we only care about the user's intention, which is to access the history of locations. The UI is responsible for providing the user with the mechanism with which to perform that action, as we will see when we get to the next chapter and cover the UI layer.

Once the request to see the connection history event fires off, the **HomeViewModel** class determines the next course of action. In this case, it informs the view that a navigation event occurred by emitting an **OnViewHistory** object (see *line 11*). As features are decoupled, the home feature does not know about the connection history feature. It therefore does not know how this navigation event will be processed. It only knows that we should be navigating away from the home screen and that the trigger for the navigation is the user requesting the history of connections. We will discuss this in greater detail when we discuss navigation in *Chapter 7, Dependency Injection and Navigation*.

Let us get back to the home screen. In the previous snippet of **HomeViewModel**, we omitted the constructor parameters. Let us explore them now:

HomeViewModel.kt (snippet)
```
7.    private val getConnectionDetailsUseCase: GetConnectionDetailsUseCase,
8.    private val connectionStateToPresentationMapper:
9.        ConnectionStateToPresentationMapper,
10.   private val saveConnectionDetailsUseCase: SaveConnectionDetailsUseCase,
11.   private val connectionDetailsToDomainMapper:
12.       ConnectionDetailsToDomainMapper,
13.   private val exceptionToPresentationMapper:
14.       ExceptionToPresentationMapper,
15.   useCaseExecutor: UseCaseExecutor
```

We start by providing our viewmodel with instances of **GetConnectionDetailsUseCase** and **ConnectionStateToPresentationMapper**. You should recognize the usecase class from the previous chapter, where we discussed the feature's Domain layer. We have not yet discussed **ConnectionStateToPresentationMapper**.

As our implementation of Clean Architecture relies on strict layer separation, our UI has no access to the Domain layer and Domain models. For this reason, it is the responsibility of the Presentation layer to convert (or map) Domain models to Presentation ones, which the UI can access. This conversion is done using **mappers**.

Mappers are a crucial part of our Clean Architecture implementation and appear in every layer but the Domain. This makes sense when we think about the Dependency Rule. Every layer could have its own models, which may need to be translated into or from models in other layers. Every layer but the Domain layer, that is, since it does not depend on any other layer.

With this understanding of mappers in mind, here is the code for **ConnectionDetailsToPresentationMapper**:

ConnectionDetailsToPresentationMapper.kt

```kotlin
1.   package com.mitteloupe.whoami.home.presentation.mapper
2.
3.   [imports...]
4.
5.   class ConnectionDetailsToPresentationMapper(
6.       private val exceptionToPresentationMapper: ExceptionToPresentationMapper
7.   ) {
8.       fun toPresentation(
9.           connectionDetails: ConnectionDetailsDomainModel
10.      ) = when (connectionDetails) {
11.          is Connected -> HomeViewState.Connected(
12.              ipAddress = connectionDetails.ipAddress,
13.              city = connectionDetails.city,
14.              region = connectionDetails.region,
15.              countryCode = connectionDetails.countryCode,
16.              geolocation = connectionDetails.geolocation,
17.              internetServiceProviderName =
18.                  connectionDetails.internetServiceProviderName,
19.              postCode = connectionDetails.postCode,
20.              timeZone = connectionDetails.timeZone
21.          )
22.
23.          Disconnected -> HomeViewState.Disconnected
24.          Unset -> HomeViewState.Loading
25.          is Error -> {
26.              HomeViewState.Error(
27.                  exceptionToPresentationMapper
28.                      .toPresentation(connectionDetails.exception)
29.              )
30.          }
31.      }
32.  }
```

Starting from the package name (*line 1*), we can see the Presentation mappers live within the **presentation** package of our app under the feature name (**home**) and in a **mapper** sub-package.

The class name for mappers is usually constructed by taking the name of the input model, stripping away the layer suffix (so, in this case, we take **ConnectionDetailsDomainModel**, strip away **DomainModel**, and we end up with **ConnectionDetails**), and adding the target layer (**Presentation** for this Presentation mapper) and the word **Mapper**. In cases where more than one input argument is required, such as an index, we replace **Mapper** with **Resolver**, as mappers are expected to have a one-to-one input-to-output ratio.

> Note: **An interesting implementation detail to note is how mappers can be nested (line 6). This makes testing our mappers much easier by reducing the number of permutations that we need to worry about. It also simplifies the implementation of each individual mapper.**

Mappers always have a single public function. The function name indicates the direction of mapping and is prefixed with **to**. In this case, we are mapping to a Presentation model, and so the appropriate function name would be **toPresentation**. We pass in the input model as an argument to this public function and name it by using the class name with the layer name suffix omitted: **ConnectionDetailsDomainModel** becomes **connectionDetails**.

Different fields are mapped differently. *Lines 12* to *20* are examples of a common pattern in our mappers. Quite often, values are mapped as-is. This is common with primitive types. *Lines 27* and *28* demonstrate how we use a nested mapper to map a custom type from our Domain layer to an appropriate Presentation model.

Now that we have explored a mapper, let us go back to our **HomeViewModel**. In our first viewmodel snippet, we looked at its constructor. Let us take another look at it:

HomeViewModel.kt (snippet)

```
5.     class HomeViewModel(...) :
6.         BaseViewModel<HomeViewState, HomePresentationNotification>(...) {
```

On *line 6*, we see the types that we provide to the **BaseViewModel** (highlighted in **bold**). To avoid confusion, note that, unlike everywhere else in this book, we are revisiting a line of code that was introduced earlier in a reformatted fashion. Let us start with the first generic type argument, the view state, which is a **sealed interface**:

HomeViewState.kt

```
1.     package com.mitteloupe.whoami.home.presentation.model
2.
3.     sealed interface HomeViewState {
4.         data object Loading : HomeViewState
```

```
 5.
 6.       data class Connected(
 7.           val ipAddress: String,
 8.           val city: String?,
 9.           val region: String?,
10.           val countryCode: String?,
11.           val geolocation: String?,
12.           val internetServiceProviderName: String?,
13.           val postCode: String?,
14.           val timeZone: String?
15.       ) : HomeViewState
16.
17.       data object Disconnected : HomeViewState
18.
19.       data class Error(val error: ErrorPresentationModel) : HomeViewState
20.   }
```

> **Note:** In the first edition of this book, I suggested using a data class for the view state. Unfortunately, this encouraged holding state in the viewmodel. The approach suggested in this edition leaves state resolution to the view. This makes more sense because the view always knows what state it is currently in. It is the source of truth for that information.

Starting from the first line, we can see that the view state is stored under the same feature package as the viewmodel class (**com.mitteloupe.whoami.home**). However, while the viewmodel resides in the **viewmodel** package, the view state resides in **model**.

Next, we have the sealed interface name (**HomeViewState**, line 3). Like the viewmodel class, the view state sealed interface is named after the *screen* (not the *feature*) whose state it holds. Since this is the view state of the home screen, its name is prefixed with **Home**. View states are always suffixed with **ViewState** to make them easy to recognize. Following these rules, our view state is named **HomeViewState**.

Since the view state is a sealed interface, it has a closed set of states. Some of its states include some fields, such as the **Connected** state (*lines 6 to 15*) and the **Error** state (*line 19*). Other states require no additional information, like the **Loading** state (*line 4*) and the **Disconnected** one (*line 17*).

On *lines 7 to 14*, we have the fields of the **Connected** state class. None of the fields has a default value because we expect them all to be provided when the state is instantiated. The second thing to note about the **HomeViewState** states is the naming of the states. Let us look at **Loading**, for example. Note that it does not specify *how* the state is presented to the user. It does not mention spinners, skeleton animations, or any other form of progress indicators. It only indicates *what* state is presented to the user, in this case, a loading state. The *how* is left to the discretion of the View.

A word about nullability. Generally, I try to avoid **null** values. They implicitly describe a state. Discovering whether that state is intentional or not requires digging through the code. A preferable alternative, in this case, could be a **sealed interface** or a **sealed class** with **Set** and **Unset** states. I opted for **null** here to save some trees (or bytes, if you are reading the digital version).

Here is how such a class might look:

```kotlin
sealed interface CityName {
    data class Set(val name: String) : CityName

    data object Unset : CityName
}
```

Looking back at **HomeViewModel**, the next generic argument is **HomePresentationNotification**. This is a sealed interface that contains the different types of notifications we may want to present to the user. As notifications are mostly used to indicate failures, we will discuss them in depth in *Chapter 11, Failures and Exceptions*.

With the **HomeViewModel** constructor out of the way, let us proceed to explore the body of the class:

HomeViewModel.kt (snippet)

```kotlin
9.    fun onEnter() {
10.        updateViewState(Loading)
11.        fetchConnectionDetails()
12.    }
13.
14.    ...
15.
47.    private fun fetchConnectionDetails() {
48.        getConnectionDetailsUseCase(
49.            onResult = ::presentConnectionDetails,
50.            onException = ::presentError
51.        )
52.    }
53.
54.    private fun presentConnectionDetails(
55.        connectionDetails: ConnectionDetailsDomainModel
56.    ) {
57.        updateViewState(
58.            connectionDetailsPresentationMapper
59.                .toPresentation(connectionDetails)
```

```
60.        )
61.    }
```

Once again, this is a partial view of the file, meant to help us cover relevant aspects of it. We now go back to *line 9*, which I left out earlier.

Since we want to know when the view is entered (or navigated to), we introduce the **onEnter()** function (*lines 9 to 12*). We expect the view to call this function as soon as it can, and *only once* every time the user enters the screen. Just like we discussed before, the function name describes an event and so starts with **on** followed by the event that occurred as a verb in its infinitive form: **Enter**.

As soon as the **onEnter()** function is called, we update the view state so that the view can present the loading state (*line 10*). We then obtain the current connection details by calling **fetchConnectionDetails()** (*line 11*). The **fetch** prefix is used to suggest that this can potentially be a long-running operation, as opposed to, for example, a **get**.

The **fetchConnectionDetails** function executes the **GetConnectionDetailsUseCase** instance's **execute** function using the **UseCaseExecutor**. This is done under the hood in **BaseViewModel**. This usecase requires no input, so we only need to pass in references to the **presentConnectionDetails(ConnectionDetailsDomainModel)** function for presenting a successful result and the **presentError(DomainException)** for reporting errors (*lines 48 to 51*). I purposely omitted the handling of errors and exceptions at this point, as this is a broad topic, and it will be covered in *Chapter 11, Failures and Exceptions*.

When the usecase executes successfully, **presentConnectionDetails** (*lines 54 to 61*) will get called with the connection details for the current connection. In this function, we map the returned Domain model, **connectionDetails**, to a Presentation model using **connectionDetailsPresentationMapper** (*lines 58 and 59*). We then update the view state with the returned state on *line 57*.

Before we wrap up the Presentation layer section, I would like to discuss the implementation process briefly.

Once the Domain layer is implemented, the development of the Presentation and Data layers can proceed simultaneously. Neither layer affects the other directly, so neither blocks the development of the other.

The order in which I would recommend implementing the Presentation layer is as follows:

1. Presentation models. This includes the view state file, Presentation notification classes, and PresentationDestination subclasses.

2. Domain to Presentation and Presentation to Domain mappers.

3. Viewmodels.

Consider taking a **test-driven development** (**TDD**) approach. If you do not want to use TDD, at the very least make sure to wrap up your implementation by writing unit tests for all your mappers (parameterized tests would be a good idea) and, most importantly, your viewmodel.

With the Presentation layer ready, we can proceed to implement the UI layer. This will be the topic of the next chapter.

Conclusion

This chapter should have given you a comprehensive view of the Presentation layer code. We discussed viewmodels, Presentation models, and mappers that translate Domain models to Presentation ones and vice versa. You should now know how to implement the code that the UI layer can be built on top of.

In the next chapter, we will move on to the UI layer. We will then be able to have a working app, at least from the user-facing aspect.

Points to remember

In this chapter, we discussed the Presentation layer in code. These are a few key takeaways:

- **The Presentation layer relies on the Domain layer**: To implement the Presentation layer, we should start with an already existing Domain layer. The Presentation layer mostly deals with Domain usecases.

- **Think of the user, not the UI**: The Presentation should not care about how the UI is implemented. Think of user actions and intents without UI details. Buttons, Views, and composables are all off-limits. We do not want to have to rewrite our Presentation when the UI implementation changes.

- **The Presentation should be stateless**: The Presentation layer is a middle layer. It is never the source of truth; true data always originates from a datasource or the UI. Having more than one source of truth is a recipe for a synchronization disaster.

- **Again, remember testing**: viewmodels should always be unit tested, with no exception. Most mappers can easily be tested, too.

Join our Discord space

Join our Discord workspace for latest updates, offers, tech happenings around the world, new releases, and sessions with the authors:

https://discord.bpbonline.com

CHAPTER 5

The UI Layer

The best interface is no interface.

- Luke Wroblewski

Introduction

Apps are not very interesting if the user cannot interact with them. So far, we have focused on the foundational parts of the app and have not exposed anything to the user. In this chapter, this is about to change. The UI layer is user-facing. This means that it will be responsible for presenting information to the user and letting the user interact with the app.

Any libraries or SDKs that are used in this chapter were chosen for the sake of demonstration, and none are binding. You are encouraged to choose any libraries or SDKs that work best for you. In fact, that is one of the reasons that we are using Clean Architecture in the first place: it should be easy for you to postpone the choice of dependencies and easily replace them later if you so choose.

Structure

In this chapter, we will cover the following topics:

- Role of the UI layer

- UI architecture code

- UI feature code

Objectives

The UI is the part of the app that the user interacts with. This chapter will explain how we should approach the UI layer and connect it to the Presentation layer. When you finish reading this chapter, you should be able to implement a functional app using Clean Architecture. It may not have a working Data layer, but it will look right and will fundamentally work.

Role of the UI layer

Android apps are designed to serve the user. To do so, they should either provide the user with information or take the user's input. Most apps do both. The user can interact with an app in many ways. They could be tapping away. They could be swiping, pinching, or using other gestures. They could be using their microphone as an interface, or even their camera. They can consume data by watching the screen, listening to the device speaker, or feeling the device vibrating. All of these and more serve as the user interface. In most cases, there is more than one way to interact with the user, and quite often, the interface gets updated. Managing the interface is the responsibility of the UI layer.

For our **WhoAmI** app, I will demonstrate a UI implementation using Jetpack Compose. However, different UI implementations can comfortably co-exist in a Clean Architecture project. In fact, the GitHub repository example demonstrates a hybrid solution with Android fragments in addition to Jetpack Compose. We will take the home screen as an example, which is a composable.

Remember that it is the role of the UI layer to protect the Presentation layer (and through it the Domain layer and all other code in the app) from UI-specific changes. We should be able to implement **Activity** classes or Compose screens by changing the UI layer alone. None of the other layers of code in our project should be affected by the change.

Following the pattern that we established earlier, we will start by looking into the architecture implementation.

The UI architecture code

Before we start breaking our implementation down, let us take a quick look at the UI architecture module structure, as shown in *Figure 5.1*:

```
∨ ⌷ architecture
    › ⌷ domain
    › ⌷ instrumentation-test
    › ⌷ presentation
    › ⌷ presentation-test
    ∨ ⌷ ui
        ∨ ⌷ src
            ∨ ⌷ main
                ∨ ⌷ java
                    ∨ ⌷ com
                        ∨ ⌷ mitteloupe
                            ∨ ⌷ whoami
                                ∨ ⌷ architecture
                                    ∨ ⌷ ui
                                        ∨ ⌷ binder
                                                 ⌦ ViewStateBinder
                                        ∨ ⌷ navigation
                                            ∨ ⌷ exception
                                                     ⌦ UnhandledNavigationException
                                            ∨ ⌷ mapper
                                                     ⌦ NavigationEventDestinationMapper
                                            ∨ ⌷ model
                                                     ⌦ UiDestination
                                        ∨ ⌷ notification
                                            ∨ ⌷ mapper
                                                     ⌦ NotificationUiMapper
                                            ∨ ⌷ model
                                                     ⌦ UiNotification
                                        ∨ ⌷ view
                                                 ⌦ BaseComposeHolder
                                                 ⌦ BaseFragment
                                                 ⌦ ScreenEnterObserver.kt
                                                 ⌦ ViewsProvider
```

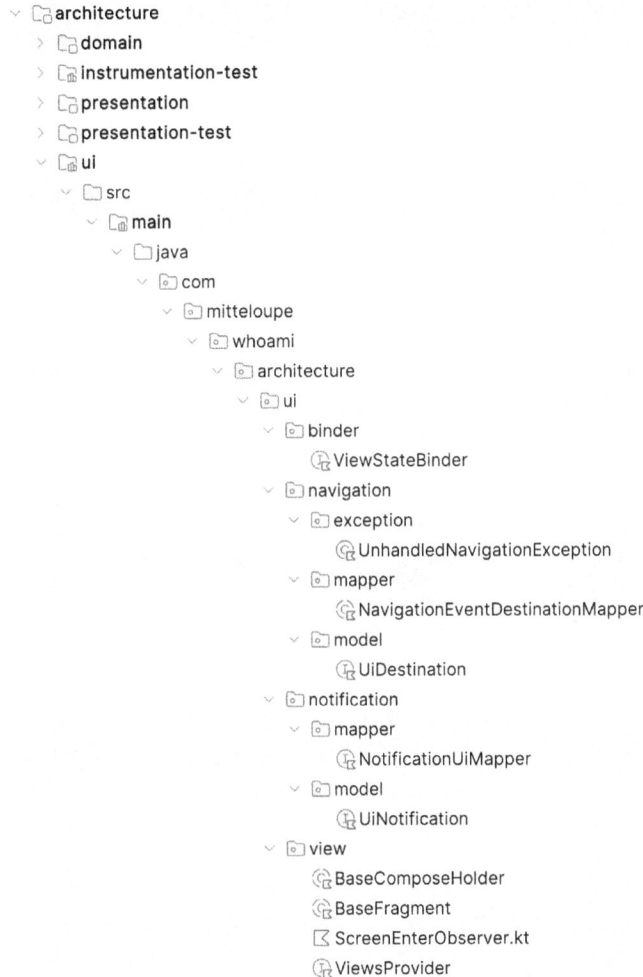

Figure 5.1: The structure of our UI architecture module

The UI architecture Gradle module is **architecture:ui**. The key class in our Compose implementation is the **BaseComposeHolder**. This class reduces our boilerplate code considerably by handling notifications and navigation of Compose screens. It also serves as the foundation for our alternative to dependency injection, which Compose offers very little support for otherwise, at least at the time of writing. We will start by covering the constructor of **BaseComposeHolder**:

BaseComposeHolder.kt

```
1.    package com.mitteloupe.whoami.architecture.ui.view
2.
3.    [imports...]
4.
```

```
 5.    abstract class BaseComposeHolder<
 6.        VIEW_STATE : Any,
 7.        NOTIFICATION : PresentationNotification
 8.    >(
 9.        private val viewModel: BaseViewModel<VIEW_STATE, NOTIFICATION>,
10.        private val navigationMapper:
11.            NavigationEventDestinationMapper<PresentationNavigationEvent>,
12.        private val notificationMapper: NotificationUiMapper<NOTIFICATION>
13.    ) {
```

Starting from the first line, we can see that the **BaseComposeHolder.kt** file belongs in the **architecture** package, under the **ui** layer package, and the **view** subpackage. It is important to remember that view in this context refers to the view in the MVVM pattern, not the Android **View** system.

The **BaseComposeHolder** abstract class has two generic types (*lines 6 and 7*), reflecting those of the Presentation layer's **BaseViewModel** class: **VIEW_STATE**, a non-null type representing, as the name suggests, the view state model type, and **NOTIFICATION**, which extends **PresentationNotification** and represents the types of notifications that the view can handle.

Let us look at the constructor parameters. First, we have the view model (*line 9*), whose generic types are the same as those of the **BaseComposeHolder** class. The second parameter is a navigation mapper (*lines 10 and 11*), used to map **PresentationNavigationEvent** instances to UI destinations. The third and final parameter is a notifications mapper. Similar to the navigation mapper, its role is to map Presentation notifications to UI ones.

Now that we have seen the constructor of the **BaseComposeHolder** class, let us dig deeper and explore the body of the **BaseComposeHolder** class:

BaseComposeHolder.kt (continued)

```
14.    @Composable
15.    fun ViewModelObserver(navController: NavController) {
16.        viewModel.notification.collectAsState(initial = null)
17.            .value?.let { notificationValue ->
18.                Notifier(notification = notificationValue)
19.            }
20.
21.        viewModel.navigationEvent.collectAsState(initial = null)
22.            .value?.let { navigationValue ->
23.                Navigator(navigationValue, navController)
24.            }
25.    }
26.
```

```
27.    @Composable
28.    private fun Notifier(notification: NOTIFICATION) {
29.        LaunchedEffect(notification) {
30.            notificationMapper.toUi(notification).present()
31.        }
32.    }
33.
34.    @Composable
35.    private fun Navigator(
36.        navigation: PresentationNavigationEvent,
37.        navController: NavController
38.    ) {
39.        LaunchedEffect(navigation) {
40.            navigationMapper.toUi(navigation).navigate(navController)
41.        }
42.    }
```

The body of **BaseComposeHolder** contains three primary composables: **ViewModelObserver**, **Notifier**, and **Navigator**. Out of these three functions, **ViewModelObserver** is the only public one, designed to be called from composable screens that are driven by viewmodels.

The **ViewModelObserver** function is responsible for observing navigation and notification events and passing them on to the **Notifier** and **Navigator** composables, respectively. Each one of these two private composables maps its input Presentation model to a UI one and executes its primary function. We will discuss the UI models and their public interfaces next.

First, let us take a look at the **UiNotification** interface:

UiNotification.kt

```
1.    package com.mitteloupe.whoami.architecture.ui.notification.model
2.
3.    fun interface UiNotification {
4.        fun present()
5.    }
```

If we start with the first line, we can see that the **UiNotification** interface is located under the **architecture** feature package, then the **ui** layer package, and finally the **notification. model** sub-package.

Implementations of the **UiNotification** functional interface must implement the **present()** function (*line 4*). The implementation is expected to notify the user of the relevant event. Possible implementations could include a system notification, a toast, a sound, or vibration, for example. Of course, a combination of methods is also possible.

The other interface we should discuss is **UiDestination**, shown as follows:

UiDestination.kt

```
1.    package com.mitteloupe.whoami.architecture.ui.navigation.model
2.
3.    import androidx.navigation.NavController
4.
5.    fun interface UiDestination {
6.        fun navigate(navController: NavController)
7.    }
```

The **UiDestination** functional interface is very similar to the **UiNotification** one. On *line 1*, we can see that it, too, resides under the **architecture** feature package, under the **ui** layer package, and then under the **navigation.model** sub-package.

Like its notifications counterpart, the **UiDestination** interface requires its implementations to implement a single function. In this case, it is **navigate(NavController)** (*line 6*).

Navigation often requires an instance of **NavController**. The navigation controller is usually unavailable during mapper construction. For this reason, we provide it to the **navigate** function. If you do not intend to use the navigation components in your navigation, you can omit this parameter.

Implementations of the **UiDestination** interface are responsible for taking the user to the destination that they represent when **navigate** is called. This could be navigating to a different screen or launching a different app, for example.

To produce an implementation of **UiNotification** or **UiDestination** from their Presentation layer counterparts, a mapper is needed. We have seen these mappers in action in **BaseComposeHolder**. Let us break down the code of these mappers, starting with **NavigationEventDestinationMapper**:

NavigationEventDestinationMapper.kt

```
1.    package com.mitteloupe.whoami.architecture.ui.navigation.mapper
2.
3.    [imports...]
4.
5.    abstract class NavigationEventDestinationMapper<
6.        in EVENT : PresentationNavigationEvent
7.    >(private val kotlinClass: KClass<EVENT>) {
8.        fun toUi(
9.            navigationEvent: PresentationNavigationEvent
10.       ): UiDestination = when {
```

```
11.              kotlinClass.isInstance(navigationEvent) ->
12.                  mapTypedEvent(navigationEvent as EVENT)
13.
14.          else -> mapGenericEvent(navigationEvent) ?:
15.              throw UnhandledNavigationException(navigationEvent)
16.      }
17.
18.      protected abstract fun mapTypedEvent(
19.          navigationEvent: EVENT
20.      ): UiDestination
21.
22.      protected open fun mapGenericEvent(
23.          navigationEvent: PresentationNavigationEvent
24.      ): UiDestination? = null
25.  }
```

Starting from the top, we can see that the navigation mapper resides under the same root package as the **UiDestination** interface: **com.mitteloupe.whiami.architecture. ui.navigation**. The difference is that **UiDestination** is under the **model** package, while the mapper is under **mapper**.

The **NavigationEventDestinationMapper** abstract class has one generic type (*line 6*), which is an implementation of **PresentationNavigationEvent**. This type determines the type of input that this mapper supports. We visited **PresentationNavigationEvent** when we covered the Presentation layer in *Chapter 4, The Presentation Layer*.

The constructor of our mapper requires a Kotlin class of the type that is supported by the mapper implementation (*line 7*). This allows us, as we will soon see, to handle feature-specific destinations as closed sets. This, in turn, lets us write exhaustive **when** statements.

Like all mappers, this navigation mapper only exposes a single function: **toUi(PresentationNavigationEvent)** (*lines 8 to 16*). This function breaks down the handling of destinations into two:

- Destinations that are of the defined generic type.

- All other destination types.

Destinations of the first group are passed to the **mapTypedEvent(EVENT)** abstract function for mapping. Destinations of the second group are passed to the **mapGenericEvent(PresentationNavigationEvent)** abstract function. This function may return **null** if it fails to find an appropriate UI destination. When this happens, we throw an **UnhandledNavigationException** (*lines 14 and 15*).

This implementation is slightly complicated, but that is because we want the mapper to support destinations external to any particular feature, too. If you do not require this capability, your mapper can be simplified. In any case, I am sure you will be relieved to see that the **NotificationUiMapper** interface is much simpler:

NotificationUiMapper.kt

```
1.    package com.mitteloupe.whoami.architecture.ui.notification.mapper
2.
3.    [imports...]
4.
5.    interface NotificationUiMapper<
6.        in PRESENTATION_NOTIFICATION : PresentationNotification
7.    > {
8.        fun toUi(notification: PRESENTATION_NOTIFICATION): UiNotification
9.    }
```

On the first line, we can see that, much like the navigation mapper and UI destination model share a common root package, the **NotificationUiMapper** interface shares a common package with the **UiNotification** interface: **com.mitteloupe.whiami.architecture. ui.notification**. The **UiNotification** interface is then saved under **model**, and the mapper is saved under **mapper**.

The **NotificationUiMapper** interface has one generic type, **PRESENTATION_NOTIFICATION**, that extends the **PresentationNotification** interface (*line 6*). This allows us to write exhaustive **when** statements in our mapper implementation. We will get to that a bit later.

This mapper, as we have learned to expect, has a single public function: **toUi(PresentationNotification)** (*line 8*). Implementations of this mapper will be responsible for translating a Presentation layer notification model to its UI equivalent.

With the mappers out of the way, our architecture UI implementation is complete. I usually have a few other files here, depending on my implementation. For example, a **BaseFragment** class can help reduce boilerplate code around binding to a view model when going the XML route. Let us proceed to explore a concrete feature: our home screen.

UI feature code

In this edition of the book, we will focus on a Jetpack Compose implementation of the UI. This is because there is a strong push at the time of writing by Google to adopt Compose.

You can see the UI feature Gradle module (**home:ui**) structure in *Figure 5.2*:

```
∨ 🗁 home
   > 🗁 data
   > 🗁 domain
   > 🗁 presentation
   ∨ 🗁 ui
      ∨ 🗁 src
         ∨ 🗁 main
            ∨ 🗁 java
               ∨ 🗁 com
                  ∨ 🗁 mitteloupe
                     ∨ 🗁 whoami
                        ∨ 🗁 home
                           ∨ 🗁 ui
                              ∨ 🗁 content
                                   🗋 ConnectedContent.kt
                                   🗋 DetailsBlock.kt
                                   🗋 DetailsRow.kt
                                   🗋 DisconnectedContent.kt
                                   🗋 ErrorContent.kt
                                   🗋 IpAddressCard.kt
                                   🗋 NavigationButton.kt
                              ∨ 🗁 di
                                   🖳 HomeDependencies
                              ∨ 🗁 mapper
                                   🖳 ConnectionDetailsUiMapper
                                   🖳 ErrorUiMapper
                                   🖳 HomeNotificationUiMapper
                                   🖳 HomeViewStateUiMapper
                              ∨ 🗁 model
                                   🖳 ConnectionDetailsUiModel
                                   🖳 DetailsUiModel
                                   🖳 HomeViewStateUiModel
                                   🖳 IconLabelUiModel
                              ∨ 🗁 view
                                 ∨ 🗁 spring
                                      🗋 EnterSpring.kt
                                 ∨ 🗁 widget
                                    ∨ 🗁 preview
                                         🖳 ErrorPreviewModel
                                         🖳 ErrorPreviewParameterProvider
                                      🗋 ConnectedContentContainer.kt
                                      🗋 DisconnectedContentContainer.kt
                                      🗋 ErrorContentContainer.kt
                                      🗋 HomeFooter.kt
                                      🗋 LoadingAnimationContainer.kt
                                      🗋 NavigationButtons.kt
                                      🗋 NotificationToast.kt
                                   🗋 HomeScreen.kt
```

Figure 5.2: The structure of our UI feature module

As Compose can lead to an explosion of composable functions, and because this book is not about developing user interfaces for Android, we will only cover the necessary parts to help you see how all the moving parts fit together.

If you remember, we started the architecture section with the **BaseComposeHolder** class. To follow the same approach, we will start our journey into the UI implementation by looking at the **HomeDependencies** class, which extends the **BaseComposeHolder** one:

HomeDependencies.kt

```
1.    package com.mitteloupe.whoami.home.ui.di
2.
3.    [imports...]
4.
5.    data class HomeDependencies(
6.        val homeViewModel: HomeViewModel,
7.        val homeViewStateUiMapper: HomeViewStateUiMapper,
8.        val connectionDetailsUiMapper: ConnectionDetailsUiMapper,
9.        private val homeNavigationMapper:
10.           NavigationEventDestinationMapper<PresentationNavigationEvent>,
11.       private val homeNotificationMapper:
12.           NotificationUiMapper<HomePresentationNotification>,
13.       val errorUiMapper: ErrorUiMapper,
14.       val analytics: Analytics
15.   ) : BaseComposeHolder<HomeViewState, HomePresentationNotification>(
16.       homeViewModel,
17.       homeNavigationMapper,
18.       homeNotificationMapper
19.   )
```

Starting from the top of the file, we can see that **HomeDependencies** is saved under the **home** feature package, under the **ui** layer package, and finally under the **di** (dependency injection) sub-package. That is because the primary responsibility of **HomeDependencies** is to provide the dependencies that our home screen composable needs to that screen. This is also the reason for its name: the **Home** prefix reflects the *screen* (not *feature*) name, and the **Dependencies** suffix tells us that it holds the dependencies for the screen.

A secondary responsibility of **HomeDependencies**, which is handled by its **BaseComposeHolder** superclass, is to provide a mechanism to bind the viewmodel to the composable. The binding is done by calling the **ViewModelObserver** composable (see earlier in this chapter).

Continuing to *line 5*, we see that **HomeDependencies** is a data class. Between *lines 6* and *14*, we see all its constructor parameters. First, we have a **HomeViewModel** instance. If you remember from the previous chapter, **HomeViewModel** sets two generic types for its **BaseViewModel** superclass: **HomeViewState** and **HomePresentationNotification**. These are precisely the same generic types that we set for **BaseComposeHolder** on *line 15*. This is important because if the generic types did not match, we would not be able to pass **homeViewModel** to **BaseComposeHolder**, and our code would not compile. Is compile-time safety not great?

Lines 7 through *13* all contain various mappers. In our case, they all map from Presentation to UI. However, if we needed mappers from UI back to Presentation, they would be here as well. Note that **homeNavigationMapper** (*lines 9* and *10*) and **homeNotificationMapper** (*lines 11* and *12*) are both private: they do not need to be accessed by our code apart from that in the **BaseComposeHolder** class.

In *line 14*, we have an instance of our analytics interface. In most cases, we use analytics tools to monitor and study user behavior. Since, as the name suggests, UI is where our app meets the user, it makes sense for the analytics interface to be found here.

Now, let us look at the UI models that we will use in the home feature:

ConnectionDetailsUiModel.kt

```
1.    package com.mitteloupe.whoami.home.ui.model
2.
3.    [import...]
4.
5.    @Parcelize
6.    data class ConnectionDetailsUiModel(
7.        val ipAddress: String,
8.        val cityIconLabel: IconLabelUiModel?,
9.        val regionIconLabel: IconLabelUiModel?,
10.       val countryIconLabel: IconLabelUiModel?,
11.       val geolocationIconLabel: IconLabelUiModel?,
12.       val postCode: IconLabelUiModel?,
13.       val timeZone: IconLabelUiModel?,
14.       val internetServiceProviderName: IconLabelUiModel?
15.   ) : Parcelable
16.
17.   @Parcelize
18.   data class IconLabelUiModel(
19.       @DrawableRes val iconResourceId: Int,
20.       val label: String
21.   ) : Parcelable
```

In the preceding code, I condensed two closely related classes. In a project, I would keep each in a separate file. However, because they both reside in the same package and because I wanted to discuss them together, they are grouped together here. In the first line, we can see that the models live in the **model** package, under the **ui** layer package, then under the **home** feature package and the app package.

Next, because these are UI packages, we can use a host of external dependencies without much worry. In this case, we use the **kotlinx.parcelize** library and its **@Parcelize** annotation (*lines 5, 17*) to allow us to persist models across configuration changes. To make it work, we also make both models implement the **Parcelable** interface (*lines 15, 21*).

Another important thing you will notice is that our models are data classes. This will help us when comparing instances, as data classes generate **equals()** and **hashCode()** pairs for us. Next, pay attention to the class name. I opted to suffix my UI models with **UiModel**. This will make distinguishing between them and Presentation models easier.

The **ConnectionDetailsUiModel** class has a relatively flat structure. Most of its fields are of the **IconLabelUiModel** type, which is a simple data class with two fields.

Looking at the **IconLabelUiModel** class, it holds an icon resource identifier and a label associated with that icon. Again, and this is important, because these are UI models, we can depend on the Android framework and so, we make it clear that **iconResourceId** expects drawable resource IDs by annotating it with the **@DrawableRes** annotation (*line 19*).

> Note: **Looking at all the model fields (lines 7 to 14 and 19, 20), one thing that you should observe straight away is that they are all immutable. It is generally a better practice because it is thread-safe, less error-prone, and easier to debug. I have yet to come across a situation where a feature required mutable models.**

The next model we will go over is the **HomeViewStateUiModel** sealed interface:

HomeViewStateUiModel.kt

```
1.    package com.mitteloupe.whoami.home.ui.model
2.
3.    [imports...]
4.
5.    @Parcelize
6.    sealed interface HomeViewStateUiModel : Parcelable {
7.        @Parcelize
8.        data object Loading : HomeViewStateUiModel
9.
10.       @Parcelize
11.       data object Connected : HomeViewStateUiModel
12.
13.       @Parcelize
14.       data object Disconnected : HomeViewStateUiModel
15.
16.       @Parcelize
17.       data object Error : HomeViewStateUiModel
18.   }
```

This sealed interface describes the different states of the screen. The screen state can be either loading (*line 8*), connected to the internet (*line 11*), disconnected from the internet (*line 14*), or in some erroneous state (*line 17*).

With the models covered, we can move on to the mappers we have seen mentioned in the **HomeDependencies** class. First, let us start with the **HomeViewStateUiMapper** class:

HomeViewStateUiMapper.kt

```
1.    package com.mitteloupe.whoami.home.ui.mapper
2.
3.    [imports...]
4.
5.    class HomeViewStateUiMapper {
6.        fun toUi(viewState: HomeViewState) = when (viewState) {
7.            is Connected -> HomeViewStateUiModel.Connected
8.            is Disconnected -> HomeViewStateUiModel.Disconnected
9.            is Error -> HomeViewStateUiModel.Error
10.           is Loading -> HomeViewStateUiModel.Loading
11.        }
12.    }
```

The first thing to note is the package name (*line 1*). Still under the **ui** layer package, we have a **mapper** package for our mappers.

You will notice a common pattern. Many mappers follow this pattern: their main mapping function (**toUi(HomeViewState)** on lines 6-11 in this case) is implemented using a single, exhaustive **when** statement. This **when** statement maps every model from one layer to its counterpart in another layer.

> Note: **It is important to note that we avoided using else. I highly recommend that you do not use else whenever possible. Avoiding it gives us compile-time safety: if we added a new state to the Presentation model, the compiler would tell us that the new state is not yet handled here.**

While many mappers follow the one-to-one pattern, not all of them do. Let us take the **ConnectionDetailsUiMapper** class as an example:

ConnectionDetailsUiMapper.kt

```
1.    package com.mitteloupe.whoami.home.ui.mapper
2.
3.    [imports...]
4.
5.    class ConnectionDetailsUiMapper {
```

```
6.          fun toUi(connectionDetails: HomeViewState.Connected) =
7.              ConnectionDetailsUiModel(
8.                  ipAddress = connectionDetails.ipAddress,
9.                  cityIconLabel = connectionDetails.city
10.                     .labelAndIcon(R.drawable.icon_city),
11.                 regionIconLabel = connectionDetails.region
12.                     .labelAndIcon(R.drawable.icon_region),
13.                 countryIconLabel = connectionDetails.countryCode
14.                     ?.toCountryName()
15.                     .labelAndIcon(R.drawable.icon_country),
16.                 geolocationIconLabel = connectionDetails.geolocation
17.                     ?.replace(",", ", ")
18.                     .labelAndIcon(R.drawable.icon_geolocation),
19.                 postCode = connectionDetails.postCode
20.                     .labelAndIcon(R.drawable.icon_post_code),
21.                 timeZone = connectionDetails.timeZone
22.                     .labelAndIcon(R.drawable.icon_time_zone),
23.                 internetServiceProviderName = connectionDetails
24.                     .internetServiceProviderName
25.                     .labelAndIcon(
26.                         R.drawable.icon_internet_service_provider
27.                     )
28.             )
29.
30.     private fun String?.labelAndIcon(
31.         @DrawableRes iconResourceId: Int
32.     ) = this?.let { IconLabelUiModel(iconResourceId, this) }
33.
34.     private fun String.toCountryName() =
35.         Locale("", this).displayCountry
36. }
```

This mapper is somewhat more complicated than **HomeViewStateUiModel**, for every input **HomeViewState.Connected** model, its **toUi(HomeViewState.Connected)** function produces an output **ConnectionDetailsUiModel** instance (*lines 6 to 28*). Let us explore it in greater detail.

The first field passed to the **ConnectionDetailsUiModel** constructor is the IP address, which is passed as-is from the input model (*line 8*).

Many of the output fields contain labels and icons (*lines 9 to 27*) encapsulated in **IconLabelUiModel** instances. The label for each output field is obtained from the corresponding field on the input model. The mapper knows which icon resource ID is required for each field, and so these values can be hardcoded. As all of these fields require a null check, **labelAndIcon(Int)**, a private helper extension function on nullable strings is introduced on *lines 30 to 32*. This function helps reduce some of the boilerplate and repetition.

Pay particular attention to **countryIconLabel** (*lines 13 to 15*) and **geolocationIconLabel** (lines *16 to 18*) because they are both different from all other label and icon fields in slightly different ways.

Let us start with **countryIconLabel**, which needs to figure out the name of a country from an ISO-3166 code to show on a label. This is done via the private extension function **toCountryName()** presented on *lines 34* and *35*. Next, we have **geolocationIconLabel**, which needs to make sure that there is a space after the provided geolocation comma. It does it by calling **replace** on *line 17*.

The next mapper provided in the **HomeDependencies** class is an instance of **NavigationEventDestinationMapper<PresentationNavigationEvent>**. It is responsible for handling navigation out of the feature. Due to that, the concrete implementation does not live in the feature package nor in any of its modules. Instead, it resides in the app module, which knows about all features. We will cover **HomeNavigationEventDestinationMapper** when we get to navigation in *Chapter 7, Dependency Injection and Navigation*.

Moving on, the **HomeDependencies** class provides an implementation of the **NotificationUiMapper** interface. Our mapper implementation class is **HomeNotificationUiMapper**:

HomeNotificationUiMapper.kt

```
1.    package com.mitteloupe.whoami.home.ui.mapper
2.
3.    [imports...]
4.
5.    class HomeNotificationUiMapper(
6.        private val context: Context,
7.        private val notificationToast:
8.            (Context, String) -> Unit = ::staticNotificationToast
9.    ) : NotificationUiMapper<HomePresentationNotification> {
10.       override fun toUi(
11.           notification: HomePresentationNotification
12.       ): UiNotification = when (notification) {
13.           is ConnectionSaved -> {
14.               connectionSavedUiNotification(
15.                   context,
16.                   notification.ipAddress,
```

```
17.                     notificationToast
18.                 )
19.             }
20.         }
21.
22.     private fun connectionSavedUiNotification(
23.         context: Context,
24.         ipAddress: String,
25.         notificationToast: (Context, String) -> Unit
26.     ) = UiNotification {
27.         val text = context.getString(
28.             R.string.home_details_saved_notification,
29.             ipAddress
30.         )
31.
32.         notificationToast(context, text)
33.     }
34. }
```

This mapper shows us yet another type of mapping implementation. As we will see shortly, the **HomeNotificationUiMapper** class maps its input to an anonymous lambda.

To name our mapper, we again take the name of the *screen* (not *feature*) whose notifications it supports (**Home**) and suffix it with **NotificationUiMapper** to produce the final name of **HomeNotificationUiMapper**.

As this mapper produces **UiNotification** instances that require an Android **Context** object to perform their job, we inject one via the mapper's constructor (*line 6*).

Lines 7, 8, and *23* warrant special attention. As you probably know, showing a toast in Android requires making a static call. Static calls make testing harder. Due to that, this implementation must adapt to be easily testable. I usually do my best to avoid changing code to satisfy tests, so this is a subtle exception. The code for presenting a toast is a straightforward one-liner, so we can comfortably allow tests to replace it with an alternative, testable mechanism. In production, we fall back to the default value for **notificationToast**, which executes the native Android code. An alternative could be to introduce a class of our own that unifies the presentation of toasts across the app.

This example only handles one notification type: **ConnectionSaved** (*line 13*). When the notification is of that type, it is mapped to a private function that returns an anonymous implementation of the **UiNotification** interface (*lines 22 to 33*). We provide it with the **Context** instance that we injected into the mapper, the IP address string that we obtain from the input notification, and the injected **notificationToast** implementation.

We declare the **UiNotification** implementations inside the mapper because the notification functions and the mapper are tightly coupled. We will never access these functions from anywhere else.

Looking at the implementation of the UI notification interface (*lines 27* to *32*), we can see that when **present()** is called, we read the notification message from the **home_details_saved_ notification** string resource, replacing its placeholder with the injected IP address (*lines 27* to *30*). In *line 32*, we call the injected **notificationToast** lambda with the injected **Context** object and the resolved string.

In short, the **HomeNotificationUiMapper** maps a **HomePresentationNotification** object to a **UiNotification** implementation. We can then call **present()** on the returned lambda to present the appropriate notification to the user.

The final mapper in the **HomeDependencies** class is an instance of the **ErrorUiMapper** class:

ErrorUiMapper.kt

```
1.    package com.mitteloupe.whoami.home.ui.mapper
2.
3.    [imports...]
4.
5.    class ErrorUiMapper(private val resources: Resources) {
6.        fun toUi(presentationError: HomeViewState.Error) =
7.            when (val error = presentationError.error) {
8.                NoIpAddress ->
9.                    string(R.string.home_error_no_ip_description)
10.               is NoIpAddressInformation -> {
11.                   resources.getString(
12.                       R.string.home_error_no_information_description,
13.                       error.ipAddress
14.                   )
15.               }
16.
17.               RequestTimeout ->
18.                   string(R.string.home_error_timeout_description)
19.               Unknown -> string(R.string.home_error_unknown_description)
20.       }
21.
22.       private fun string(@StringRes stringResourceId: Int) =
23.           resources.getString(stringResourceId)
24.   }
```

The **ErrorUiMapper** class is responsible for mapping **HomeViewState.Error** instances to error strings. To perform this mapping, it applies a **when** statement to the error field, producing a resource-based string for each case. Most cases do not have placeholders and can leverage the syntactic sugar **string(Int)** function introduced on *lines 22* and *23*. An exception is **NoIpAddressInformation**, because it does replace a string placeholder with the IP address provided via the input error model.

With the mappers all covered, we can continue to the most exciting part of our UI: the screen composable. We will skip the analytics class implementation because it can widely differ between implementations and is therefore outside of the scope of this book.

Due to the complexity of Compose, we will only explore the stateful container of our screen. Beyond that, it is down to you to implement concrete screens. So, without further ado, here is the **Home** composable:

HomeScreen.kt

```
1.    package com.mitteloupe.whoami.home.ui.view
2.
3.    [imports...]
4.
5.    @Composable
6.    fun HomeDependencies.Home(
7.        navController: NavController,
8.        modifier: Modifier = Modifier
9.    ) {
10.       fun relaySavingToViewModel(connectionDetails: HomeViewState) {
11.           require(connectionDetails is HomeViewState.Connected) {
12.               "Unexpected click, not connected."
13.           }
14.           homeViewModel.onSaveDetailsAction(connectionDetails)
15.       }
16.
17.       ScreenEnterObserver {
18.           analytics.logScreen("Home")
19.           homeViewModel.onEnter()
20.       }
21.
22.       ViewModelObserver(navController)
23.
24.       val viewState by homeViewModel.viewState
25.           .collectAsState(HomeViewState.Loading)
26.
```

```
27.          val connectionDetails by rememberSaveable(viewState) {
28.              mutableStateOf(
29.                  (viewState as? HomeViewState.Connected)
30.                      ?.let(connectionDetailsUiMapper::toUi)
31.              )
32.          }
33.          val errorMessage by rememberSaveable(viewState) {
34.              mutableStateOf((viewState as? HomeViewState.Error)
35.                  ?.let(errorUiMapper::toUi).orEmpty())
36.          }
37.          val uiState by rememberSaveable(viewState) {
38.              mutableStateOf(homeViewStateUiMapper.toUi(viewState))
39.          }
40.
41.          HomeContents(...)
42.      }
```

The first thing to note is that the file name, **HomeScreen.kt**, does not align with the composable name, **Home**. The home screen contains at least two composable functions: the stateful composable (**Home**, listed previously) and the stateless one (**HomeContent**, mentioned on *line 41*). It makes sense to name the file to reflect the idea that these composables share. That idea is the home screen, and thus the file is named **HomeScreen.kt**.

Moving on to the contents of the file, the first thing we see is the package name. Located under the app package (**com.mitteloupe.whoami**), we have the feature named package (**home**), followed by the layer named one (**ui**), and we have the **view** package. The **view** name in this context comes from the MVVM pattern, not the Android term of the same name.

The next important thing to note is that our **Home** composable is not a standard function. Instead, it is an extension function on **HomeDependencies**. This gives us easy access to the objects held in **HomeDependencies**. As I mentioned earlier, this is our way of working around the absence of a DI solution in Jetpack Compose.

The Home function has two parameters: a **NavController** instance (*line 7*) and a **Modifier** one (*line 8*). The **NavController** instance is expected to be the one that is used by the outer **NavHost** composable. The **Modifier** instance is there because it is a Compose best practice to always pass one in to composables.

The **relaySavingToViewModel(HomeViewState)** function at the top of the **Home** composable (*lines 10 to 15*) is a convenience one. It ensures that when a save action is triggered, the view state is **Connected** and then conveys the saving event and the state, as presented to the user, to the **homeViewModel** object.

The first call in the **Home** composable is to the **ScreenEnterObserver** (*lines 17 to 20*). This observer takes the lambda argument and only executes it, as its name suggests, the first time the composable is composed. We use this mechanism to record the user entering the home screen (*line 18*) and to notify the **viewmodel** of the event (*line 19*). Here is the **ScreenEnterObserver** composable for completeness:

ScreenEnterObserver.kt

```
1.    package com.mitteloupe.whoami.architecture.ui.view
2.
3.    [imports...]
4.
5.    @Composable
6.    fun ScreenEnterObserver(onEntered: () -> Unit) {
7.        var entered by rememberSaveable { mutableStateOf(false) }
8.
9.        LaunchedEffect(entered) {
10.            if (!entered) {
11.                entered = true
12.                onEntered()
13.            }
14.        }
15.    }
```

There really is not much to **ScreenEnterObserver**. It is a part of the architecture UI module and remembers when it is composed for the first time, executing the provided **onEntered** argument. It uses **rememberSaveable** to ensure that it survives configuration changes. This prevents it from executing the **onEntered()** lambda every time the configuration changes.

Let us get back to our Home composable. On *line 22*, we call the **ViewModelObserver** composable with the **navController** object. We discussed **ViewModelObserver** when we looked at **BaseComposeHolder**, where the **ViewModelObserver** composable is declared. It is here that we bind the viewmodel handling of navigation and notifications.

We continue to collect view state updates from the viewmodel on *lines 24* and *25*. This means that the **viewState** variable will hold the latest Presentation view state. To access the data, we want to map it to UI models, which is exactly what we do on *lines 27* to *39*. The **connectionDetails** variable will hold connection details when the **viewState** value has such information, and **null** otherwise (*lines 27* to *32*). The **errorMessage** variable will behave the same way, but based on any error messages in the **viewState** value (*lines 33* to *36*). Finally, **uiState** will hold the general view state: loading, connected, disconnected, or in error (*lines 37* to *39*). All these variables rely on mappers, which we have seen earlier, to resolve their values.

Finally, the resolved values are passed on to the stateless **HomeContents** composable for display (*line 41*).

Note: **A quick word about abstraction. Whether it is an analytics library or an image loading library, never, and I emphasize, never, access code from these libraries directly from your code. Always abstract it away. Wrap it in a class that implements an interface. Make sure the interface does not expose any library-specific code. I really cannot stress how important this is enough. Some developers prefer to use extension functions for this kind of abstraction. I advise against it because mocking or stubbing extension functions is not as straightforward, nor does it make the dependency as explicitly clear as interface dependencies do.**

At this point, assuming that we called our feature composable function from somewhere in our app, we should be able to run our code and see the feature screen. The feature is fundamentally working. Depending on the order in which we implemented our layers, we may already have a working Data layer, too. If so, we are done with the feature. Otherwise, all we have left to do is implement the Data layer. However, not having a complete Data layer is not preventing us from running and interacting with the feature.

The order in which I would recommend implementing the UI layer is as follows:

1. **UI models**. The ones you are most likely to need are the navigation and notification ones. You should be able to tell which other UI models you would need based on the Views in your layout. Every composable may justify a new UI model or fields in an existing one.

2. **Mappers**. For every UI model, implement relevant mappers from Presentation to UI. If you need to send models back to the view model, implement Presentation to UI mappers. You can follow **test-driven development** (**TDD**) or write tests after the fact. Either way, do not neglect the tests.

3. Extend `BaseComposeHolder` to provide the feature composable with any required dependencies.

4. The feature's **stateful composable**. Remember to call `ViewModelObserver` and `ScreenEnterObserver`, as appropriate. Define any input arguments that your composable would need, and a mechanism to navigate to it.

In the next chapter, we will focus on making sure that the data that the feature is working with is real.

Conclusion

This chapter covered the different parts of the UI layer. It showed you how the UI handles user actions and presents data to the user, all while protecting the Presentation layer. We discussed the different mappers that the UI layer utilizes to bridge the gap between the user and the Presentation layer. We saw how the UI layer can leverage its exposure to SDKs and libraries. We also explored a Jetpack Compose implementation example.

In the next chapter, we will explore a different part of the architecture: the one responsible for persisting and providing the app with data. Namely, we will go over the Data and DataSource layers.

Points to remember

There are a few important rules that I suggest you keep in mind when implementing the UI layer:

- **The UI technology does not matter**: At the time of writing, Google is pushing developers to Jetpack Compose. Before Compose, we had XML layouts and custom views. Voice is another interface that is gaining momentum again with the rise of AI and **large language models** (**LLMs**) in particular. Regardless of what your choice of interface is, the options available to the user remain the same. Clean Architecture lets us switch interfaces without affecting other layers.

- **Represent the user**: It is the responsibility of the UI layer to inform the Presentation layer of user actions and to convey feedback back to the user.

- **Individual components have UI models**: The UI layer receives and sends Presentation models to the viewmodel, but maps them to UI models for its own components.

- **Configuration changes**: Handling configuration changes is the responsibility of the UI layer, not the Presentation layer. Only the UI knows what is actually shown to the user.

- **Remember testing**: The UI is harder to unit test. However, some parts of the UI layer are perfect candidates for testing. Take mappers, for example. Navigation mappers in particular are worth testing.

Join our Discord space

Join our Discord workspace for latest updates, offers, tech happenings around the world, new releases, and sessions with the authors:

https://discord.bpbonline.com

CHAPTER 6

The DataSource and Data Layers

Without data, you're just another person with an opinion.

- William Edwards Deming

Introduction

So far, we have covered the implementation of the Domain layer and the business logic within it. We continued to discuss the Presentation layer that relies on it and, in turn, the UI layer that relies upon the latter. Along the way, I mentioned that once the Domain layer was implemented, we could also start working on the Data side of things. This will be the topic of this chapter.

I mentioned this in the previous chapter, but it is true for this one as well: the libraries that are used in this chapter were chosen for demonstration. You may want to choose other libraries, and that would be fine. In any case, your choices are not binding. That is why we are using Clean Architecture. You can change your mind later with minimal impact on the project.

Structure

In this chapter, we will cover the following topics:

- The DataSource layer
- The Data layer

Objectives

In *Chapter 3, The Domain Layer*, we started covering the implementation details of a Clean Architecture Android app. In this chapter, we aim to wrap up the required information for implementing a complete feature. By the end of this chapter, you should be able to implement an end-to-end working feature.

The DataSource layer

In the first edition of this book, we treated the separation between the Data and DataSource layers with caution. In this edition, I draw a clear line between the two. For that reason, the DataSource layer must be implemented *before* the Data layer can be implemented. Otherwise, the Data layer has no way of sending or receiving data.

The advantage of the DataSource layer is that, much like the Domain layer, it is highly independent and can be implemented independently and as early as we want. Conveniently, its development can also be postponed until very late in the process. The point in time at which we absolutely must develop the DataSource layer is when the Domain, Presentation, and UI layers are all implemented. At that point, not having a working DataSource layer would prevent us from implementing the Data layer and would therefore be the only thing preventing us from releasing a fully working feature.

It is important to mention that datasources are not coupled with features. This means that a datasource will be used by one or more features, and its name will often not reflect any feature's name (if it does, it is incidental).

Let us explore the DataSource layer implementation.

The DataSource architecture code

In *Figure 6.1,* you can see the structure of the DataSource architecture module:

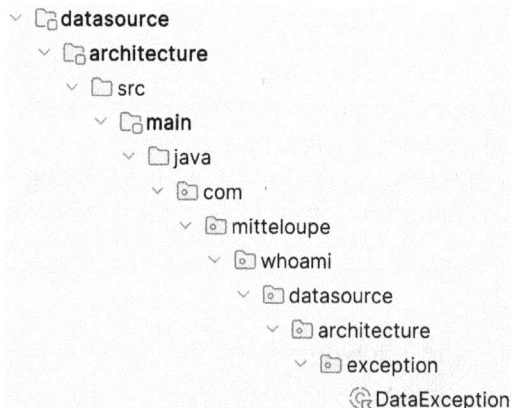

```
∨  datasource
   ∨  architecture
      ∨  src
         ∨  main
            ∨  java
               ∨  com
                  ∨  mitteloupe
                     ∨  whoami
                        ∨  datasource
                           ∨  architecture
                              ∨  exception
                                    DataException
```

Figure 6.1: The structure of our DataSource architecture module

As you can see, the architecture Gradle module (**datasource:architecture**) for the DataSource layer is very minimal, and besides the obvious **build.gradle.kts** file (which was omitted from all module structure figures) only has a single abstract class: **DataException**:

DataException.kt

```
1.    package com.mitteloupe.whoami.datasource.architecture.exception
2.
3.    abstract class DataException(cause: Throwable? = null) :
4.        Exception(cause)
```

Let us look at the package name first. As we can see, the app package (**com.mitteloupe. whoami**) is followed by **datasource**. We are used to seeing features at this level, but datasources are in their own category and are feature agnostic. Under the **datasource** package, we have **architecture**, which tells us that this package is usable across all datasources. Finally, we have **exception**, which is our package for storing… well, exceptions.

The **DataException** class itself is quite straightforward: any subclasses can pass in an optional **Throwable** object as the **cause** argument (*line 3*), which is passed on to the **Exception** constructor (*line 4*). The purpose of this class and its subclasses is to expose exceptions to repositories in the Data layer in a meaningful way. What does this mean? Let me explain.

Instead of throwing an **IOException** or other exceptions that are tied to concrete implementation details, such as the network, disk access, or a Bluetooth device, it allows us to convey what went wrong in an implementation-agnostic way. Imagine that we tried to save the user details and failed. It could be due to a network issue, or maybe the storage was full. What the repository cares about is that the saving failed unexpectedly, but not necessarily why (although that information may be available via the **cause** field).

While the **DataException.kt** file is a simple one, it highlights another important fact about the DataSource layer: it shows us that this layer exposes an interface to the Data layer, and that we refer to classes that are a part of this interface, like exceptions or models, as Data classes. We will get back to this point when we explore the DataSource feature implementation next.

The DataSource implementation code

You may find the title of this section confusing because it contains the word *implementation*, while in earlier chapters, sections that followed the architecture code sections mention *feature* instead. I contemplated naming this section consistently, but opted for correctness over consistency. Remember that datasources are feature agnostic. *The DataSource feature code* would have simply been incorrect.

When we get to the Data layer later in this chapter and discuss the feature repository, you will see that our feature example depends on multiple datasources. We will not be able to cover all of them in this book. Instead, we will focus on one to give you an idea of what concrete datasources look like.

A challenge that we have to tackle when implementing datasources is the fact that the Data layer is platform independent and can therefore be a Java or Kotlin module (as opposed to an Android one). This means that the Data layer modules cannot access platform-specific implementations, which is precisely what our datasources contain. So, how do we solve this problem?

We solve it by introducing a datasource interface in a Java (or Kotlin) module. We then implement the datasource interface in a separate Android module. Finally, we provide the implementation using dependency injection in the app module (we cover this in the next chapter, *Chapter 7, Dependency Injection and Navigation*).

Let us start with the **datasource:source** module, which is the Java module. You can see its structure in *Figure 6.2*:

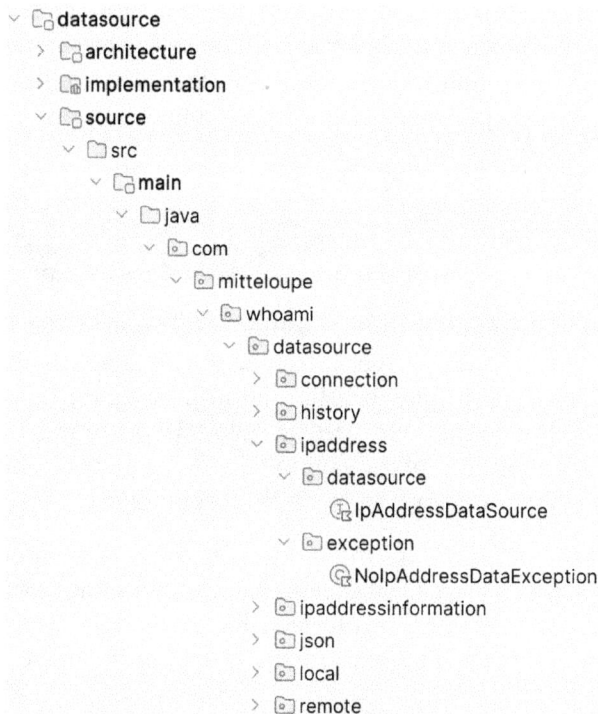

```
∨ ⌷ datasource
    > ⌷ architecture
    > ⌷ implementation
    ∨ ⌷ source
        ∨ ⌷ src
            ∨ ⌷ main
                ∨ ⌷ java
                    ∨ ⌷ com
                        ∨ ⌷ mitteloupe
                            ∨ ⌷ whoami
                                ∨ ⌷ datasource
                                    > ⌷ connection
                                    > ⌷ history
                                    ∨ ⌷ ipaddress
                                        ∨ ⌷ datasource
                                                ⌷ IpAddressDataSource
                                        ∨ ⌷ exception
                                                ⌷ NoIpAddressDataException
                                    > ⌷ ipaddressinformation
                                    > ⌷ json
                                    > ⌷ local
                                    > ⌷ remote
```

Figure 6.2: The structure of the DataSource source module

First, we will take a look at the **IpAddressDataSource** interface:

IpAddressDataSource.kt

```kotlin
1.   package com.mitteloupe.whoami.datasource.ipaddress.datasource
2.
3.   import com.mitteloupe.whoami...NoIpAddressDataException
4.
5.   interface IpAddressDataSource {
```

```
6.        @Throws(NoIpAddressDataException::class)
7.        fun ipAddress(): String
8.    }
```

As we can see, datasources reside under the app package, then under **datasource**, which groups the datasource code. Within that package, we have a package for the specific resource in question, which is **ipaddress** in our case. Finally, we have a second **datasource** package. This second package is for grouping relevant datasource code for the IP address resource.

The **IpAddressDataSource** interface has a single function, **ipAddress()**, which returns an IP address as a string and can throw a **NoIpAddressDataException** exception (*lines 6 and 7*). Datasources can, and often do, have more than one function. These functions usually allow you to get, add, remove, and update resources.

For completeness, this is the **NoIpAddressDataException** class, which also resides in the **datasource:source** module:

NoIpAddressDataException.kt

```
1.    package com.mitteloupe.whoami.datasource.ipaddress.exception
2.
3.    import com.mitteloupe.whoami.datasource...DataException
4.
5.    class NoIpAddressDataException : DataException()
```

As we can see in *line 1*, the exception is under the **ipaddress** resource package and is saved under the **exception** package. The exception class itself is a plain class extending the **DataException** abstract class.

This wraps up the Java module part of our implementation. Now, let us take a look at the Android module, where we have the **IpAddressDataSource** implementation.

The concrete, Android library part of the DataSource layer is saved in the **datasource:implementation** package. You can see how our DataSource implementation module looks in *Figure 6.3*:

```
∨ ⌂ datasource
    › ⌂ architecture
    ∨ ⌂ implementation
        ∨ ⌂ src
            ∨ ⌂ main
                ∨ ⌂ java
                    ∨ ⌂ com
                        ∨ ⌂ mitteloupe
                            ∨ ⌂ whoami
                                ∨ ⌂ datasource
                                    › ⌂ connection
                                    › ⌂ history
                                    ∨ ⌂ ipaddress
                                        ∨ ⌂ datasource
                                            IpAddressDataSourceImpl
                                        ∨ ⌂ mapper
                                            IpAddressDataMapper
                                        ∨ ⌂ model
                                            IpAddressApiModel
                                        ∨ ⌂ service
                                            IpAddressService
                                    › ⌂ ipaddressinformation
                                    › ⌂ json
                                    › ⌂ remote
```

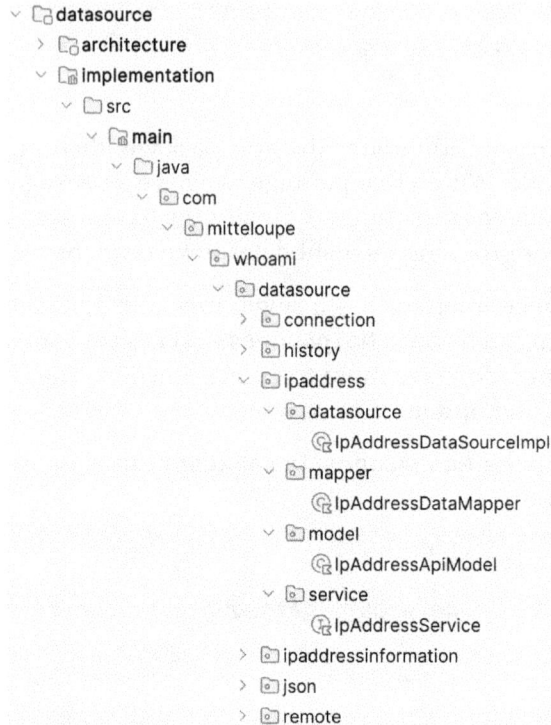

Figure 6.3: The structure of our Data module

Our example uses **Retrofit**. In your own projects, you could easily swap it for **Ktor**[1] or any other networking solution. You could be storing all data locally and using **Realm, Room, SQLite,** or even **SharedPreferences**. There may even be cases where keeping the data in memory suffices. In fact, the important thing to note here is that this decision can come at the very last minute, and changing our minds would have a very limited impact on our codebase. We can delay this decision until we implement our datasource class.

The datasource class will be responsible for retrieving and storing models stored locally or remotely. As part of performing this responsibility, it will use mappers to translate the stored models to and from Data models, which our repositories understand.

If we do not yet have the actual storage solution in place, we can introduce a stub datasource, just like we did with the repository when working on the Domain layer.

For our concrete implementation of **IpAddressDataSource**, we must first declare a **Retrofit** service. This is the **IpAddressService** service:

IpAddressService.kt

```
1.    package com.mitteloupe.whoami.datasource.ipaddress.service
2.
```

1 **https://ktor.io/**

```
3.    [imports...]
4.
5.    interface IpAddressService {
6.        @GET("?format=json")
7.        fun ipAddress(): Call<IpAddressApiModel>
8.    }
```

We will not dig too much into the Retrofit implementation, but I will explain this interface briefly. First, note the package name on the first line. Again, we store the file under the datasource IP address resource package (**com.mitteloupe.whoami.datasource.ipaddress**). This time, we have a **service** subpackage, where we can store all Retrofit services that we may need for managing the IP address resource.

Retrofit takes interfaces as the contract between its code and a remote API, and by convention, the names of these interfaces are suffixed with **Service** (*line 5*). The network call for obtaining the user's IP address is an HTTP GET request that is made to the server address (not shown here), with the **"?format=json"** query string appended to it (*line 6*). The query string tells this specific service that we want to receive the response in the JSON format. The **ipAddress()** function then returns an **IpAddressApiModel** response object wrapped in an object implementing the Retrofit **Call** interface (*line 7*). This is a simplification of how Retrofit works. Retrofit will obtain the JSON response from the server as a string and decode it into an **IpAddressApiModel** instance.

IpAddressApiModel is an API model and represents data originating from a remote API. This is the code for this API model:

IpAddressApiModel.kt
```
1.    package com.mitteloupe.whoami.datasource.ipaddress.model
2.
3.    [imports...]
4.
5.    @JsonClass(generateAdapter = true)
6.    data class IpAddressApiModel(
7.        @Json(name = "ip")
8.        val ipAddress: String
9.    )
```

As we can see on *line 1*, the API model resides in the **model** subpackage of the IP address resource package (**com.mitteloupe.whoami.datasource.ipaddress**).

The **@JsonClass** annotation (*line 5*) is a **Moshi**[2] annotation that tells the **Kotlin Symbol Processor** (**KSP**) to generate an adapter between a JSON string and the subsequent **IpAddressApiModel** class.

2 Moshi is a JSON library for Android. See here: **https://github.com/square/moshi**

The **@Json** annotation tells KSP that the JSON key for the **ipAddress** field is **"ip"**, rather than the default **"ipAddress"** that it would have otherwise derived from the field name on *line 8*.

It is a good idea to have local models regardless of the origin of the data. Many storage solutions tend to have annotations for aliasing, indexing, and so forth. These annotations are specific to a particular solution (a networking library, a database library, and so on). As such, we do not want to tie any models to any one solution other than those that are directly used to interact with that solution.

To return a Data model as our interface dictates, our datasource implementation needs to map the API model to a Data one. Our mapper that performs this operation looks like this:

IpAddressDataMapper.kt

```
1.    package com.mitteloupe.whoami.datasource.ipaddress.mapper
2.
3.    import com.mitteloupe.whoami.datasource.ipaddress...IpAddressApiModel
4.
5.    class IpAddressDataMapper {
6.        fun toData(ipAddress: IpAddressApiModel) = ipAddress.ipAddress
7.    }
```

Starting from the first line, we can see that our mapper is still under the IP address resource package (**com.mitteloupe.whoami.datasource.ipaddress**). Under that package, we have the **mapper** package, in which we store mappers that map Data objects to storage type ones (such as an API, a database, an SDK, and so on) and vice versa.

Mapper names (*line 5*) start with the model they are mapping (**IpAddress**), followed by the destination type (**Data**), and the **Mapper** suffix. This is consistent with all mapper names across the different layers.

> Note: **We may often opt to flatten the structure of models. A nested structure that may work well for the storage solution might be adding unnecessary complexity to the rest of our app. Flattening the model removes the need for nested mappers and reduces the overall number of models. In this case, we decided to map a data class to a primitive string (line 6).**

Note that the function name, **toData**, reflects the destination of mapping.

The mapping from model to string reminds us of an important fact: the API may not match our expectations; the API response may have additional fields that we do not currently care about. It may be missing fields, forcing us to come up with default values. It may be breaking down the data in a way that is not convenient for us. This is where mappers and the layer separation shine and help us protect our code from external changes.

Of course, we should always remember to unit-test our mappers. If we followed TDD, the tests would already be in place. Otherwise, we should write them now. This will reduce the chances of copy and paste or typing errors. It will also serve as live documentation going forward.

With the mappers in place, we can implement our datasource:

IpAddressDataSourceImpl.kt
```
1.    package com.mitteloupe.whoami.datasource.ipaddress.datasource
2.
3.    [imports...]
4.
5.    class IpAddressDataSourceImpl(
6.        private val lazyIpAddressService: Lazy<IpAddressService>,
7.        private val ipAddressDataMapper: IpAddressDataMapper
8.    ) : IpAddressDataSource {
9.        private val ipAddressService by lazy {
10.            lazyIpAddressService.value
11.        }
12.
13.        override fun ipAddress(): String = ipAddressDataMapper.toData(
14.            ipAddressService.ipAddress().fetchBodyOrThrow {
15.                NoIpAddressDataException()
16.            }
17.        )
18.    }
```

The **IpAddressDataSourceImpl** class lives under the same **datasource.ipaddress.datasource** subpackage (*line 1*) as the interface it implements. The interface it implements is **IpAddressDataSource** (*line 8*), which we declared in the **datasource:source** module.

Our implementation name matches the interface name, with the word **Impl** as a suffix to indicate this is the concrete source (*line 5*). We are not too worried about this name not being pretty, because it will only be used once: in our dependency injection code. If you ever end up with more than one implementation of the datasource, consider replacing **Impl** with meaningful names to distinguish between the different implementations.

In datasource implementations, we tend to find two specific types of constructor arguments: **sources** and **mappers**.

Sources may include Retrofit services (see *line 6*), **SharedPreferences** instances, and SDK instances, to name a few. Making the service lazy in this case allows us to postpone the service instantiation until we need to make the first network call.

Mappers are there to provide, as I am sure you have guessed, mapping from the different sources to Data models and back. In our example, on *line 7*, we have the mapper from an API IP address model to an IP address string. Remember that in many cases, the output of a mapper would be a model and not a primitive value.

In *lines 9* to *11*, we have some syntactic sugar to make **ipAddressService** easier to access later.

Our **ipAddress(): String** implementation (*lines 13* to *17*) reads an IP address model from the provided **ipAddressService** (*lines 14* to *16*). If the service fails to fetch an IP address for any reason, we throw a **NoIpAddressDataException** object. We will cover the handling of such exceptions in *Chapter 11, Failures and Exceptions*.

Once we have an IP address API model, we use the **ipAddressDataMapper** instance to map it to a string, which we return (*line 13*).

As mentioned earlier, the implementation of **IpAddressDataSource** and its related mappers could have been postponed in favor of a quick stub implementation. We only really needed the datasource interface to be able to implement our repository. So, with the datasource in place, we can proceed to the Data layer.

The order in which I recommend implementing the DataSource layer is as follows:

- Local, API, or SDK models.
- Configure your storage and network libraries and implement the code that they require.
- Data models and exceptions.
- DataSource interfaces.
- Mappers for local, API, or SDK to Data and vice versa.
- DataSource implementations.

Remember your unit test coverage. Mappers and datasource implementations are worth testing.

The Data layer

As we leave the DataSource layer behind and proceed to discuss the Data layer, we are back in the world of features. The Data layer is feature-specific, like the Domain, Presentation, and UI layers that we covered in the previous chapters.

Unlike all other layers, the Data layer is not split into two modules. It is implemented in a single module per feature.

Looking back at **WhoIAm**, when we implemented the Domain layer, we were stubbing our repository implementation. This allowed us to move forward with the implementation of the Presentation layer and eventually the UI layer without waiting for the Data layer implementation. Depending on our team size, we may want to tackle the Presentation and Data layers at the same time, or we may choose to implement them sequentially. Either way works. That is one of the benefits of implementing Clean Architecture in our app.

The Data module is stored in a feature-specific Gradle module, in our case, it is the `home:data` one. You can observe the structure of the module in *Figure 6.4*:

```
home
  data
    src
      main
        java
          com
            mitteloupe
              whoami
                home
                  data
                    mapper
                      ConnectionDetailsDataMapper
                      ConnectionDetailsDomainResolver
                      ThrowableDomainMapper
                    repository
                      ConnectionDetailsRepository
                      ConnectionHistoryRepository
```

Figure 6.4: *The structure of the Data module*

Before we get to the repository implementation, we have one more class that we need to implement: the Data to Domain mapper. Without it, the repository would have no way of converting the Data model obtained from the datasource to the Domain model that the usecase expects.

If you remember, when we first encountered mappers, I mentioned that they were a pattern for translating one model to another. As we work on Clean Architecture projects, we sometimes find that our input needs to be more than just one model. For example, to translate a Presentation model to a UI model, you may want to add an index to each UI model. Another example is when you are obtaining data from multiple datasources and want to translate that data into a single Data model.

A mapper is not the right pattern for this kind of conversion, unless you introduce a new input model that combines the different data elements. Another option that we have is to not name the class a mapper to avoid the contradiction between naming and implementation, and instead call it something different. I often use the name *resolver* for this kind of scenario. This is the case with **ConnectionDetailsDomainResolver**, shown as follows:

ConnectionDetailsDomainResolver.kt

```
1.    package com.mitteloupe.whoami.home.data.mapper
2.
3.    [imports...]
4.
5.    class ConnectionDetailsDomainResolver {
6.        fun toDomain(
7.            connectionState: ConnectionStateDataModel,
8.            ipAddress: String?,
9.            ipAddressInformation: IpAddressInformationDataModel?
10.       ): ConnectionDetailsDomainModel = when (connectionState) {
11.           Connected -> {
12.               requireNotNull(ipAddress)
13.               ConnectionDetailsDomainModel.Connected(
14.                   ipAddress = ipAddress,
15.                   city = ipAddressInformation?.city,
16.                   region = ipAddressInformation?.region,
17.                   countryCode = ipAddressInformation?.country,
18.                   geolocation = ipAddressInformation?.geolocation,
19.                   internetServiceProviderName = ipAddressInformation
20.                       ?.internetServiceProviderName,
21.                   postCode = ipAddressInformation?.postCode,
22.                   timeZone = ipAddressInformation?.timeZone
23.               )
24.           }
25.
26.           Disconnected -> ConnectionDetailsDomainModel.Disconnected
27.           Unset -> ConnectionDetailsDomainModel.Unset
28.       }
29.   }
```

There are three points that are worth highlighting about this Data to Domain resolver:

- The resolver is stored under the Data layer package of the feature name (**home**). Like mappers, the resolver is saved under the **mapper** package (*line 1*). There is no value in distinguishing between mappers and resolvers when it comes to the package name, since they serve the same logical role of translating models from one layer to another.

- The mapper name reflects its direction—prefixed with the output model name **ConnectionDetails**, followed by the destination (**Domain**). The resolver name ends with a **Resolver** suffix, giving us the complete name of **ConnectionDetailsDomainResolver**.

- Lastly, the function name reflects the destination (**toDomain**, *line 6*). It takes three Data models as its input and returns a new corresponding Domain model.

The resolver maps every connection state to its Data interpretation. The connected state is mapped to the **Connected** data class (*lines 11 to 24*), and the disconnected and unset states are mapped to the **Disconnected** and **Unset** objects, respectively (*lines 26 and 27*).

We can see that the IP address and the IP address information are only used if the connection state is connected (*lines 11 to 24*). We must have an IP address if we are connected, and so we require that it is not **null** (*line 12*) when the device is connected. All of the IP address information fields are optional (*lines 15 to 22*).

Again, remember to always consider having unit test coverage for your mappers.

We now have everything that we need to implement our repository:

ConnectionDetailsRepository.kt

```
1.    package com.mitteloupe.whoami.home.data.repository
2.
3.    [imports...]
4.
5.    private const val RETRY_DELAY_MILLISECONDS = 1000L
6.
7.    class ConnectionDetailsRepository(
8.        private val ipAddressDataSource: IpAddressDataSource,
9.        private val ipAddressInformationDataSource:
10.           IpAddressInformationDataSource,
11.       private val connectionDataSource: ConnectionDataSource,
12.       private val connectionDetailsDomainResolver:
13.           ConnectionDetailsDomainResolver,
14.       private val throwableDomainMapper: ThrowableDomainMapper
15.   ) : GetConnectionDetailsRepository {
16.       override fun connectionDetails():
17.           Flow<ConnectionDetailsDomainModel> =
18.           connectionDataSource.observeIsConnected()
19.               .map { connectionState ->
20.                   val (optionalIpAddress, ipAddressInformation) =
21.                       when (connectionState) {
22.                           Connected -> {
23.                               val ipAddress = ipAddressDataSource
24.                                   .ipAddress()
25.                               ipAddress to try {
26.                                   ipAddressInformationDataSource
```

```
27.                                    .ipAddressInformation(ipAddress)
28.                               } catch (
29.                                   _: NoIpAddressInformationDataException
30.                               ) {
31.                                   null
32.                               }
33.                           }

35.                           Disconnected, Unset -> null to null
36.                       }
37.                   connectionDetailsDomainResolver.toDomain(
38.                       connectionState,
39.                       optionalIpAddress,
40.                       ipAddressInformation
41.                   )
42.               }.retryWhen { cause, _ ->
43.                   emit(Error(throwableDomainMapper.toDomain(cause)))
44.                   delay(RETRY_DELAY_MILLISECONDS)
45.                   true
46.               }
47.       }
```

Starting from the package name, we can see that the repository implementation lives under our Data layer **data** sub-package of the **home** feature package, and finally under the **repository** package.

In *line 5*, we have a constant that is used to control the duration of the delay between retries upon failure. We suffix its name with **_MILLISECONDS** to indicate the unit type that it stores.

When naming our repository implementation, consider its current and future purpose. This repository will implement all connection details-related repository interfaces. Right now, it is implementing the **GetConnectionDetailsRepository** interface (see *line 15*). However, going forward, it may be implementing related interfaces, such as maybe **SaveConnectionDetailsRepository**. It makes sense, then, that we will name it to represent the overarching idea of these interfaces. We take the **ConnectionDetails** subject and use it as a prefix and suffix the name with **Repository** to indicate this is the app implementation, ending up with **ConnectionDetailsRepository** (*line 7*).

The concrete connection details repository implementation depends on an **IpAddressDataSource** instance (*line 8*) and a **ConnectionDetailsDomainResolver** (*lines 12 and 13*), both of which we covered earlier. It relies on additional datasources to determine the current connection state and to obtain the details for an IP address (*lines 9 to 11*). Finally, it relies on a mapper of Throwable objects from the Data layer to Domain error objects (*line 14*). We did not go over these implementations, since they repeat the patterns that we have covered with the **IpAddressDataSource** and **ConnectionDetailsDomainResolver** implementations.

The **connectionDetails(): Flow<ConnectionDetailsDomainModel>** implementation (*lines 16* to *46*) observes the connection state via the **observeIsConnected()** function of the **connectionDataSource** object (*line 18*). Every time a new connection state object is emitted, it checks if the device is connected (*line 22*). If it is not (*line 35*), no IP address is available, nor are there any other connection details. When a connection is available, the code obtains the IP address from the **ipAddress()** function of the **ipAddressDataSource** object (*lines 23* and *24*). It continues to try, and obtain the information for that IP address, falling back to **null** if this fails (*lines 25* to *32*). Once done with resolving the connection information, it uses the **connectionDetailsDomainResolver** object to map all the collected information to a Domain model (*lines 37* to *41*). If an uncaught exception was thrown, it emits an error Domain model with a mapped exception (*line 43*), waits for a fixed number of milliseconds (*line 44*), and retries.

With the repository implemented, our usecase now returns real values. With the Presentation and UI layers implemented, our feature is now complete.

You can implement the Data layer in the following order:

1. Data to Domain and Domain to Data mappers.

2. Repository implementations.

Unit-test your concrete repositories and your mappers.

Conclusion

You should now have a clear understanding of how our Clean Architecture implementation is built. We have covered all the key files in every layer, from the Domain to the Presentation, the UI, and the Data. We discussed how we could introduce a DataSource layer as well. We covered how the different classes play essential roles within their corresponding layers to make our app work while keeping the innermost layers protected from external changes. We also saw how each part of the app that holds logic can be isolated, which helps with testing.

In the next chapter, we will see how to instantiate all the different classes in our architecture and how to connect features to the app and to one another using navigation.

Points to remember

There are a few important rules I suggest you keep in mind when implementing your app:

• **Datasources do not belong to a feature**: Remember that datasources represent a resource and may be used by more than one feature. Design them with this in mind.

- **Datasources can be developed in isolation**: Datasources have no dependencies anywhere in the project. This means that you can develop them in parallel to the Domain layer or at any point until the Data layer is required.

- **Design for flexibility**: Your library choices of today may change tomorrow. Memory caching may be good enough today, but tomorrow you may want to use a database. These changes should be isolated to the DataSource layer.

- **The Data layer glues datasources and Domain Repository interfaces**: It depends on both the Domain and the DataSource layers. They provide it with all the contracts and models that it needs.

- **Remember testing**: Do not neglect your unit tests. The Data and DataSource layers contain enough logic to justify tests.

Join our Discord space

Join our Discord workspace for latest updates, offers, tech happenings around the world, new releases, and sessions with the authors:

https://discord.bpbonline.com

CHAPTER 7

Dependency Injection and Navigation

One day, Alice came to a fork in the road and saw a Cheshire cat in a tree. "Which road do I take?" she asked. "Where do you want to go?" was his response. "I don't know," Alice answered. "Then," said the cat, "it doesn't matter".

- Lewis Carroll, Alice in Wonderland

Introduction

If we followed the previous chapters, we now have a working feature. Sort of. If we tried running the app, we would not be able to see our feature. What is wrong?

Well, two critical things. For a feature to truly work, it first needs some code to construct all its dependencies. The mappers, repositories, usecases, viewmodels, and other classes all need to be instantiated. We need a **dependency injection (DI)** solution.

The second thing that is missing is a navigation solution to let us navigate to any new screens introduced by this new feature.

This chapter will help you understand the roles and implementation details of both DI and navigation in a Clean Architecture app.

Note: **You can find an appendix at the end of the book covering the setup of a new project. While the topic is related to this chapter, I felt it was not directly related to Clean Architecture, and so, it is best kept separate.**

Structure

In this chapter, we will cover the following topics:

- Overview of the app module
- Implementing and arranging the DI solution
- Implementing navigation

Objectives

This chapter should give you a clear idea of how to integrate a newly completed feature into a Clean Architecture app. When you have finished reading it, you should be comfortable with implementing dependency injection for your new feature. You should also be able to implement navigation into and out of the feature.

Overview of the app module

For an application to work, it needs one central place that *glues* everything together. Beyond the Application entry point, the project needs to be set up to run. Whether it is the code from different features or the navigation between them, there should be a place where it all comes together. We call that place in our Android project the **dirty main**, and it lives in the **app** Gradle module. The responsibility of the dirty main is to handle the DI for the project and the concrete navigation functionality.

We will tackle DI first. If you are not familiar with DI, it is a technique of providing functionality to our classes without altering their code, which is a way of following the SOLID **dependency inversion** principle, represented by the letter *I*.

In the next section, we will discuss the implementation of DI in our Android app.

Implementing and arranging the DI solution

We contain our DI solution in a package within the main **app** module. I usually name that package **di** (refer to *Figure 7.1*), although you can use a different name if you have one that you are more comfortable with. Whatever you do, though, avoid naming it after a third-party library such as Dagger, Hilt[1], or Koin. This is because we want to keep our DI solution, like every other part of our app, abstract and open to change. While a package renamed at a later time may not have a significant impact, avoiding using specific solution names is a good habit to adopt.

---

1 **https://dagger.dev/hilt/**

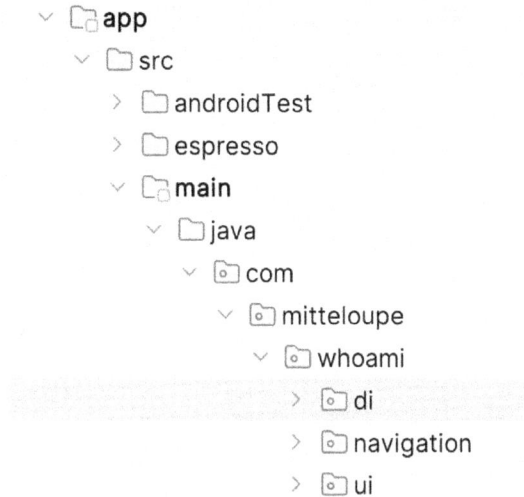

Figure 7.1: *The dirty main package, with di (highlighted) and navigation*

The structure within the DI package will vary depending on the complexity of your app and the DI solution that you choose. While we called this area of the code our *Dirty Main*, there is nothing stopping us from trying to keep it tidy. I will share with you the approach that served me well before.

I will assume that you are using **Hilt**. At the time of writing, it is one of the most convenient DI solutions for Android. When using Hilt, you would need to have Dagger modules.

You can start with a single module to hold all your dependencies. Let us call the module class **AppModule**. Quite quickly, **AppModule** grows and becomes harder to manage. In addition, while you are likely to start with the **SingletonComponent**, you may end up having to use different components, too. At that point, I usually start breaking the module down into feature modules. One such module could be a **HomeModule** object. This new module will hold all the dependencies specific to the home feature.

Over time, the feature modules can grow beyond maintainability, too. This is when I start breaking them down by layer. I will now have a **HomeUiModule** object and a **HomeDataModule** one, shown as follows:

```
 ∨  ▣ di
       🗃AnalyticsModule
       🗃AppDependenciesModule
       🗃ArchitectureModule
       🗃ConnectionDataSourceModule
       🗃ConnectionHistoryModule
       🗃HistoryModule
       🗃HistoryUiModule
       🗃HomeDataModule
       🗃HomeModule
       🗃HomeUiModule
       🗃IpAddressDataSourceModule
       🗃IpAddressHistoryDataSourceModule
       🗃IpAddressInformationDataSourceModule
       🗃JsonProcessing
       🗃LocalPersistenceModule
       🗃NetworkModule
       🗃NetworkUrlModule
       🗃ResourcesModule
       🗃TimeModule
```

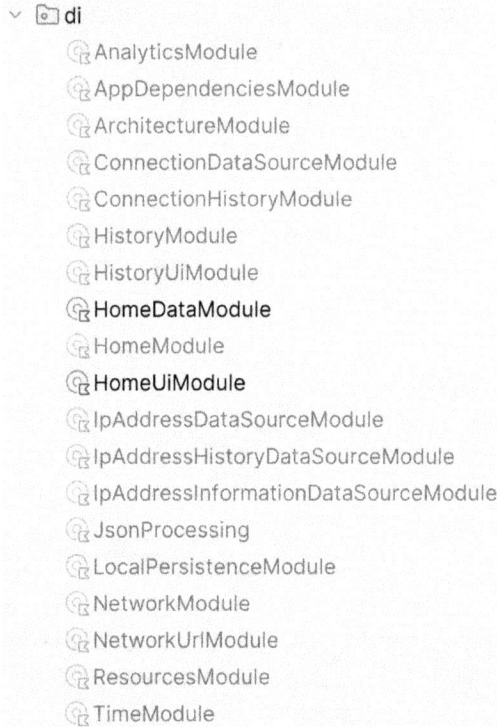

Figure 7.2: The dependency injection modules for WhoAmI

Over time, the DI modules tend to mirror the features and architecture layers that we covered in the previous chapters.

To give you an idea of what a single module file may look like, here is **HomeUiModule.kt**:

HomeUiModule.kt

```
1.   package com.mitteloupe.whoami.di
2.
3.   [imports...]
4.
5.   @Module
6.   @InstallIn(ActivityComponent::class)
7.   object HomeUiModule {
8.       @Provides
9.       fun providesHomeViewStateUiMapper() = HomeViewStateUiMapper()
10.
11.      @Provides
12.      @JvmSuppressWildcards
13.      fun providesHomeNavigationEventDestinationMapper(
14.          analytics: Analytics,
```

```
15.             @ActivityContext context: Context
16.         ): NavigationEventDestinationMapper<
17.             HomePresentationNavigationEvent
18.         > = HomeNavigationEventDestinationMapper(analytics, context)
19.
20.         @Provides
21.         fun providesHomeNotificationUiMapper(
22.             @ActivityContext context: Context
23.         ) = HomeNotificationUiMapper(context)
24.
25.         @Provides
26.         fun providesErrorUiMapper(resources: Resources) =
27.             ErrorUiMapper(resources)
28.
29.         @Provides
30.         fun providesConnectionDetailsUiMapper() =
31.             ConnectionDetailsUiMapper()
32.
33.         @Provides
34.         fun providesHomeDependencies(
35.             homeViewModel: HomeViewModel,
36.             homeViewStateUiMapper: HomeViewStateUiMapper,
37.             connectionDetailsUiMapper: ConnectionDetailsUiMapper,
38.             homeNavigationMapper: @JvmSuppressWildcards
39.             NavigationEventDestinationMapper<
40.                 HomePresentationNavigationEvent
41.             >,
42.             homeNotificationMapper: HomeNotificationUiMapper,
43.             errorUiMapper: ErrorUiMapper,
44.             analytics: Analytics
45.         ) = HomeDependencies(homeViewModel, ..., analytics)
46.     }
```

As you can see, the **HomeUiModule** object is responsible for providing the UI with concrete instances of its dependencies: Presentation to UI mappers and a **HomeDependencies** object. As none of these classes hold state, we do not have reason to make any of them reusable or singletons.

The most granular breakdown of modules is the result of end-to-end test requirements. Often, our tests require that we replace some classes. For example, we may want to use a dummy analytics library in our tests. I then extract the relevant classes into their own module object, making them easy to swap out.

Constructing all the different objects and values that we need to run our app is one part of getting the app to work. Another, no less important part, is connecting the different screens within the app. That is the responsibility of our navigation solution. We will cover navigation next.

Implementing navigation

Figure 7.3 shows the file structure for our navigation solution:

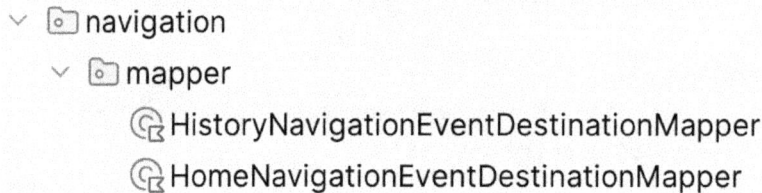

> ∨ ▣ navigation
>> ∨ ▣ mapper
>>> ⒢ HistoryNavigationEventDestinationMapper
>>> ⒢ HomeNavigationEventDestinationMapper

Figure 7.3: *The navigation package for WhoAmI*

Most apps span more than one screen. An app screen does not have to cover the whole screen of the device. It could be a fragment, a dialog, or a card, too. A screen is any user-facing interface that either conveys information to the user or provides the user with a mechanism to input data, or both. Screens are built in our UI layer.

For an app to work, these screens need to be connected somehow. This is what we refer to as *navigation*. In the Android world, we currently have a couple of common mechanisms of navigation:

- **Native navigation**: Launching Activities via Intents, using `FragmentManager` objects to present Fragments, and launching dialogs directly (commonly using an `AlertDialog.Builder`).

- **The Navigation framework**: *Google* offers a framework for navigation. Historically, it relied on XML navigation graphs. More recently, Google added support for navigating within Jetpack Compose (version 1.0.0-alpha01 was released on October 28, 2020). This is an ongoing Google project at the time of writing.

At the time of writing this book, Google released an alpha version of their new navigation library, **Navigation 3**[2]. Since it is too early to adopt it, we will not. However, it is worth noting that navigation solutions do change over time, and this is another example.

In Clean Architecture, we consider these different options as *details*. This means that using one over the other or swapping one for another should have little impact on the project as a whole. This is very similar to our DataSource layer, where one data storage solution can be swapped for another with limited impact.

---

2 You can read more about Navigation 3 here: **https://developer.android.com/guide/navigation/navigation-3**

To achieve this level of freedom, we need to abstract our navigation. In its simplest form, a navigation system is a collection of actions having an origin and a destination. Each such action can hold a payload with some metadata that provides context for the destination.

For example, when navigating from a screen with a list of dishes in a menu to a particular dish details screen, our origin is the list of dishes (or menu) screen. Our destination is the dish details screen (**OnViewDishDetails** could be an appropriate name for such a Presentation destination). Our payload is likely to be the unique identifier of the dish in question.

From a Presentation perspective, each feature must have at least one *entry point*, and it can have more. These entry points are characterized by their associated payloads.

Each feature can also have one or more *exit points* (it can have none, too). As we want to keep our features independent, it is important to perceive these exit points by the action or event that triggered them, rather than by their expected destination. For example, **OnDishDetailsSaved** is a better destination description than **BackToDishDetails**. This distinction gives us the freedom to later reuse features in different contexts.

In his book *Clean Architecture, Robert C. Martin* suggests having a *dirty main* function. It is this function that *glues* all the different classes together. We mentioned this concept earlier in this chapter. The *dirty main* function is replaced in Android with DI solutions such as **Hilt** or **Koin**. There is another aspect to *gluing* everything together. Indeed, I am referring to the navigation solution. The only component that should know how the features come together is the app itself.

Let us look at a concrete example from our **WhoAmI** app.

Navigation is triggered by the Presentation layer. More specifically, it starts with a viewmodel. In *Chapter 4, The Presentation Layer*, we saw that the **BaseViewModel** exposed a **navigationEvent** field of the type **Flow<PresentationNavigationEvent>**. We also observed the **emitNavigationEvent(PresentationNavigationEvent)** protected function that updated that field.

So, let us say that the user has a **Save Details** button on the home screen, which is expected to save the current connection details. What happens when the user taps that button? Let us break it down:

First, our view would inform our **HomeViewModel** object of the event by calling the **onSaveDetailsAction(HomeViewState.Connected)** function, passing in the connected state that was presented to the user at the time at which they tapped the button.

Then, the viewmodel would inform the view that it should navigate to the next screen by calling the **emitNavigationEvent** function, passing in the **OnSavedDetails** implementation of the **HomePresentationNavigationEvent** sealed interface. Let us take a short detour and inspect this interface:

HomePresentationNavigationEvent.kt

```
1.   package com.mitteloupe.whoami.home.presentation.navigation
2.
3.   import com...presentation.navigation.PresentationNavigationEvent
4.
5.   sealed interface HomePresentationNavigationEvent :
6.       PresentationNavigationEvent {
7.       data object OnViewHistory :
8.           HomePresentationNavigationEvent
9.
10.      data class OnSavedDetails(
11.          val savedIpAddress: String
12.      ) : HomePresentationNavigationEvent
13.
14.      data object OnViewOpenSourceNotices :
15.          HomePresentationNavigationEvent
16.  }
```

Starting with the package name (*line 1*), we see the **PresentationNavigationEvent** implementations for the home feature are kept under the **presentation** sub-package of the **home** feature sub-package, and finally, the **navigation** sub-package.

The **HomePresentationNavigationEvent** sealed interface for the home feature (*line 5*) confines the list of accepted events and helps us with writing exhaustive when statements in our Presentation to UI mapper, as we will see next.

The **OnSavedDetails** class (*lines 10 to 12,* in bold) implements the **PresentationNavigationEvent** interface indirectly by implementing **HomePresentationNavigationEvent**. Since it holds navigation data, it is declared as a data class. Its navigation data is a single argument, **savedIpAddress** (*line 11*). This argument represents the information that we need to enter the target destination.

> Note: **Note that despite potentially having more information about the saved connection, we settle for just enough information to identify it. This makes our destination considerably easier to reuse; it is much easier to obtain an IP address than all the fields that the destination could have potentially required (think city, country code, or time zone, for example). Remember that models can grow quite complex. Passing an identifier frees the origin from having to do any heavy lifting or obtaining data it does not need otherwise. It also protects us from tightly coupling features via common models.**

We can now get back to our navigation flow. Once the **navigationEvent** field of the viewmodel is updated, the observing view can proceed with navigation. In our **BaseComposeHolder** code in *Chapter 5, The UI Layer*, this was achieved by using a **NavigationEventDestinationMapper** to map the event to a destination. Once we obtained a UI destination object, we executed its **navigate(NavController)** function.

Let us take a quick look back at **HomeDependencies** from the same chapter. Remember, this is the home screen subclass of **BaseComposeHolder**. One of its fields is of type **NavigationEvenDestinationMapper<HomePresentationNavigationEvent>**. This abstract class is extended by the **NavigationEventDestinationMapper** class, which is implemented in the **app** module:

HomeNavigationEventDestinationMapper.kt

```
1.   package com.mitteloupe.whoami.navigation.mapper
2.
3.   [imports...]
4.
5.   class HomeNavigationEventDestinationMapper() :
6.       NavigationEventDestinationMapper
7.           <HomePresentationNavigationEvent>(
8.       HomePresentationNavigationEvent::class
9.   ) {
10.      override fun mapTypedEvent(
11.          navigationEvent: HomePresentationNavigationEvent
12.      ): UiDestination = when (navigationEvent) {
13.          is OnSavedDetails ->
14.              history(navigationEvent.savedIpAddress)
15.      }
16.
17.      private fun history(
18.          highlightedIpAddress: String?
19.      ): UiDestination = UiDestination { navController ->
20.          navController.navigate(History(highlightedIpAddress))
21.      }
22.  }
```

The **com.mitteloupe.whoami.navigation** package (*line 1*) is an app-wide package where we store all our navigation mappers. For consistency, we keep the mappers under the **mapper** subpackage. This is where feature-specific Presentation navigation events are mapped to UI destinations. These UI destinations can navigate to other features within the app or even outside of it.

Each screen's Presentation navigation event to UI destination mapper implementation is named by taking the screen name (**Home**) and appending **NavigationEventDestinationMapper** to it. If multiple features have screens with the same name, we can prefix the mapper name with the feature name. So, the home screen **NavigationEventDestinationMapper** implementation is named **HomeNavigationEventDestinationMapper** (line 5).

Our mapper has no constructor parameters (*line 5*). However, it is quite common to have constructor parameters in the navigation mappers. We often need an Android **Context** instance, for example, to launch activities or intents.

The core functionality of our Presentation to UI destination mapper lies in its **mapTypedEvent** implementation (*lines 10 to 15*). The input of this function is a **HomePresentationNavigationEvent** instance (*line 11*). This instance is a screen-specific destination. As **HomePresentationNavigationEvent** is a sealed interface, we can write an exhaustive when statement to handle all cases (*lines 12 to 15*). This is a simplified mapper, and additional destinations from the home screen were omitted for this book.

Within each Presentation to UI destination mapper, we define concrete implementations for every UI destination. *Lines 17 to 21* show the **history(String?)** destination function. Let us break it down.

The first thing to notice is that the implementation is private (*line 17*). This is because no code outside of the mapper should know or care about the concrete UI destination implementation. We have achieved this level of abstraction by leveraging polymorphism through the public **UiDestination** interface and its **navigate(NavController)** function. Thanks to this function, we do not care what **UiDestination** instance we have. When we want to navigate to a destination, we simply execute the **navigate(NavController)** function.

Still on *line 16*, note that we used a function to tidy up our code. The function accepts a nullable IP address string (*line 18*) and returns an anonymous **UiDestination** implementation (*lines 19 to 21*). The nullability here is interesting. The **highlightedIpAddress** argument will be **null** when we navigate to the history screen without first saving an IP address (this case is not shown here). The last thing that is worth noting on *line 16* is the function name. We try to keep things simple: since this function returns a destination that navigates to the history screen, the name **history** will do.

To navigate to the history screen, our UI destination implementation needs a **NavController** instance, which the **navigate(NavController)** function receives (*line 19*).

The actual navigation behavior of our UI destination, including the navigation target, is defined on *line 20*. In this case, it is a simple call to the **navigate(Any)** function of the **NavController** instance, passing in the **History** route. For completeness, this is the **Routes.kt** file, saved in the **app** Gradle module under the **ui** package:

Routes.kt

```
1.    package com.mitteloupe.whoami.ui.main.route
2.
3.    import kotlinx.serialization.Serializable
4.
```

```
5.    @Serializable
6.    object Home
7.
8.    @Serializable
9.    data class History(val highlightedIpAddress: String?)
```

The **Routes.kt** file holds a couple of routes used for type-safe navigation in a Compose project. You can read more about it here:

https://developer.android.com/guide/navigation/design/type-safety

Depending on your individual navigation solution choices, you may have to provide other dependencies to your mapper and the concrete destinations. The pattern will remain the same whether you use Google's XML-based Navigation components, Intent-based navigation, or any other navigation approach.

To test our Presentation to UI destination mappers, we can use a parameterized test. The input would be the Presentation destination model. Since the UI destination models are private, we would instead execute the **navigate(NavController)** function of the mapper output and verify that the expected navigation took place.

When we looked at the **NavigationEventDestinationMapper** abstract class, we saw that when a mapper failed to handle a Presentation navigation event, it threw an **UnhandledNavigationException** object. In case you were wondering, the following code shows its implementation, which helps you figure out what Presentation navigation event was not handled successfully:

UnhandledNavigationException.kt

```
1. package com.mitteloupe.whoami.architecture.ui.navigation.exception
2.
3. import com...architecture.model.presentation.PresentationDestination
4.
5. class UnhandledNavigationException(
6.     event: PresentationNavigationEvent
7. ) : IllegalArgumentException(
8.     "Navigation event ${event::class.simpleName} was not handled."
9. )
```

This exception lives in the **architecture:ui** module. We keep it under the same **ui.navigation** subpackage used by the **NavigationEventDestinationMapper** class and the **UiDestination** interface. We then place it under the **exception** subpackage (*line 1*).

The constructor takes a **PresentationNavigationEvent** as an argument (*line 6*). This helps us debug any app crashes caused by trying to handle an unsupported navigation event (see *line 8*).

`UnhandledNavigationException` extends `IllegalArgumentException` (*lines* 7 to 9), passing in a meaningful error message including, as we have just covered, the event class name. Remember that with obfuscation, the event class name may be lost. Consider excluding navigation events from obfuscation if this is a concern.

Conclusion

Having read this chapter, you should now have a good grasp of how our Clean Architecture app is put together. You should know how to instantiate all the different classes that are required by individual features. You should also have a clear understanding of how navigation within the app and between screens and features is managed.

In the next chapter, we will shift our focus to testing. More specifically, we will see how each of the classes that were mentioned in the last few chapters to be testable gets thoroughly tested.

Points to remember

When it comes to dependency injection and navigation, these are the key things you should remember:

- **Start simple**: When you implement a DI solution, do not rush to break down your solution into small components. Start with one central place and break it down as the need arises.

- **Group dependencies by feature, then layer**: As you break down your DI solution into smaller components, focus on breaking it down by feature first. If you need to break it down further, break it down by layer. This keeps related dependencies close together.

- **Isolate features**: Remember that features should generally not know about each other. While there are exceptions to this rule, try to keep each feature separate from the others, with the app dealing with the integration.

- **Navigation at the feature level is abstract**: Remember that features report the user's intent. They should not know where the user would end up after they leave the feature.

- **Testing, testing, testing**: Good DI solutions will usually fail during compilation if implemented incorrectly. Navigation, on the other hand, should be tested. Parameterized tests can help.

CHAPTER 8
Unit Testing

I have to keep testing myself.

- Eartha Kitt

Introduction

A clear benefit of having an architecture that breaks the responsibilities down into small classes with clear responsibilities is testability. Clean Architecture is especially useful in this regard, since most of the code, by design, does not rely on any third-party constraints. This makes unit testing significantly easier.

In this chapter, we will not go into **test-driven development** (**TDD**) because how you choose to write your unit tests is up to you. We will, however, see what code needs testing and how those tests should look.

Structure

In this chapter, we will cover the following topics:

- The value of unit tests
- Testing the Domain layer
- Testing the Presentation layer

- Testing the Data layer

- Testing the DataSource layer

- The fallacy of test coverage

Objectives

Unit tests are important. This chapter shares the reasons why and provides concrete examples of unit tests within a Clean Architecture project. By the end of it, you will have a clear idea of what to unit test and how. You should also have a clear understanding of why you should never neglect your unit tests.

The value of unit tests

When we develop an app, we write production code. Our code presents data to the user, takes user input, processes it, and feeds data back to the user. None of these responsibilities requires tests to work. *Why bother with tests, then?*

In fact, there are at least three good reasons for writing tests:

- Documentation

- Validation

- Protection against regression and accidental changes

The first reason for writing tests is *documentation*. If you adopt the Clean Code approach, you are likely to have very few comments in your codebase. Comments will usually be replaced by better-named classes, functions, variables, and so forth. While these explain *what* the code does, they do not explain what the expectations of the code are, or the *why*.

If we consider a mapper as an example, the production code would tell us what values *are* translated into what. A test would tell us what we *expect* to be translated into what. The distinction is important. A well-written test describes our expectations of the code. It does not concern itself with the *how*, or the internal details of the implementation (well, no more than it must).

The second reason for writing tests is *validation*. For the same reason that accountants use double bookkeeping to ensure that they do not make errors, we write tests, at the risk of repeating ourselves, to make certain that our expectations match the actual behavior of the code.

The third reason is protection against *regressions* and *accidental changes*. Imagine changing your code in the process of development to experiment with certain behavior. Imagine that by the time you are done with the piece of work, you forget the quick and dirty hack that you introduced to check a certain state and commit it. Your tests are there to flag such errors. If your change was intentional, you would have updated the tests as well.

These are by no means the only reasons to write unit tests. I cannot tell you the number of times when I had to work on unfamiliar code, and existing tests gave me confidence that I was not breaking the code when refactoring. This is a common industry phenomenon: projects grow in complexity over time, and team members come and go. Having the reassurance of written unit tests becomes priceless.

The bottom line is this: respect your tests. Writing tests may cost you time, but I guarantee that those tests will save you a lot more time than they cost in the long run.

So, what do we test and how? In the next section, we will start breaking it down.

Testing the Domain layer

In the previous chapters, we said that the development of a feature should start at the Domain. It is only natural, then, that we would cover the testing of the Domain layer first.

The main entity of the Domain layer is the usecase. Usecases are usually very straightforward classes and so are quite simple to test. Let us take the **GetConnectionDetailsUseCase** class from *Chapter 3, The Domain Layer*, as an example. Here is a quick reminder:

GetConnectionDetailsUseCase.kt

```
1.    package com.mitteloupe.whoami.home.domain.usecase
2.
3.    [imports...]
4.
5.    class GetConnectionDetailsUseCase(
6.        private val repository: GetConnectionDetailsRepository,
7.        coroutineContextProvider: CoroutineContextProvider
8.    ) : ContinuousExecutingUseCase<Unit, ConnectionDetailsDomainModel>(
9.        coroutineContextProvider
10.   ) {
11.       override fun executeInBackground(request: Unit) =
12.           repository.connectionDetails()
13.   }
```

In our example, we will use JUnit 4. I will leave choosing your preferred test framework to you.

This usecase has one public function: **executeInBackground**. While it is true that it also has an **execute** function inherited from the **ContinuousExecutingUseCase** class, we are not interested in testing the functionality of that function every time we test a usecase. Furthermore, it is not implemented or modified in **GetConnectionDetailsUseCase**, so there is no value in testing it here. For these reasons, we test **executeInBackground** directly. This is what a test file for the above usecase would look like:

GetDishDetailsUseCaseTest.kt

```
1.    package com.mitteloupe.whoami.home.domain.usecase
2.
3.    [imports...]
4.
5.    @RunWith(MockitoJUnitRunner::class)
6.    class GetConnectionDetailsUseCaseTest {
```

Going from top to bottom, the first thing to note is that the package name of our unit test matches that of the class under test[1], **GetConnectionDetailsUseCase**, i.e., **com.mitteloupe. whoami.home.domain.usecase**. The file will be stored in the **home:domain** module under **[PROJECT_ROOT]/app/src/test/java/com/mitteloupe/whoami/home/domain/usecase**. Note that since these are unit tests, they are stored under **test**, not **androidTest**.

In case you are not used to writing tests, it may be worth to briefly cover what **mocks** are. In a unit test, we want to test *a single class* in isolation. This means that we do not want to execute any code that lives *outside of that class* or within its injected dependencies. This is where mocks come into the picture.

Mocks are dummy instances of classes. Instead of relying on the real behavior of real class instances, we stub, or fake, the expected behavior using such dummy instances. This allows us to test the class in question without worrying about any logic that is external to it. We work on the assumption that the dependencies of the class that is being tested are themselves tested in isolation. This allows us to set expectations. We can configure the mock to respond in a certain way to certain function calls without that class doing any actual work.

At least two popular libraries exist for mocking in Kotlin: **Mockito** and **MockK**. We will use Mockito going forward. Most of the principles we will discuss are not library-specific.

Having said that, a few words of advice specifically related to **Mockito**: since we need to mock some dependencies, we use the **MockitoJUnitRunner** class (*line 5*). Out of the options that Mockito provides for instantiating mocks (including a JUnit rule, a static function call, and in-place instantiation), this is the option that I would recommend using whenever possible. The only case in which you should fall back to using the JUnit rule would be when you would want to use a different JUnit runner, such as the **Parameterized** or **Suite** runners.

The reason is simple: when using the **MockitoJUnitRunner** runner, you get reliable automatic validation of your Mockito usage on top of the mock instantiation. While using the rule offers the same benefits, it is not as succinct. Whether you prefer to use the runner or the rule is your choice, but avoid calling **MockitoAnnotations.initMocks** directly, as you will lose the reliable framework validation if you do.

---

1 The term class under test is a common way to refer to the class that is being unit tested. Other common names are the cut acronym of the same term and subject.

The name of the test class is, by convention, the same as that of the class under test but with a **Test** suffix (*line 6*). So, for **GetConnectionDetailsUseCase**, we end up with **GetConnectionDetailsUseCaseTest**. Let us continue with the test file:

GetConnectionDetailsUseCaseTest.kt (continued)

```
 7.    private lateinit var classUnderTest: GetConnectionDetailsUseCase
 8.
 9.    @Mock
10.    private lateinit var getConnectionDetailsRepository:
11.        GetConnectionDetailsRepository
12.
13.    @Mock
14.    private lateinit var coroutineContextProvider:
15.        CoroutineContextProvider
```

The first field that we define is that of our class under test (which is **GetConnectionDetailsUseCase**, see *line 7*). I always prefer calling this field **classUnderTest**. This makes all my tests consistent and predictable, as well as making the most important class in the test stand out. It is a **lateinit var** because we want to instantiate it in the **setUp()** function later. We know that we will fulfill the promise that **lateinit** makes, and the field will be initialized by the time it is first accessed. The first access would be in a test, which only happens after the **setUp()** function is finished. Since the field does not need to be accessed from outside the test class, it is declared private.

The next fields that we define are our mocks (*lines 9 to 15*). As each field is annotated with the **@Mock** annotation (*lines 9, 13*), both fields will be initialized by the Mockito runner. Therefore, mocks are also defined as **lateinit var** fields. Like the class under test, our mocks are private.

I tend to name my fields by the class type that they hold. The field for a **GetConnectionDetailsRepository** object is therefore named **getConnectionDetailsRepository**, and that of the **CoroutineContextProvider** is named **coroutineContextProvider**. I make an exception when two or more instances of the same type are needed. In that case, I try to give each instance a meaningful name that would give me a quick indication of which instance is used for what purpose. Let us continue with the test file:

GetDishDetailsUseCaseTest.kt (continued)

```
17.    @Before
18.    fun setUp() {
19.        classUnderTest = GetConnectionDetailsUseCase(
20.            getConnectionDetailsRepository,
21.            coroutineContextProvider
```

```
22.          )
23.          }
```

Next, we have the initialization block (*lines 17* to *23*). It is declared by annotating a function with the **@Before** annotation (*line 17*). By convention, the function is named **setUp** (*line 18*). The function is expected to have no arguments. This function sets the stage before every individual test. Every such test starts by executing the **@Before** annotated function (if it is present) and once the test completes, it finishes by executing the optional **@After** annotated function to tidy up after itself. I rarely find myself needing to tidy up after the tests, as you can see from this example. This is because I try to avoid depending on, and therefore having to set and clear, any global state.

The most common responsibility of the **setUp** function is to instantiate the **classUnderTest**, providing it with any constructor dependencies, which are commonly mocks (see *lines 19* to *22*). This can sometimes be replaced by annotating the **classUnderTest** with **@InjectMocks**[2]. However, covering that option is outside of the scope of this book. The other kind of code that you are likely to find in a **setUp** function is that which configures the mocks to behave a certain way across all tests (this is known as stubbing).

Let us imagine, for example, that we are injecting a configuration mock into our class under test. Let us assume that the configuration mock has a field that tells us whether we are in debug mode. In our test, we may only be interested in testing the code that is not debug-related. In this case, we can configure our mock to always return false when queried for the debug mode state. This will be done in the **setUp** function because it applies to every test.

Another example could be a factory mock, which we always expect to produce the same mocked instance. This, too, can be done in the **setUp** function.

Let us get back to our test:

GetDishDetailsUseCaseTest.kt (continued)

```
25.    @Test
26.    fun `Given connection details when executeInBackground then returns
       connection details`() = runBlocking {
27.        // Given
28.        val expectedConnectionDetails =
29.            ConnectionDetailsDomainModel.Disconnected
30.        given { getConnectionDetailsRepository.connectionDetails() }
31.            .willReturn(flowOf(expectedConnectionDetails))
32.
33.        // When
34.        val actualValue = classUnderTest.executeInBackground(Unit)
35.            .lastOrNull()
```

2 **https://www.javadoc.io/doc/org.mockito/mockito-core/latest/org/mockito/InjectMocks.html**

```
36.
37.        // Then
38.        assertEquals(expectedConnectionDetails, actualValue)
39.    }
```

After setting up the stage for our tests, we can implement our actual test (*lines 25 to 39*). We annotate each test with the **@Test** annotation (*line 25*). This tells JUnit that the following function describes a test. A nice feature of Kotlin is that it allows you to name your function as a sentence by putting it between backticks (`` `...` ``). We name our test by following the **behavior-driven development** (**BDD**) paradigm. This means our test name starts with a **Given**, which is the context of the test, or where we configure the test scenario. The name follows up with a **when**, which describes the action taken, the action that we are testing. Finally, it describes the acceptance criteria, or the verification of the outcome in the form of a **then**. This is how we end up with the expressive function name `` `Given connection details when executeInBackground then returns connection details` `` (*line 26*). Do not worry about the long name, we are happy that it describes the test well.

Still on *line 26*, we can see that our test is wrapped in a **runBlocking** block because it needs to execute a suspending function.

We break our test down into three sections following the same BDD paradigm. We mark each section appropriately using a comment (this is one of the only cases where I rely on comments) and so, we have three comments, one for each section: **// Given**, **// When**, and **// Then**.

Under **Given** (*lines 28 to 31*), we declare all our constants and stubs. We also perform any actions required to configure the initial state for the test scenario. In our example, we declare the expected connection details model (*lines 28 and 29*), which can represent any state. This is the value that we expect to get back from the call to **executeInBackground**. Next, on *lines 30 and 31*, we stub the **getConnectionDetailsRepository connectionDetails()** function call so that it would return the expected connection details that we declared earlier.

Under **When** (*lines 34-35*), we execute the **executeInBackground** call, passing in **Unit**. This is the behavior that we are testing. We call **lastOrNull()** to collect the latest value emitted from the tested class. This is the suspending function that required the earlier **runBlocking** wrapper. We store the result in **actualValue**. I usually prefix any results returned from the class under test with **actual**, highlighting that these are the values that I am interested in validating.

So, under **Then**, I validate that the value of the **actualValue** variable matches the expected connection details (*line 38*). Note that when using **assertEquals**[3] we should provide the expected value first, followed by the value we are testing against. The order of arguments matters because it makes the error message in case of failure meaningful. When the fields are reversed, the error message is confusing.

---

3 assertEquals belongs to the Assert class that comes bundled with the Junit framework. Alternative assertion libraries, such as Hamcreset, Kluent and kotlin.test exist. Since this is down to personal preference, the examples in this book will use the Junit Assert functions.

Some usecases do not return values. When testing these usecases, I usually use the **verify** function to make sure that the relevant repository function was called.

This wraps up our usecase test. Since usecases are quite simple in nature, so are their tests. Since there is very little logic in the Domain layer, this concludes the Domain section of this chapter. We will look into testing the Presentation layer next.

Testing the Presentation layer

In our Presentation layer, we have our viewmodels (or presenters if we have an MVP architecture). These are important classes to test as they hold our Presentation logic. For our viewmodels or presenters to pass data that is provided by the Domain layer to the UI, as well as from the UI to the Domain, they require mappers. Mappers are equally important in terms of testing because they are the bridges using which data travels across the layer boundaries.

As mappers are an important part of our implementation, let us start our Presentation layer test coverage with testing a mapper. Specifically, we will be testing **ConnectionDetailsDomainToPresentationMapper**. I have not shown you this class before, so here it is:

ConnectionDetailsPresentationMapper.kt

```
1.    package com.mitteloupe.whoami.home.presentation.mapper
2.
3.    [imports...]
4.
5.    class ConnectionDetailsPresentationMapper(
6.        private val exceptionPresentationMapper:
7.            ExceptionPresentationMapper
8.    ) {
9.        fun toPresentation(
10.            connectionDetails: ConnectionDetailsDomainModel
11.        ) = when (connectionDetails) {
12.            is Connected -> HomeViewState.Connected(
13.                ipAddress = connectionDetails.ipAddress,
14.                city = connectionDetails.city,
15.                region = connectionDetails.region,
16.                countryCode = connectionDetails.countryCode,
17.                geolocation = connectionDetails.geolocation,
18.                internetServiceProviderName =
19.                    connectionDetails.internetServiceProviderName,
20.                postCode = connectionDetails.postCode,
21.                timeZone = connectionDetails.timeZone
```

```
22.              )
23.
24.              Disconnected -> HomeViewState.Disconnected
25.              Unset -> HomeViewState.Loading
26.              is Error -> {
27.                  HomeViewState.Error(
28.                      exceptionPresentationMapper.toPresentation(
29.                          connectionDetails.exception
30.                      )
31.                  )
32.              }
33.          }
34.      }
```

I picked this mapper because it depends on another mapper (an instance of **ExceptionPresentationMapper**), making for a slightly more interesting test. Here it is, starting with the first few lines:

ConnectionDetailsPresentationMapperTest.kt

```
1.    package com.mitteloupe.whoami.home.presentation.mapper
2.
3.    [imports...]
4.
5.    @RunWith(Parameterized::class)
6.    class ConnectionDetailsPresentationMapperTest(
7.        private val givenConnectionDetails: ConnectionDetailsDomainModel,
8.        private val expectedViewState: HomeViewState,
9.        private val stubMapper: ExceptionPresentationMapper.() -> Unit
10.   ) {
```

The first thing that is worth noting about this test is its runner. We are using the **Parameterized** runner (*line 5*). Given an iterable of arrays of arguments (phew, that is a mouthful!), this runner runs the same test (or tests) once for every such array of arguments. This makes it perfect for testing mappers, where we only need to test that given some input, we receive the expected output, and we want to ensure that it works for different inputs and outputs.

In *lines 7* to *9*, we can see the arguments that the test relies on. The first parameter is **givenConnectionDetails**, which holds a **ConnectionDetailsDomainModel** object. The second is the **expectedViewState** parameter, which holds a **HomeViewState** object. The third and last argument is **stubMapper**, a lambda that is an extension on the **ExceptionPresentationMapper** class. It allows us to stub expected behavior on the mapper per test case. Let us continue with the test class:

ConnectionDetailsPresentationMapperTest.kt (continued)

```
11.         companion object {
12.             @JvmStatic
13.             @Parameters(name = "Given {0} then returns {1}")
14.             fun data(): Iterable<Array<*>> = setOf(
15.                 connectedTestCase(
16.                     ipAddress = "1.2.3.4",
17.                     city = null,
18.                     region = null,
19.                     country = null,
20.                     geolocation = null,
21.                     internetServiceProviderName = null,
22.                     postCode = null,
23.                     timeZone = null
24.                 ),
25.                 connectedTestCase(
26.                     ipAddress = "4.3.2.1",
27.                     city = "New York",
28.                     region = "New York",
29.                     country = "United States",
30.                     geolocation = "1.0,1.0",
31.                     internetServiceProviderName = "Whistle",
32.                     postCode = "A123456",
33.                 timeZone = "EST"
34.                 ),
35.                 testCase(Disconnected, HomeViewState.Disconnected),
36.                 testCase(Unset, HomeViewState.Loading),
37.                 errorTestCase(
38.                     UnknownDomainException(),
39.                     ErrorPresentationModel.Unknown
40.                 )
41.             )
```

We continue by introducing a companion object for the parameterized test static setup code.

In the companion object, we declare our test cases as collections of input/output arguments. To generate the static parameter-providing function required by the **Parameterized** runner in Java, we annotate the **data()** function with the **@JvmStatic** annotation (*line 12*).

Next, we annotate the parameters function with the **@Parameters** annotation, which tells our runner that this is its parameters function. We provide the optional **name** argument to construct an identifiable name for each test case. This is helpful when debugging failed cases. **{0}** and

{1} are placeholders that are later replaced by the constructor arguments in the corresponding order. If you feel that the **toString()** values of your input and output variables are too verbose or unclear, you can provide additional arguments for the sake of clearer identification and labeling of test cases. I sometimes provide a string value for this purpose.

Lastly, we name our parameters function **data()** (*line 23*). We could name it anything that we want, but **data** is the name that is used in the JUnit documentation, and seems like a sensible name.

The data function returns an **Iterable<Array<Any>>**. Specifically, we return a set of test cases, each item of which is an array holding a value for each constructor argument of the test class. To streamline the test cases, we implement the private **connectedTestCase**, **testCase**, and **errorTestCase** functions. We will get into these functions next. For now, note how every test case is represented by a function call (see *lines 15 to 40*).

Moving on, we can see what the **connectedTestCase**, **testCase**, and **errorTestCase** functions look like:

ConnectionDetailsPresentationMapperTest.kt (continued)

```
43.          private fun testCase(
44.              connectionDetails: ConnectionDetailsDomainModel,
45.              viewState: HomeViewState,
46.              stubMapper: ExceptionPresentationMapper.() -> Unit = {}
47.          ) = arrayOf(connectionDetails, viewState, stubMapper)
48.
49.          private fun connectedTestCase(
50.              ipAddress: String,
51.              city: String?,
52.              region: String?,
53.              country: String?,
54.              geolocation: String?,
55.              internetServiceProviderName: String?,
56.              postCode: String?,
57.              timeZone: String?
58.          ) = testCase(
59.              Connected(
60.                  ipAddress,
61.                  city,
62.                  region,
63.                  country,
64.                  geolocation,
65.                  internetServiceProviderName,
66.                  postCode,
```

```
67.                       timeZone
68.                   ),
69.               HomeViewState.Connected(
70.                   ipAddress,
71.                   city,
72.                   region,
73.                   country,
74.                   geolocation,
75.                   internetServiceProviderName,
76.                   postCode,
77.                   timeZone
78.               )
79.           )
80.
81.       private fun errorTestCase(
82.           domainException: DomainException,
83.           presentationError: ErrorPresentationModel
84.       ) = testCase(
85.           Error(domainException),
86.           HomeViewState.Error(presentationError)
87.       ) {
88.           given { toPresentation(domainException) }
89.               .willReturn(presentationError)
90.       }
91.   }
```

On *lines 43 to 47*, we have the first **testCase(…)** function that we just mentioned. It is a convenience function designed to group all the arguments required by a test case and provide type safety. In our case, its parameters are a **ConnectionDetailsDomainModel** object, a **HomeViewState** object, and an extension lambda on **ExceptionPresentationMapper** for stubbing the behavior of its instance. The lambda does nothing by default. These arguments mirror the test class constructor parameters (on *lines 7 to 9* earlier).

As constructing a concrete **ConnectionDetailsDomainModel** instance can get quite verbose, and because the fields in some of its states are expected to be returned in the **HomeViewState** instance as-is, we have two additional private **testCase** functions: **connectedTestCase** (*lines 49 to 79*) and **errorTestCase** (*lines 81 to 90*). The responsibility of these functions is easy to identify because both have names ending with **TestCase**. Both functions have parameters that reflect the models that they need to produce. They construct the required given and expected models and let the **testCase** function (on *line 43*) glue them together using an array, to satisfy the expectations of the **data()** function. The **errorTestCase** function takes care of stubbing the **ExceptionPresentationMapper** object, too (*lines 88 and 89*).

The arguments for the extended test case functions (**connectedTestCase** and **errorTestCase**) include an argument for each value that we rely on to construct our models. This creates a flattened structure for providing the arguments. An added value of having test case convenience functions is that we can define default values. Imagine that we wanted each test case to modify only one of the fields. If we define default values for all fields, we could omit all values but the one in question per test case. We could then test changes to **ipAddress**, **city**, **region**, **country**, and so on in isolation. Remember that in our case, the actual value of **ipAddress** does not really matter, as any value that is passed in and returned as-is would make the test pass.

Let us move on:

ConnectionDetailsPresentationMapperTest.kt (continued)

```
93.        @get:Rule
94.        val mockitoRule: MethodRule = MockitoJUnit.rule()
95.
96.        private lateinit var classUnderTest:
97.            ConnectionDetailsPresentationMapper
98.
99.        @Mock
100.       private lateinit var exceptionPresentationMapper:
101.           ExceptionPresentationMapper
102.
103.       @Before
104.       fun setUp() {
105.           classUnderTest = ConnectionDetailsPresentationMapper(
106.               exceptionPresentationMapper
107.           )
108.       }
```

As we are using the **Parameterized** runner, we use a **MockitoRule** object to instantiate our mocks (*lines* 93 and 94). It makes sense to name the rule **mockitoRule** to have a consistent name across our tests that differentiates it from other rules that we may have.

We continue to declare our class under the test field on *lines* 96 and 97. We also declare an instance of the **ExceptionPresentationMapper** class that our class under test depends on as a mock on *lines* 99 to 101.

Our **setUp()** function is annotated with the **@Before** annotation to tell the test runner that it should be executed before every test. The function instantiates our class under test using the mocked **ExceptionPresentationMapper** instance (*lines* 105 to 107).

Next, we will get to the test function:

ConnectionDetailsPresentationMapperTest.kt (continued)

```
110.     @Test
111.      fun `When toPresentation`() {
112.          // Given
113.          exceptionPresentationMapper.stubMapper()
114.
115.          // When
116.          val actualValue = classUnderTest
117.              .toPresentation(givenConnectionDetails)
118.
119.          // Then
120.          assertEquals(expectedViewState, actualValue)
121.      }
122.  }
```

The last part of the test class is the test itself (*lines 110* to *121*). Remember, this test will run once for every test case that we declared earlier. Before each test, **setUp()** will execute, constructing a new instance of the class under test.

Just as with our usecase test, the test itself must be annotated with the **@Test** annotation (*line 110*). *Do not forget this annotation.* You will get no warnings or errors if you do. The class will compile and run. The test will simply not run and will not report any results. When this is your only test, it will be very noticeable. However, once you start having tens, hundreds, or even thousands of unit tests, it will become increasingly easy to miss the accidental omission.

Since we named the individual cases with a **Given** and a **then** (see *line 13* earlier), our function name can describe the function by simply specifying the name of the function it will execute, preceded by **When** (*line 111*), completing the given/when/then BDD paradigm.

Under the **Given** section (*line 113*), we stub the **exceptionPresentationMapper** object using the constructor-provided **stubMapper** lambda extension function. You can remind yourself of its declaration on *line 9* and the concrete implementation on *lines 88* and *89*.

> **Note:** One common shortcut that developers take is to rely on calling the any() function as the input matchers instead of specifying the input argument directly. The any() function tells Mockito to stub any call to the stubbed function by returning the expected value regardless of the input value. My advice to you: avoid any() as much as possible. In most cases, we know precisely what data should be used to execute the stubbed function. By validating that the expected value was used, we are adding value to our test: it now protects us from accidentally passing the wrong value to the call.

Going back to *lines 88* to *90*, let us say that we used the **any()** function in our stubbing instead of the **domainException** variable. Imagine that we had two exception models: **domainException1** and **domainException2**. Now imagine that we accidentally mapped **domainException1** into **presentationException2** and **domainException2** into **presentationException1**. Our test may fail because the models will not match. What if we swapped the order in which we used the presentation models? We could make the test pass. Why is this a problem? Due to our stubbing no longer reflecting the expected production behavior. This means that we will have production bugs with passing tests. Of course, the tangle of mappings will also make maintenance of the code extremely difficult.

The preceding scenario can be mitigated by avoiding the use of **any()** and explicitly specifying both the expected input and the expected output of each stubbed call.

Back to our test, we continue to implement our When section, where we execute the **toPresentation(ConnectionDetailsDomainModel)** function, passing in the **givenConnectionDetails** value of our current test case (*lines 116* and *117*). We store the result in the **actualValue** variable.

Finally, to verify that our mapper works as expected, we compare the value of the **actualValue** variable against the value stored in the **expectedViewState** variable for this test case.

This concludes our mapper test. All mapper tests for all mappers across the different Clean Architecture layers are very similar and follow the principles that were laid out previously. We will therefore avoid going over any other mapper tests. I will mention them where relevant, but please refer to the explanations above when in doubt.

The second class type that we want to have test coverage for in our Presentation layer is the viewmodel. It is extremely important that we test this class, as it holds our Presentation logic.

Before we dive into a concrete viewmodel test, let us go over a base class for our viewmodel tests, which reduces the boilerplate code in individual tests. The version provided in this book is stripped down to the bare minimum required, but you can scale it up as the need arises:

BaseViewModelTest.kt

```
1.    package com.mitteloupe.whoami.architecture.presentation.viewmodel
2.
3.    [imports...]
4.
5.    abstract class BaseViewModelTest<
6.        VIEW_MODEL :
7.            BaseViewModel<out Any, out PresentationNotification>
8.        > {
9.        private val testScheduler = TestCoroutineScheduler()
10.
11.        private val testDispatcher =
12.            UnconfinedTestDispatcher(testScheduler)
13.
```

```
14.        protected lateinit var classUnderTest: VIEW_MODEL
15.
16.        @Mock
17.        protected lateinit var useCaseExecutor: UseCaseExecutor
18.
19.        @Before
20.        fun coroutineSetUp() {
21.            Dispatchers.setMain(testDispatcher)
22.        }
23.
24.        @After
25.        fun coroutineTearDown() {
26.            Dispatchers.resetMain()
27.        }
28.
29.        protected fun <RESULT> UseCase<Unit, RESULT>
30.            .givenSuccessfulExecution(result: RESULT) {
31.            willAnswer { invocationOnMock ->
32.                val onResult: (RESULT) -> Unit =
33.                    invocationOnMock.getArgument(1)
34.                onResult(result)
35.            }.given(useCaseExecutor).execute(
36.                useCase = eq(this@givenSuccessfulExecution),
37.                onResult = any(),
38.                onException = any()
39.            )
40.        }
41.    }
```

The **BaseViewModelTest** abstract class is part of the architecture pseudo-feature's Presentation layer. It will be used to test individual viewmodels, and as such will always be coupled to a specific viewmodel per test class. We use the **VIEW_MODEL** generic type (*lines 6 and 7*) to help us declare a typed **classUnderTest** variable.

A second common pattern when testing viewmodels that we extracted to the **BaseViewModelTest** class is the setting of a test main dispatcher for coroutines. As you can see, this involves a lot of boilerplate code (*lines 9, 11, 12, 19 to 22, and 24 to 27*).

A third bit of common code that we introduced in **BaseViewModelTest** is the mocking of a **UseCaseExecutor** instance (*lines 16 and 17*).

The fourth and final block of reusable code is the **givenSuccessfulUseCaseExecution** function (*lines 29 to 40*). This function uses Mockito to stub usecase execution to execute the

onResult(RESULT) lambda that is provided when the usecase is executed. You may have noticed that, after passionately advising you to avoid the use of the **any()** function, I am using it myself. When an argument passed to a function is an anonymous lambda, we have no choice but to use the **any()** function, because we have no way to match the exact lambda.

Looking back at the **HomeViewModel** class, it had two public functions that we want to test: **onEnter()** and **onViewHistoryAction**. Note that we are not interested in testing private functions directly. First, let us quickly remind ourselves of what **HomeViewModel** looked like:

HomeViewModelTest.kt

```
1.    package com.mitteloupe.whoami.home.presentation.viewmodel
2.
3.    [imports...]
4.
5.    class HomeViewModel(
6.        private val getConnectionDetailsUseCase:
7.            GetConnectionDetailsUseCase,
8.        private val connectionDetailsPresentationMapper:
9.            ConnectionDetailsPresentationMapper,
10.       private val exceptionPresentationMapper:
11.           ExceptionPresentationMapper,
12.       useCaseExecutor: UseCaseExecutor
13.   ) : BaseViewModel<HomeViewState, HomePresentationNotification>(
14.       useCaseExecutor
15.   ) {
16.       fun onEnter() {
17.           updateViewState(Loading)
18.           fetchConnectionDetails()
19.       }
20.
21.       fun onViewHistoryAction() {
22.           emitNavigationEvent(OnViewHistory)
23.       }
24.
25.       private fun fetchConnectionDetails() {
26.           getConnectionDetailsUseCase(
27.               onResult = ::presentConnectionDetails,
28.               onException = ::presentError
29.           )
30.       }
31.
```

```
32.        private fun presentConnectionDetails(
33.            connectionDetails: ConnectionDetailsDomainModel
34.        ) {
35.            updateViewState(connectionDetailsPresentationMapper
36.                    .toPresentation(connectionDetails))
37.        }
38.
39.        private fun presentError(exception: DomainException) {
40.            updateViewState(Error(
41.                exceptionPresentationMapper.toPresentation(exception)
42.            ))
43.        }
44.    }
```

Remember, this is a simplified version of the **HomeViewModel** class that is used to demonstrate key concepts.

Now, let us take a look at **HomeViewModelTest.kt**, the test file for the **HomeViewModel** class:

HomeViewModelTest.kt

```
1.     package com.mitteloupe.whoami.home.presentation.viewmodel
2.
3.     [imports...]
4.
5.     @RunWith(MockitoJUnitRunner::class)
6.     class HomeViewModelTest :
7.         BaseViewModelTest<HomeViewModel>() {
8.         @Mock
9.         private lateinit var getConnectionDetailsUseCase:
10.            GetConnectionDetailsUseCase
11.
12.        @Mock
13.        private lateinit var connectionDetailsPresentationMapper:
14.            ConnectionDetailsPresentationMapper
15.
16.        @Mock
17.        private lateinit var saveConnectionDetailsUseCase:
18.            SaveConnectionDetailsUseCase
19.
20.        @Mock
21.        private lateinit var connectionDetailsDomainMapper:
```

```
22.              ConnectionDetailsDomainMapper
23.
24.        @Mock
25.        private lateinit var exceptionPresentationMapper:
26.              ExceptionPresentationMapper
```

As we have covered some of the basics of our unit tests before, we can scan through the first lines of the code briefly. On *line 7*, we can see that the **HomeViewModelTest** class extends the **BaseViewModelTest** abstract class that we discussed earlier. It sets its viewmodel generic type to **HomeViewModel**, which is the viewmodel class that we intend to test.

We continue to declare the mocks that our viewmodel relies on (*lines 8 to 26*). We will use these mocks to construct our viewmodel class under test, as we will see as follows:

HomeViewModelTest.kt (continued)

```
28.        @Before
29.        fun setUp() {
30.        classUnderTest = HomeViewModel(
31.              getConnectionDetailsUseCase,
32.              connectionDetailsPresentationMapper,
33.              saveConnectionDetailsUseCase,
34.              connectionDetailsDomainMapper,
35.              exceptionPresentationMapper,
36.              useCaseExecutor
37.          )
38.        }
```

When constructing our class under test, we simply pass in all our mocks. The only argument that was not explicitly mocked in the **HomeViewModelTest** class is **useCaseExecutor**, which was mocked in **BaseViewModelTest**. Next, we get to see our first test:

DishDetailsViewModelTest.kt (continued)

```
40.        @Test
41.        fun `Given disconnected when onEnter then presents disconnected
           state`() = runTest {
42.            // Given
43.            val givenConnectionState = Disconnected
44.            givenSuccessfulUseCaseExecution(
45.                getConnectionDetailsUseCase,
46.                givenConnectionState
47.            )
48.            val expectedViewState = HomeViewState.Disconnected
```

```
49.            given { connectionDetailsPresentationMapper
50.                .toPresentation(givenConnectionState)
51.            }.willReturn(expectedViewState)
52.            val deferredViewState = async(start = UNDISPATCHED) {
53.                classUnderTest.viewState.take(2).toList()
54.            }
55.
56.            // When
57.            classUnderTest.onEnter()
58.            val actualValue = deferredViewState.await()
59.
60.            // Then
61.            assertEquals(Loading, actualValue[0])
62.            assertEquals(expectedViewState, actualValue[1])
63.        }
```

Our first test is declared on *lines 40* to *63*. In it, we test the **onEnter()** function. As the test name (*line 41*) suggests, we want to verify that given a disconnected state, when we call the **onEnter** function, the viewmodel presents that disconnected state.

We start by declaring the given connection state of **Disconnected** (*line 43*). We proceed to stub the mocked **getConnectionDetailsUseCase** object to return that state (*lines 44 to 47*).

We then declare the expected domain state that we expect our viewmodel to return (*line 48*). We continue to stub the **connectionDetailsPresentationMapper** object to return the expected view state when called to map the given connection state (*lines 49 to 51*).

The last variable that we declare in the **Given** section is a deferred view state collector (*lines 52 to 54*). The **async** function call takes an optional **CoroutineStart** argument, which we set to **UNDISPATCHED**. This means that the provided coroutine block will execute immediately in the current thread until it first suspends. The second argument to the **async** function is a suspending block. The block suspends on the call to the **toList()** function on *line 53*.

Now all that is left is to call **onEnter** (*line 57*), collect the view state (*line 58*), and assert that the emitted view states match our expectations (*line 61* and *62*). Note that we also check for a loading state before receiving the final disconnected view state.

With the **onEnter()** function covered, we continue to test interactions with our viewmodel and wrap up the test class:

DishDetailsViewModelTest.kt (continued)

```
64.     @Test
65.     fun `When onViewHistoryAction then emits OnViewHistory event`() =
        runTest {
```

```
66.              val deferredNavigationEvent = async(start = UNDISPATCHED) {
67.                  classUnderTest.navigationEvent.first()
68.              }
69.              val expectedNavigationEvent = OnViewHistory
70.
71.              // When
72.              classUnderTest.onViewHistoryAction()
73.              val actualNavigationEvent = deferredNavigationEvent.await()
74.
75.              // Then
76.              assertEquals(
77.                  expectedNavigationEvent,
78.                  actualNavigationEvent
79.              )
80.          }
81.      }
```

To test the **onViewHistoryAction** function, we follow a similar pattern to that presented in our first test. The test name (*line 65*) reflects the structure of the test: we have no prerequisites, and thus no **When** part. When we call the **onViewHistoryEvent** function, we expect the viewmodel to emit an **OnViewHistory** event object.

We start by setting up a deferred navigation event collector, similar to how we set up the deferred view state collector in the previous test (*lines 66 to 68*). We then declare our expected navigation event on *line 69*.

To test the **onViewHistoryAction** function, we call it (*line 72*) and collect any emitted navigation event objects (*line 73*).

Finally, we assert that the emitted navigation event object is the one that we expected on *lines 76 to 79*.

Looking back at the viewmodel test, it is worth setting up your expectations. Your real viewmodel test is likely to be considerably more thorough. We could test any emitted notifications. We could test the unhappy paths (when our usecase fails to execute, for example). Your tests will scale up as your viewmodel does.

With the Domain and Presentation layers tested, the layers that we have left to test are the UI and Data layers. We rarely unit test the UI except for its mappers (end-to-end tests are better suited for most cases), so we are left with the Data layer. We will look into it next.

Testing the Data layer

Having covered the unit testing of the Presentation layer, we have a rough idea of how the Data layer unit tests would look. In many ways, the Data layer mirrors the Presentation layer.

Like the Presentation layer, it is a bridge between the Domain layer and the world outside of our app. Like the Presentation layer, it requires mappers to move data across.

Data layer mappers convert Domain models to Data models and vice versa. These mappers should be unit-tested. Their unit tests would look precisely like those of the Presentation layer mappers. For that reason, we will not explore testing them further in this section. Instead, we will explore the unit testing of repositories.

Here is our **ConnectionDetailsLiveRepository**, as a quick reminder:

ConnectionDetailsRepository.kt

```
1.    package com.mitteloupe.whoami.home.data.repository
2.
3.    [imports...]
4.
5.    private const val RETRY_DELAY_MILLISECONDS = 1000L
6.
7.    class ConnectionDetailsRepository(
8.        private val ipAddressDataSource: IpAddressDataSource,
9.        private val ipAddressInformationDataSource:
10.           IpAddressInformationDataSource,
11.       private val connectionDataSource: ConnectionDataSource,
12.       private val connectionDetailsDomainResolver:
13.           ConnectionDetailsDomainResolver,
14.       private val throwableDomainMapper: ThrowableDomainMapper
15.   ) : GetConnectionDetailsRepository {
16.       override fun connectionDetails():
17.           Flow<ConnectionDetailsDomainModel> =
18.           connectionDataSource.observeIsConnected()
19.               .map { connectionState ->
20.                   val (optionalIpAddress, ipAddressInformation) =
21.                       when (connectionState) {
22.                           Connected -> {
23.                               val ipAddress = ipAddressDataSource
24.                                   .ipAddress()
25.                               ipAddress to try {
26.                                   ipAddressInformationDataSource
27.                                       .ipAddressInformation(ipAddress)
28.                               } catch (
29.                                   _: NoIpAddressInformationDataException
30.                               ) {
31.                                   null
```

```
32.                                }
33.                              }
34.
35.                     Disconnected, Unset -> null to null
36.                   }
37.                 connectionDetailsDomainResolver.toDomain(
38.                     connectionState,
39.                     optionalIpAddress,
40.                     ipAddressInformation
41.                 )
42.             }.retryWhen { cause, _ ->
43.                 emit(Error(throwableDomainMapper.toDomain(cause)))
44.                 delay(RETRY_DELAY_MILLISECONDS)
45.                 true
46.             }
47.     }
```

Our repository has a single public function. Given a valid connection, it simply fetches the connection details. Most repositories would be similar in function. Of course, as our app grows, we may implement more repository interfaces in our repository. This will mean more mappers and more functions, but should generally not mean greater complexity.

In the following test, we will use MockK, to demonstrate a different mocking library. Here is how the test for this repository looks:

ConnectionDetailsRepositoryTest.kt

```
1.   package com.mitteloupe.whoami.home.data.repository
2.
3.   [imports...]
4.
5.   private val defaultIpAddressInformation =
6.       IpAddressInformationDataModel(...)
7.
8.   class ConnectionDetailsRepositoryTest {
9.       private lateinit var classUnderTest:
10.          ConnectionDetailsRepository
11.
12.      @MockK
13.      private lateinit var ipAddressDataSource:
14.          IpAddressDataSource
15.
16.      @MockK
```

```
17.         private lateinit var ipAddressInformationDataSource:
18.             IpAddressInformationDataSource
19.
20.     @MockK
21.         private lateinit var connectionDataSource:
22.             ConnectionDataSource
23.
24.     @MockK
25.         private lateinit var connectionDetailsDomainResolver:
26.             ConnectionDetailsDomainResolver
27.
28.     @MockK
29.         private lateinit var throwableDomainMapper:
30.             ThrowableDomainMapper
31.
32.     @Before
33.     fun setUp() {
34.             MockKAnnotations.init(this)
35.
36.             classUnderTest = ConnectionDetailsRepository(
37.                 ipAddressDataSource,
38.                 ipAddressInformationDataSource,
39.                 connectionDataSource,
40.                 connectionDetailsDomainResolver,
41.                 throwableDomainMapper
42.             )
43.         }
```

When we move on to the test class itself, the first part requires little explanation: we have already covered the package name for tests, the class name, the class under test field, the mocks, and the **setUp()** function. These all follow the same principles as all our other tests. Subtle differences can be found where the MockK library is used: the **@Mock** annotations are replaced by **@MockK** ones. The mocks are initialized by calling the **init** function on the **MockKAnnotations** object, passing in the **ConnectionDetailsRepositoryTest** test object (*line 34*). This replaces the runnable used by Mockito.

At the top of the test file, right after the imports (*lines 5* and *6*), we have a static IP address object to save us the trouble of instantiating multiple such objects in our tests.

Since this requires little further explanation, let us proceed with the test itself:

ConnectionDetailsRepositoryTest.kt (continued)

```
45.        @Test
46.        fun `Given unset connection when connectionDetails then returns
           unset state`() = runBlocking {
47.            // Given
48.            val givenState = ConnectionStateDataModel.Unset
49.            givenConnectionState(givenState)
50.            val expectedState = ConnectionDetailsDomainModel.Unset
51.            givenConnectionDetailsDomainResolverMaps(
52.                givenState,
53.                expectedState
54.            )
55.
56.            // When
57.            val actualValue = classUnderTest.connectionDetails()
58.                .toList()
59.
60.            // Then
61.            assertEquals(listOf(expectedState), actualValue)
62.        }
```

As with every test, we remember to annotate our test with the **@Test** annotation (line 45). We continue to name our test following the BDD paradigm of given, when, and then (line 46). Our **given** is an unset connection. Our **when** is the execution of the **connectionDetails()** function of our class under test. Our **then** is the unset connection state returned.

Under the **Given** comment (*line 47*), we set our prerequisites. First, we declare the given datasource state (*line 48*) and the expected returned repository state (*line 50*). We stub the mocks on *line 49* and *lines 51* to *54*, we will see the declaration of the **givenConnectionState** and **givenConnectionDetailsDomainResolverMaps** functions used for stubbing later in this chapter.

Moving on to the code under the **When** comment (*line 56*), we read the current value of the **connectionDetails()** function, converting the returned flow to a list by calling the **toList()** suspending function.

Finally, under **Then**, we can assert that the actual returned value equals the expected value (*line 61*).

In summary, our test ensures that the correct datasource function is called, and that its response is correctly mapped from Data to Domain before getting returned to us.

The next test is almost identical. Instead of testing the *unset* state, it tests the *disconnected* one:

ConnectionDetailsRepositoryTest.kt (continued)

```
64.        @Test
65.        fun `Given disconnected when connectionDetails then returns
           disconnected state`() = runBlocking {
66.            // Given
67.            val givenState = ConnectionStateDataModel.Disconnected
68.            givenConnectionState(givenState)
69.            val expectedState = ConnectionDetailsDomainModel.Disconnected
70.            givenConnectionDetailsDomainResolverMaps(
71.                givenState,
72.                expectedState
73.            )
74.
75.            // When
76.            val actualValue = classUnderTest.connectionDetails()
77.                    .toList()
78.
79.            // Then
80.            assertEquals(listOf(expectedState), actualValue)
81.        }
```

As we said, this second test is the same as the first one. The difference can be observed on *lines 67* and *69*, where the **Unset** object was replaced by the **Disconnected** one. Since nothing else has changed, we can proceed to the next test:

ConnectionDetailsRepositoryTest.kt (continued)

```
83.        @Test
84.        fun `Given connected when connectionDetails then returns connected
           state`() = runBlocking {
85.            // Given
86.            val givenState = ConnectionStateDataModel.Connected
87.            givenConnectionState(givenState)
88.            val givenIpAddress = "1.2.3.4"
89.            givenIpAddress(givenIpAddress)
90.            every {
91.                ipAddressInformationDataSource
92.                    .ipAddressInformation(givenIpAddress)
93.            } returns defaultIpAddressInformation
94.            val expectedState = ConnectionDetailsDomainModel.Connected(
```

```
95.                ipAddress = givenIpAddress,
96.                city = "Paris",
97.                region = "Paris",
98.                countryCode = "France",
99.                geolocation = "0.0,0.0",
100.               internetServiceProviderName = "Le ISP",
101.               postCode = "12345",
102.               timeZone = "GMT +1"
103.           )
104.       givenConnectionDetailsDomainResolverMaps(
105.               givenState,
106.               expectedState
107.           )
108.
109.           // When
110.           val actualValue = classUnderTest.connectionDetails().toList()
111.
112.           // Then
113.           assertEquals(listOf(expectedState), actualValue)
114.       }
```

The third test (the preceding one) tests the *connected* state. It starts like the first two tests by stubbing the given connection state (*lines 86* to *87*). After that, the tests diverge. When we have a connection, we also have an IP address. We stub an IP address on *lines 88* and *89*. As with the other stubbing functions, we will get to the **givenIpAddress** function later in this chapter.

We continue to stub the datasource to return the **defaultIpAddressInformation** object that we declared earlier when requested to return the IP address information for our given IP address (lines 90 to 93).

On lines 94 to 107, we are back in line with the other tests, stubbing the state that the Data to Domain resolver returns. The blocks commented **When** and **Then** are identical to the same blocks in our first two tests.

Our final test in the **ConnectionDetailsRepositoryTest** class tests the error state:

ConnectionDetailsRepositoryTest.kt (continued)

```
116.       @Test
117.       fun `Given throwable, connected when connectionDetails then
               returns error, connected`() =
118.           runBlocking {
119.               // Given
120.               val givenState = ConnectionStateDataModel.Connected
```

```
121.              givenConnectionState(givenState)
122.              val givenIpAddress = "1.1.1.1"
123.              givenIpAddress(givenIpAddress)
124.              val throwable = Throwable()
125.              every {
126.                  ipAddressInformationDataSource
127.                      .ipAddressInformation(givenIpAddress)
128.              } throws throwable andThen defaultIpAddressInformation
129.
130.              val expectedDomainException = UnknownDomainException(
131.                  throwable
132.              )
133.              every {
134.                  throwableDomainMapper.toDomain(throwable)
135.              } returns expectedDomainException
136.              val expectedState1 = ConnectionDetailsDomainModel
137.                  .Error(expectedDomainException)
138.              val expectedState2 =
139.                  ConnectionDetailsDomainModel.Connected(...)
140.              givenConnectionDetailsDomainResolverMaps(
141.                  givenState,
142.                  expectedState2
143.              )
144.
145.              // When
146.              val actualValue = classUnderTest.connectionDetails()
147.                  .toList()
148.
149.              // Then
150.              assertEquals(
151.                  listOf(expectedState1, expectedState2),
152.                  actualValue
153.              )
154.          }
```

The preceding test starts similarly to the connected state tests, by stubbing a connected state and an IP address (*lines 120 to 123*). After that, things get interesting. Instead of stubbing the datasource to return the default IP address information object, we declare a generic throwable object (*line 124*) and stub the datasource to return this error on the first call to **ipAddressInformation** before returning the IP address information on the second call (*lines 125 to 128*). The second response is set to avoid an infinite retry loop.

On *lines 130 to 135*, we declare the expected Domain exception object. The exception object keeps a reference to the original **throwable** object. We continue to stub the **throwableDomainMapper** mock object to return that Domain exception when **toDomain** is called with the original throwable.

We continue to declare the two expected connection details states on *lines 136 to 139*. We expect the connection details repository to return an error state, followed by a connected state (fields are omitted for brevity). We wrap up our **Given** commented section with a stub of the Data to Domain mapper that maps the given **Connected** Data state to its Domain equivalent.

The **When** commented section (*lines 146 to 147*) is the same as in the previous tests.

Under the **Then** comment, on *lines 150 to 153*, we have our assertion: we expect the returned connection details list to contain an error state followed by a connected state.

Before we wrap up the connection details repository test, I promised you that we would take a look at the stubbing functions that were used in the preceding tests. Here they are:

ConnectionDetailsRepositoryTest.kt (continued)

```
156.        private fun givenConnectionState(
157.            givenState: ConnectionStateDataModel
158.        ) {
159.            every {
160.                connectionDataSource.observeIsConnected()
161.            } returns flow { emit(givenState) }
162.        }
163.
164.        private fun givenConnectionDetailsDomainResolverMaps(
165.            givenState: ConnectionStateDataModel,
166.            expectedState: ConnectionDetailsDomainModel
167.        ) {
168.            every {
169.                connectionDetailsDomainResolver
170.                    .toDomain(eq(givenState), any(), any())
171.            } returns expectedState
172.        }
173.
174.        private fun givenIpAddress(givenIpAddress: String) {
175.            every {
176.                ipAddressDataSource.ipAddress()
177.            } returns givenIpAddress
178.        }
179.    }
```

Starting with the **givenConnectionState(ConnectionStateDataModel)** function (*lines 156 to 162*), we can see that it is responsible for ensuring that when **observeIsConnected()** is called, the **connectionDataSource** mock object returns a flow that emits the value of the **givenState** argument.

Next, we have the **givenConnectionDetailsDomainResolverMaps(ConnectionStateDataModel, ConnectionDetailsDomainModel)** function (*lines 164 to 172*). This function stubs the **connectionDetailsDomainResolver** mock object to return the value of **expectedState** argument when **toDomain** is invoked with the **givenState** argument. For the sake of simplicity, we accept any values for the IP address and the IP address information parameters (hence the two **any()** capturing function calls on *line 180*). You should pass in concrete values instead for more thorough validation.

The final private function is **givenIpAddress(String)** (*lines 174 to 178*). It makes sure that when **ipAddress()** is called on the mock **ipAddressDataSource** object, it returns the value of the **givenIpAddress** argument.

With the repository tested, the last remaining component in our Clean Architecture implementation that needs testing is the datasource.

Testing the DataSource layer

Before we move on to test our datasource, remember that the DataSource layer contains mappers that need testing, too. We will not dwell on them, though, as we have covered the testing of mappers already. Instead, let us start by reminding ourselves of how our datasource class looks:

IpAddressDataSourceImpl.kt

```
1.    package com.mitteloupe.whoami.datasource.ipaddress.datasource
2.
3.    [imports...]
4.
5.    class IpAddressDataSourceImpl(
6.        private val lazyIpAddressService: Lazy<IpAddressService>,
7.        private val ipAddressDataMapper: IpAddressDataMapper
8.    ) : IpAddressDataSource {
9.        private val ipAddressService by lazy {
10.            lazyIpAddressService.value
11.       }
12.
13.       override fun ipAddress(): String = ipAddressDataMapper.toData(
14.            ipAddressService.ipAddress().fetchBodyOrThrow {
15.                NoIpAddressDataException()
```

```
16.            }
17.         )
18.    }
```

Let us see the test for this datasource:

IpAddressDataSourceImplTest.kt

```
1.    package com.mitteloupe.whoami.datasource.ipaddress.datasource
2.
3.    [imports...]
4.
5.    @RunWith(MockitoJUnitRunner::class)
6.    class IpAddressDataSourceImplTest {
7.        private lateinit var classUnderTest: IpAddressDataSourceImpl
8.
9.        private lateinit var lazyIpAddressService: Lazy<IpAddressService>
10.
11.        @Mock
12.        private lateinit var ipAddressService: IpAddressService
13.
14.        @Mock
15.        private lateinit var ipAddressDataMapper: IpAddressDataMapper
16.
17.        @Before
18.        fun setUp() {
19.            lazyIpAddressService = lazy { ipAddressService }
20.            classUnderTest = IpAddressDataSourceImpl(
21.                lazyIpAddressService,
22.                ipAddressDataMapper
23.            )
24.        }
```

If you read the earlier test explanations, the first 24 lines should be clear. The only exception worth noting is *line 19*. As our datasource class requires the service object to be provided lazily, we wrap the **ipAddressService** mock object in a **Lazy** object using the **lazy** function. Let us continue to the first test:

IpAddressDataSourceImplTest.kt (continued)

```
26.        @Test
27.        fun `Given server response when ipAddress then returns IP address`
           () {
```

```
28.          // Given
29.              val ipAddress = "8.8.8.8"
30.              val givenIpAddressResponse = IpAddressApiModel(ipAddress)
31.              val givenResponse: Response<IpAddressApiModel> = mock {
32.                  on { body() } doReturn givenIpAddressResponse
33.              }
34.              val givenServerResponse: Call<IpAddressApiModel> = mock {
35.                  on { execute() } doReturn givenResponse
36.              }
37.              given { ipAddressService.ipAddress() }
38.                  .willReturn(givenServerResponse)
39.              given { ipAddressDataMapper.toData(givenIpAddressResponse) }
40.                  .willReturn(ipAddress)
41.
42.          // When
43.              val actualValue = classUnderTest.ipAddress()
44.
45.          // Then
46.              assertEquals(ipAddress, actualValue)
47.      }
```

Our test starts on *line 27* and is preceded by the **@Test** annotation. The BDD-structured test name tells us that we have a server response, and when we call **ipAddress** we expect to get an IP address back.

On *lines 29* to *38*, we set up the returning of an IP address. We start by declaring an IP address variable. We continue to wrap that variable in an **IpAddressApiModel** object. This is the same model that represents the successful responses of the server, and indeed, we then create a mock server response, setting its **body()** function to return the **IpAddressApiModel** object that we constructed. Finally, we create yet another mock, this time implementing the **Call<IpAddressApiModel>** interface, returning the response that we mocked earlier when **execute()** is called. With this last mock, we can stub the **ipAddressService** mock object's **ipAddress()** function.

We also need to stub the **ipAddressDataMapper** mock object (*lines 39* and *40*). We set it to return the IP address that we declared earlier when requested to map the **IpAddressApiModel** object to the Data layer representation. Remember that in this case, the Data representation is a primitive string.

We continue to execute the **ipAddress()** function and store its response in the **actualValue** variable (*line 43*).

Finally, we assert the actual returned value matches the expected value.

This concludes the happy path scenario. However, what if something went wrong with our request? We will test this scenario next:

IpAddressDataSourceImplTest.kt (continued)

```
49.        @Test(expected = NoIpAddressDataException::class)
50.        fun `Given null server response when ipAddress then throws
           NoIpAddressDataException`() {
51.            // Given
52.            val givenResponse: Response<IpAddressApiModel> = mock {
53.                on { body() } doReturn null
54.            }
55.            val givenServerResponse: Call<IpAddressApiModel> = mock {
56.                on { execute() } doReturn givenResponse
57.            }
58.            given { ipAddressService.ipAddress() }
59.                .willReturn(givenServerResponse)
60.
61.            // When
62.            classUnderTest.ipAddress()
63.
64.            // Then throws NoIpAddressDataException
65.        }
```

To declare our exception test, we start by setting the **expected** property of the **@Test** annotation to **NoIpAddressDataException::class** (*line 49*). This tells JUnit that we expect our code to throw an instance of this exception. This test will only pass if an exception of this type is thrown.

As the name of the test (*line 50*) suggests, if the server response is **null**, when we call **ipAddress** on our datasource object, we expect the above exception to be thrown.

Under the **Given** comment, as you would expect, we mock a response that returns **null** when its **body()** function is called (*lines 52 to 54*). We proceed to create a **Call** mock that returns the mock **Response** object when **execute()** is called (*lines 55 to 57*). We wrap the prerequisites section by stubbing the **ipAddress** function of our mock **ipAddressService** object to return the mock **Call** object (*lines 58 and 59*).

With the mocking and stubbing done, we can call the **ipAddress()** function on *line 62*.

As the comment on *line 64* suggests, we expect an exception of the right type to be thrown at this point. If we get here and an exception of the expected type is not thrown, our test will fail.

We now know that our class under test behaves as expected when the body of the server response is **null**. What else could go wrong? Well, for one, the socket can time out while we are waiting for the server to respond. Let us test this scenario:

IpAddressDataSourceImplTest.kt (continued)

```
67.        @Test(expected = RequestTimeoutDataException::class)
68.        fun `Given socket timeout exception when ipAddress then throws
           RequestTimeoutDataException`() {
69.            // Given
70.            val givenServerResponse: Call<IpAddressApiModel> = mock {
71.                on { execute() } doThrow SocketTimeoutException()
72.            }
73.            given { ipAddressService.ipAddress() }
74.                .willReturn(givenServerResponse)
75.
76.            // When
77.            classUnderTest.ipAddress()
78.
79.            // Then throws NoIpAddressDataException
80.        }
81.    }
```

This test shares a lot in common with the previous test. It, too, expects an exception to be thrown (see *lines 67* and *79*). To emulate a request timeout, we create a mock **Call** object that throws a **SocketTimeoutException** object when its **execute()** function is called (*lines 70* to *72*). We then stub the **ipAddressService** mock object to return the mocked **Call** object when its **ipAddress()** function is called.

When we call **ipAddress()** on our class under test (*line 77*), we expect an object of type **SocketTimeoutException** to be thrown. If it is, our tests will pass.

Have we covered every possible scenario? Probably not. However, we covered the most common ones. When writing tests for your code, try to challenge yourself. *What assumptions have you made? Will those assumptions always be true? Can we end up with values at the boundaries?* An empty collection, a string longer than the expected length, and **Int.MAX_VALUE** are all examples of such boundaries. *Are we getting the right exceptions when we expect them?* Try to make sure that we are.

Having tested the datasource, we have completed the unit test coverage of our Clean Architecture components across all layers. Next, we will discuss what is worth testing, what is not, and how to maintain our tests over time.

The fallacy of test coverage confidence

Many companies focus on test coverage as a metric for the quality of tests. This metric is misleading. Not every line of code is worth testing, and having code covered by a test does not guarantee that it will never fail.

One of the most obvious examples of code that could do without unit tests is simple getters and setters. Writing tests for these functions, which we never expect to change or introduce problems, may simply be bloating your test code without offering any meaningful value. These are known as *trivial tests*.

Focus your test efforts on code that contains logic. Conditional statements, switches, collection access, are all examples that would justify testing. If you are not sure whether code justifies a test, by all means, err on the side of caution and write a test.

The important point is that we should not blindly be writing tests to satisfy some arbitrary metric. Our code coverage should be high because we cover all our important logic, not because every line must be visited by a test.

Furthermore, as I mentioned above, merely visiting a line of code does not guarantee that the line is thoroughly tested. It might only be visited in a certain state. Visiting that line in another state could lead to a bug that the tests missed.

This leads me to my second point: maintaining your tests. When a bug is found (this is inevitable. Expect it to happen, sooner or later), write a test that reproduces the bug. With the failing test in place, fix the bug and make sure that the test passes. This benefits you twice: first, you have proof that the bug is fixed. Second, your code has a test covering it in case the bug is ever reintroduced.

Do not neglect your tests. Keep them updated, and they will serve you as documentation and as insurance.

Conclusion

Unit testing is a powerful tool. Clean Architecture helps us apply that tool in a structured way, which allows us to have *meaningful* test coverage. Our test documents the expectations of our different classes and functions and provides an added layer of protection against bugs, current and future.

Writing and maintaining your unit tests leverages one of Clean Architecture's greatest strengths, its high testability. Once you get into the habit of writing these tests, the effort involved becomes negligible, especially compared to the returns of having those tests in place.

In the next chapter, we will cover testing the parts that we cannot test easily (or at all) using unit tests. Namely, we will be testing the UI and the integration of all our components into a working app.

Points to remember

When it comes to unit testing your code, these are a few points worth keeping in mind:

- Unit-test your usecases, mappers, viewmodels, repositories, and datasources.

- Unit-test every other class that you create and holds logic.

- Try to think of different scenarios when writing your tests. What happens if the input is not what you expected? What if a returned value is not what you expected? Consider data boundaries and edge cases.

- When fixing a bug, always update your tests to cover that scenario. Write new tests before fixing the bug.

Join our Discord space

Join our Discord workspace for latest updates, offers, tech happenings around the world, new releases, and sessions with the authors:

https://discord.bpbonline.com

CHAPTER 9
End-to-end Testing

Quality is not an act, it is a habit.

- Aristotle

Introduction

Testing the UI of an app is a hard problem. The UI changes often, which can lead to tests breaking. You have to worry about things like the UI state, scrolling to elements, overlaying elements blocking gestures, and the complexity of validating the output of the app. You need to run these tests in a real environment or one that closely mimics it. Life is even harder in the Android world, where we have significant fragmentation[1] and the Android lifecycle to worry about.

Nevertheless, testing the UI is important. It is also impossible to call a test a real end-to-end test without it covering the UI. We will discuss why end-to-end tests are important and how to approach them in this chapter. As end-to-end testing is architecture-agnostic, this chapter will not be specific to Clean Architecture. I included it in this book for completeness, as you should really have end-to-end test coverage for every feature that you develop.

---

1 In other words, there are many, many android devices. these devices vary in screen size, OS version and hardware capabilities.

Structure

In this chapter, we will cover the following topics:

- The value of end-to-end tests
- The robot pattern
- Testing the home screen

Objectives

Our app is a collection of moving parts. Most of these parts can, and should, be tested in isolation. However, not every part or scenario can be covered by unit tests. Some issues can only be validated, and some bugs can only be reproduced, by testing the system as a whole. Unit tests cannot test integration. Furthermore, testing the UI using unit tests can be quite hard, partly because it often requires spinning up or faking the entire Android environment.

Before we proceed, let us agree on what we mean by end-to-end tests, because the term is somewhat charged. Some consider end-to-end tests as tests that include real network calls, interaction with Bluetooth devices, and every other external dependency of the app. This is not the definition that we will work with.

Our definition of end-to-end tests is *tests that test our app in its entirety*: from the UI to locally persisted data, including all data manipulation in between. We do not include external dependencies in our scope. Network calls and external dependencies will all be faked to act as we would expect actual dependencies to behave. This helps stabilize our tests significantly by removing external failures and delays from the equation. It also speeds up our tests by a noticeable margin. Finally, it helps us test scenarios that could be quite challenging to reproduce with real external dependencies.

At the end of this chapter, you should have an idea about how to tackle end-to-end tests and overcome some of the challenges that they introduce.

The value of end-to-end tests

Our goal when developing an app is to have a bug-free working system. For a system to work correctly, its individual parts must work correctly. We can validate this is the case for most parts of our app using unit tests.

Things get tricky when we want to test our UI. We can unit-test our UI, to an extent, using libraries such as **Robolectric**[2]. However, those tests do not offer as good coverage as running tests on a device or an emulator. Running tests in an Android environment floats issues related to animations, the effects of opening or closing the keyboard, and font sizes, to name a few. These issues can be missed if we only use Robolectric.

---

2 Robolectric is a unit-testing framework for Android. It runs on the workstation JVM and so does not require a running device or emulator. You can read more about it here: **https://robolectric.org/**

There is another reason to test the UI using an end-to-end solution. Our unit tests do not provide us with integration confidence. That is, unit tests do not guarantee that our components, which work perfectly in isolation, play well together.

With end-to-end tests, we have confidence that our app compiles, runs, and performs the tasks that we expect it to. We have confidence that the app works.

End-to-end tests are not perfect, though. They are slow to run. It is not always easy to stabilize them so that they consistently pass when your app is perfectly fine (or consistently fail when it is not). That is why end-to-end tests are just a part of our safety net. We still need our unit tests to give us that extra bit of confidence that all parts of our system are behaving as expected.

End-to-end tests are also notorious for being hard to write. In the next section, we will explore a pattern that makes writing, reading, and maintaining end-to-end tests considerably easier.

The robot pattern

In order to test our UI and our end-to-end functionality, we need to be able to describe user journeys through the app. Let us take the login journey of an imaginary app as an example. You can see the relevant screens for this scenario in *Figure 9.1*. The user should be able to:

1. Launch the app.

2. See the landing screen, which includes a form with username and password fields and a button labeled **Login**.

3. Type in their username and password.

4. Tap the **Login** button.

5. See the home screen of the app. This screen may have a title, navigation, or other components that allow the user to know that they have successfully logged in.

There are a few things to notice here. First, note how we break the relevant journey down into two relevant screens: the *landing screen* and the *home screen*. Each screen has components that the user can observe or interact with. Second, note that this is only testing the *happy path*. That is, we are not describing any failure scenarios, such as when the username is not specified or the credentials are wrong. Those would be separate paths, tested independently. Refer to the following figure:

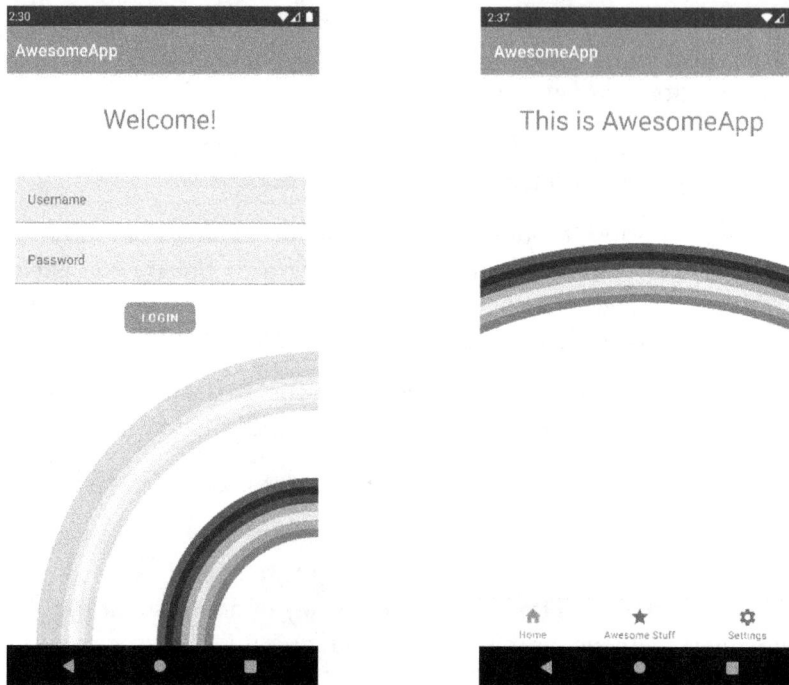

Figure 9.1: *A landing screen (left) and home screen (right)*

The third thing to notice is that the user's behavior is easy to describe when expressed in plain English. *Would it not be great if we could maintain this level of clarity when writing our tests?* I present to you the **robot pattern**.

First introduced in 2016 by *Jake Wharton*[3], the robot pattern is an adaptation of *Martin Fowler's Page Object Pattern*[4] from 2013, previously called the Windows Driver API[5] (2004). So, the robot pattern is not a new idea.

The premise of the robot pattern is simple: we design an interface that allows us to mimic a user, or a robot, going through the app to accomplish specific tasks.

To do this, we break the app down into *screens*. Every activity, every fragment, every dialog, every composable container becomes a screen. Each screen is represented by a class in our tests.

These screen classes abstract away the UI details behind functions that describe intent. Doing so gives our test code stability. If a screen allows us to type in a number, we should not care if the UI involves a button for every digit like a calculator does, or if it offers a single input field that we could type the value into (see *Figure 9.2*). We should not care if the implementation details changed, either. We simply need a function that takes in the number that we want to

3 **https://jakewharton.com/testing-robots/**
4 **https://martinfowler.com/bliki/PageObject.html**
5 **https://martinfowler.com/eaaDev/WindowDriver.html**

feed into the UI and takes care of the typing details for us. A good name for such a function could be **enterNumber(Int)**.

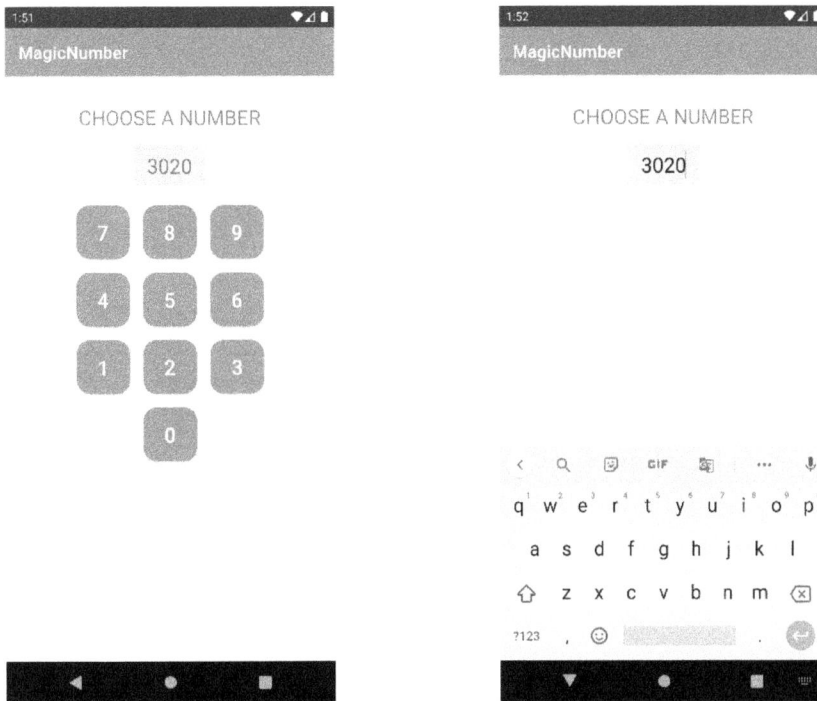

Figure 9.2: Input via numeric buttons (left) and input field (right)

A robot in our context has two distinct capabilities:

- It can *see* (or observe, if you prefer), which is essentially the equivalent of making an assertion.

- It can *interact* (touch, type, toggle, or even wait, for example) with the user interface.

The robot (or page object) pattern is open to interpretation. The implementation suggested here is one that evolved during my work with many talented colleagues from several different companies. It has served me well and proved easy even for testers with no prior programming experience to adopt.

Since the Hilt-related boilerplate may change over time, any explanation provided here may quickly grow outdated. Instead, I suggest that you follow the steps documented online[6] to get your end-to-end instrumented testing framework up and running. Instead of wasting words on repeating the documentation, I will focus on the implementation of specific test types. This will give you an idea of how the robot pattern looks. We will start with an activity test.

---

6 Hilt setup: **https://developer.android.com/training/dependency-injection/hilt-testing# end-to-end**
Espresso setup: **https://developer.android.com/training/testing/espresso/setup# set-up-environment**

Testing the home screen

Before we explore testing screens, take a look at *Figure 9.3* for an idea about the package structure of our testing solution:

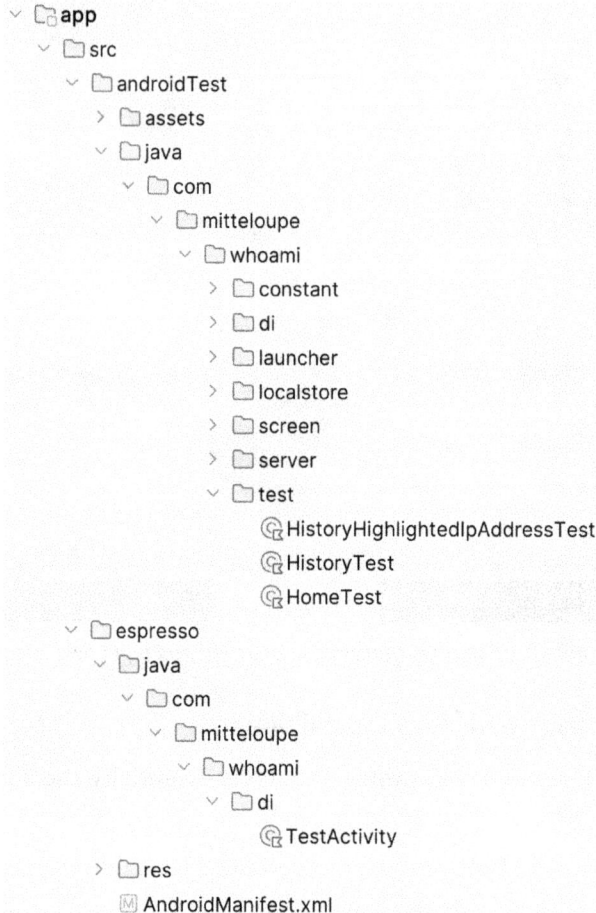

```
∨ ⌐ app
    ∨ ☐ src
        ∨ ☐ androidTest
            › ☐ assets
            ∨ ☐ java
                ∨ ☐ com
                    ∨ ☐ mitteloupe
                        ∨ ☐ whoami
                            › ☐ constant
                            › ☐ di
                            › ☐ launcher
                            › ☐ localstore
                            › ☐ screen
                            › ☐ server
                            ∨ ☐ test
                                    ⒼⒶ HistoryHighlightedIpAddressTest
                                    ⒼⒶ HistoryTest
                                    ⒼⒶ HomeTest
        ∨ ☐ espresso
            ∨ ☐ java
                ∨ ☐ com
                    ∨ ☐ mitteloupe
                        ∨ ☐ whoami
                            ∨ ☐ di
                                    ⒼⒶ TestActivity
            › ☐ res
                  Ⓜ AndroidManifest.xml
```

Figure 9.3: The package structure of our end-to-end testing solution

In the structure, you can see some of the app-specific structure of our solution, which we keep in the **app** module. We keep it there to refer to concrete app screens or activities. To make our test framework reusable, we isolate as much of its reusable code as possible in the **architecture:instrumentation-test** module (see *Figure 9.4*):

```
              ∨ 🗁 architecture
                > 🗁 domain
                ∨ 🗁 instrumentation-test
                    ∨ 🗁 src
                        ∨ 🗁 main
                            > 🗁 assets
                            ∨ 🗁 java
                                ∨ 🗁 com
                                    ∨ 🗁 mitteloupe
                                        ∨ 🗁 whoami
                                            ∨ 🗁 test
                                                > 🗁 action
                                                > 🗁 annotation
                                                > 🗁 assertion
                                                > 🗁 asset
                                                > 🗁 idlingresource
                                                > 🗁 launcher
                                                > 🗁 localstore
                                                > 🗁 matcher
                                                > 🗁 rule
                                                > 🗁 server
                                                > 🗁 test
```

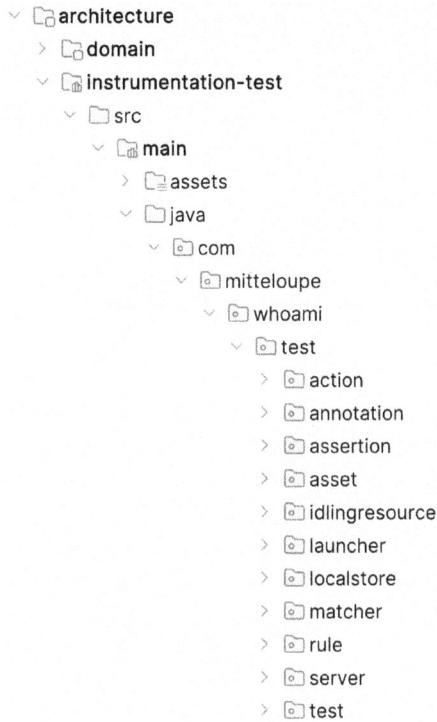

Figure 9.4: The reusable code in the architecture:instrumentation-test module

Throughout the chapter, I will mention what code goes in which of the two modules.

When testing our home screen, we want to make sure that we see the first app screen. No interaction is required from the user to see that screen beyond launching the app. Therefore, our test can be quite simple:

HomeTest.kt

```
1.   package com.mitteloupe.whoami.test
2.
3.   [imports...]
4.
5.   @HiltAndroidTest
6.   class HomeTest : BaseTest() {
7.       override val composeTestRule =
8.           createAndroidComposeRule<TestActivity>()
9.
10.      override val startActivityLauncher by lazy {
11.          FromScreen(composeTestRule, Home)
12.      }
```

```
13.
14.          @Inject
15.          lateinit var homeScreen: HomeScreen
16.
17.          @Test
18.          @ServerRequestResponse(
19.              [
20.                  REQUEST_RESPONSE_GET_IP,
21.                  REQUEST_RESPONSE_GET_IP_DETAILS
22.              ]
23.          )
24.          fun givenConnectedWhenStartingAppThenIpAddressPresented() {
25.              with(composeTestRule) {
26.                  with(homeScreen) {
27.                      seesIpAddressLabel()
28.                      seesIpAddressSubtitleLabel()
29.                  }
30.              }
31.          }
32.      }
```

End-to-end tests are stored in the **app** module and under **app/src/androidTest**. I tend to store tests under the **test** subpackage, as can be seen in *line 1* (**com.mitteloupe.whoami. test** in this case).

Since we are using Hilt, every test must be annotated with the **@HiltAndroidTest** annotation (*line 5*). This allows us to inject dependencies, as we will see shortly. Our **HomeTest** extends **BaseTest** (*line 6*), which we will also explore shortly.

When testing an app that utilizes Jetpack Compose, we need an implementation of the **ComposeContentTestRule** interface to find and interact with composables. The **createAndroidComposableRule** function returns an Android-specific **AndroidComposeRule** object, which is an implementation of the **ComposeContentTestRule** interface. We call this function on *lines 7* and *8* with the generic type set to the **TestActivity** class and assign the returned object to the **composeTestRule** variable.

The **TestActivity** class is an empty subclass of the **AppCompatActivity** class. The **TestActivity** class replaces the **MainActivity** one and avoids loading the **Home** composable before every test. We add it to our **espresso** variant of the **app** Gradle module so that it is deployed with the app in end-to-end tests. Of course, we remember to include it in the **AndroidManifest.xml** file of the **espresso** variant.

Each test needs to declare the user's entry point into the app. In our case, we will be testing the home screen, and so we will use the **FromScreen** class, passing in the value of the

composeTestRule field and the **Home** route object (*line 11*). We will discuss **FromScreen** when we look into **BaseTest**.

As mentioned above, thanks to the **@HiltAndroidTest** annotation, we can inject dependencies into our test. On *lines 14* and *15,* we inject a **HomeScreen** object. This is the only screen that we care about in this test. We will discuss **HomeScreen** in depth later.

The single test that is currently in our test class is quite short (*lines 17* to *31*). We start by annotating the test with the **@Test** annotation so that it is identified as a test, just like we do with unit tests (*line 17*). We also annotate it with our custom **@ServerRequestResponse** annotation, specifying the IDs of request and response pairs that we want stubbed (*lines 18* to *23*). I will expand on this annotation when we discuss stubbing remote server responses. We continue to name our test in a BDD fashion (Given/when/then, see *line 24*).

When writing tests for composable screens, we must utilize the **AndroidComposeRule** object that we instantiated earlier. We achieve this by making all functions of all screen classes into extension functions on the **ComposeContentTestRule** interface. We will see this when we explore a screen class. To access these extension functions, we wrap our entire test in a **with** block, passing in the value of the **composeTestRule** variable (*line 25*).

We bound each screen interaction in a **with** block, too (*lines 26* to *29*). This helps emphasize transitions between screens and reduces the amount of code within each such block.

On *lines 27* and *28*, we can see our assertions in this test. Thinking of the robot pattern here, our robot can *see* and *interact*. In this case, since no action is required from the user, we will simply assert that the IP address and subtitle labels that we expect to see on the home screen are present.

In most cases, we will assume that the screen is at an expected state at any given point in time and will not rely on assertions. Instead, we will interact with the interface under that assumption. We will fall back to assertions when no user interaction makes sense.

To get a better understanding of how our test works under the hood, let us start by looking at **BaseTest**:

BaseTest.kt

```
1.    package com.mitteloupe.whoami.test.test
2.
3.    [imports...]
4.
5.    typealias TypedAndroidComposeTestRule<ACTIVITY> =
6.        AndroidComposeTestRule<ActivityScenarioRule<ACTIVITY>, ACTIVITY>
7.
8.    abstract class BaseTest {
```

BaseTest.kt is saved under **architecture/instrumentation-test/src/main** and in the **architecture:instrumentation-test** gradle module. As it is a part of our testing foundation, it is stored under the **test** subpackage. As it is specific to single tests, it is stored under the second **test** subpackage (*line 1*).

We start by declaring the **TypedAndroidComposeTestRule** type alias that will tidy up our code (*lines 5* and *6*). Remember it, we will get back to it later.

BaseTest is an abstract class (*line 8*) because instantiating it on its own is meaningless. This class contains no actual test code. It merely declares the foundation for all end-to-end tests to build on.

Let us jump into the **BaseTest** class itself:

BaseTest.kt (continued)

```
 9.        private val hiltAndroidRule by lazy { HiltAndroidRule(this) }
10.
11.        protected abstract val composeTestRule: ComposeContentTestRule
12.
13.        @get:Rule
14.        val testRules: RuleChain by lazy {
15.            RuleChain
16.                .outerRule(hiltAndroidRule)
17.                .around(HiltInjectorRule(hiltAndroidRule))
18.                .around(composeTestRule)
19.        }
```

The first line in the **BaseTest** class (*line 9*) creates a **HiltAndroidRule** instance. Two things are worth noting here: first, that we instantiate the rule lazily. This is because instantiating it immediately will lead to **this** being leaked from the constructor of our Java-generated code. Lint will warn us about this if we forget, so it is easy to spot the potential bug. The second thing to note is that we do not annotate this field with the **@get:Rule** annotation, as we often do with test rules. This is intentional. We want this rule to be applied with controlled order, as we will see shortly.

The second rule that we declare is a **ComposeContentTestRule** object. The field that holds this test object is declared **protected** and **abstract** because test classes are expected to instantiate it. We do it this way because the actual instantiation, as we have seen in **HomeTest** earlier, requires a **ComponentActivity** class. We do not know which **ComponentActivity** class the concrete test will use.

This leads us to *lines 13* to *19*, where we declare our **RuleChain** object. A **RuleChain** object is a wrapper around test rules, which guarantees that the rules will be applied in an explicit order. This makes rule-processing predictable. Some rules should be executed before others; one such rule is the one stored in the **hiltAndroidRule** field. The execution of the **HiltInjectorRule** object's **apply** function depends upon the **apply** function of the **hiltAndroidRule** object getting executed first. Note that the **testRules** field is lazy. If it were not, it would evaluate **hiltAndroidRule** immediately, too, which would negate our earlier precaution against leaking **this**.

Our outer rule, which is the first to be applied and the last to be cleared (see *line 16*), is the **HiltAndroidRule** object that we declared on *line 9*.

The next rule in our rule chain is a **HiltInjectorRule** object (*line 17*). This is a simple rule that performs the actual injection for us. We will cover its implementation later on.

The last rule that we include in the chain is a **ComposeContentTestRule** object (*line 18*) that will be applied last (and thus cleared first).

As our tests evolve, we will likely want to introduce more rules to our chain. Examples may include setting up our mock web server (the **HomeTest** class relies on this, and we will discuss it in a later section of this chapter), clearing our shared preferences, or setting up a mechanism to take screenshots when tests fail. The suggested chain shown here is a minimal one.

In the first edition of this book, we also had a **DisableAnimationsRule** object in the **BaseTest** class. This rule was responsible for ensuring, as the name suggested, that animations were disabled on our test device or emulator. It is vital that we disable animations before running our tests. This speeds up tests and removes flakiness caused by animation delays. In this edition, I recommend updating your app's **build.gradle.kts** file as follows instead, because it requires considerably less code:

build.gradle.kts

```
android {
    ...
    testOptions {
        animationsDisabled = true
    }
}
```

If you are interested in the code for **DisableAnimationsRule**, it will be covered towards the end of the book.

The following lines wrap up our **BaseTest** class:

BaseTest.kt (continued)

```
21.     protected abstract val startActivityLauncher: AppLauncher
22.
23.     @Before
24.     fun setUp() {
25.         startActivityLauncher.launch()
```

```
26.          }
27.    }
```

After our rule chain, we declare an abstract **AppLauncher** variable (*line 18*). We saw a concrete assignment to this field in our **HomeTest** class. We will expand on the **AppLauncher** interface shortly and then again when exploring the testing of a **Fragment**. The launcher field is **protected** because no class outside of our tests should have access to it. It is abstract because it is down to individual tests to assign an appropriate launcher object to it.

Before each test is run, we want to launch an activity for the tested UI to live in. This is exactly what we do on *lines 23 to 26*. Note the **@Before** annotation (*line 23*), which tells our test runner to execute this function before each test. By convention, just like with our unit tests, we call this function **setUp** (*line 24*). On *line 25*, we see that before each test executes, the **launch** function of our **AppLauncher** instance is called, ensuring that the UI is launched.

Next, let us see what the **AppLauncher** interface looks like:

AppLauncher.kt
```
1.    package com.mitteloupe.whoami.test.launcher
2.
3.    fun interface AppLauncher {
4.        fun launch()
5.    }
```

This is the **AppLauncher** functional interface. Implementations of this interface will provide us with different ways of launching a screen. For Compose, we only need one implementation, namely the **fromComposable** function:

FromComposable.kt
```
1.    package com.mitteloupe.whoami.test.launcher
2.
3.    [imports...]
4.
5.    fun <ACTIVITY : ComponentActivity> fromComposable(
6.        composeContentTestRule: TypedAndroidComposeTestRule<ACTIVITY>,
7.        composable: @Composable (ACTIVITY) -> Unit
8.    ) = AppLauncher {
9.        val activity = composeContentTestRule.activity
10.       activity.findViewById<ViewGroup>(android.R.id.content)
11.           ?.let { root ->
12.               runBlocking(Dispatchers.Main) {
13.                   root.removeAllViews()
14.               }
```

```
15.                }
16.           composeContentTestRule.setContent { composable(activity) }
17.    }
```

The **fromComposable** function has one generic type, **ACTIVITY** (*line 5*), that is of the type **ComponentActivity**. This generic type allows us to specify the class of the **ComponentActivity** type in which the composable will be launched.

The function takes two arguments (*lines 6 and 7*):

- An instance of the **AndroidComposeTestRule** class (remember that we declared the **TypedAndroidComposeTestRule** type alias for it in **BaseTest.kt**).

- A composable to inflate in the available activity. This will be the composable that we want to test. It accepts the current activity as an argument to streamline the composable argument, as you will see shortly.

The **fromComposable** function returns an **AppLauncher** instance (*lines 8 to 17*). This **AppLauncher** implementation accesses the current activity from the **AndroidComposeTestRule** instance. It then finds the root view of this activity and removes all its child views (*lines 9 to 15*). This ensures that the activity is empty and ready for the new composable. With the activity ready, it sets its content to the provided composable, passing in the current activity. Note that the composable is wrapped in an anonymous composable because the **setContent** function would not accept a composable with parameters.

We can use the **fromComposable** function directly to test any composable. Since our project has a navigation host, we can introduce another function that removes much of the boilerplate of constructing the composable for us:

FromScreen.kt

```
1.    package com.mitteloupe.whoami.launcher
2.
3.    [imports...]
4.
5.    fun <ACTIVITY : AppCompatActivity> fromScreen(
6.        composeContentTestRule: TypedAndroidComposeTestRule<ACTIVITY>,
7.        startDestination: Any
8.    ) = AppLauncher {
9.        fromComposable(composeContentTestRule) { activity ->
10.            WhoAmITheme {
11.                with(
12.                    testAppDependenciesEntryPoint(activity)
13.                        .appNavHostDependencies
14.                ) {
```

```
15.                     AppNavHost(
16.                         activity.supportFragmentManager,
17.                         startDestination
18.                     )
19.                 }
20.             }
21.         }.launch()
22.     }
```

The **fromScreen** function resides in the app module because it needs to have access to the **WhoAmITheme** and **AppNavHost** composables. It takes two arguments:

- An **AndroidComposeTestRule** object.

- A start destination object.

The function returns an **AppLauncher** object that wraps around a **fromComposable** function call. It passes its **AndroidComposeTestRule** argument directly to the **fromComposable** function.

For the composable argument, it composes a **WhoAmITheme** theme wrapper. In this wrapper, it obtains an instance of **appNavHostDependencies** via a Hilt entry point (*lines 12* and *13*). We will discuss this once we finish covering the **fromScreen** function. With the obtained instance, it can call the **AppNavHost** extension composable, passing in the current activity's **FragmentManager** instance and the start destination object as arguments (*lines 15 to 18*).

Finally, because the entire block that is implementing the **AppLauncher** function interface (*lines 9 to 21*) will only be executed when the **AppLauncher** interface's **launch** function gets called, we delegate that call to **fromComposable** by calling **launch** on *line 21*.

Working around the DI constraints that Jetpack Compose currently has is outside of the scope of this book, but I will include the code for the **testAppDependenciesEntryPoint** function that was mentioned above to give you a complete picture of the implementation:

TestAppDependenciesModule.kt

```
1.    package com.mitteloupe.whoami.di
2.
3.    [imports...]
4.
5.    @EntryPoint
6.    @InstallIn(ActivityComponent::class)
7.    interface TestAppDependenciesEntryPoint {
8.        val appNavHostDependencies: AppNavHostDependencies
9.    }
10.
```

```
11.    fun testAppDependenciesEntryPoint(activity: Activity) =
12.        EntryPoints.get(
13.            activity,
14.                TestAppDependenciesEntryPoint::class.java
15.        )
```

This file leverages Hilt to provide an **AppNavHostDependencies** instance given an Android **Activity** instance. The **AppNavHostDependencies** class holds dependencies for the individual screens of the WhoAmI app. At the time of writing, it holds the dependencies for the home screen.

Let us go back to the **AppLauncher** interface before moving on. In the first edition of this book, it was named **TestLauncher** and provided mechanisms for launching activities and fragments. These implementations will not be mentioned here since this edition focuses on Jetpack Compose. I will include them towards the end of the book, since activities and fragments are still important in the Android world.

We can now look at the test rules that we used in our **BaseTest**. Specifically, let us explore the **HiltInjectorRule** class:

HiltInjectorRule.kt

```
1.    package com.mitteloupe.whoami.test.rule
2.
3.    [imports...]
4.
5.    class HiltInjectorRule(
6.        private val hiltAndroidRule: HiltAndroidRule
7.    ) : TestRule {
8.        override fun apply(
9.            base: Statement,
10.            description: Description
11.        ): Statement = object : Statement() {
12.            override fun evaluate() {
13.                hiltAndroidRule.inject()
14.                base.evaluate()
15.            }
16.        }
17.    }
```

HiltInjectorRule is a test rule responsible for injecting our dependencies before the test is run. It is important to have this rule run before later test rules that rely on injected instances.

To inject our dependencies, we need access to an **HiltAndroidRule** instance. We obtain one by adding it as a constructor parameter (*line 6*).

To implement a test rule, we need to implement the apply function. Our implementation (*lines 8 to 16*) is an anonymous **Statement** class. When the **evaluate** function of this **Statement** class (*lines 12 to 15*) executes, it injects the dependencies (*line 13*) before continuing the test execution on *line 14*.

This is an example of how simple a test rule can be in some cases. Hopefully, this motivates you to write your own when appropriate.

Let us get back to our home screen test. We saw that it depends on a **HomeScreen** class. Let us explore it:

HomeScreen.kt

```
1.    package com.mitteloupe.whoami.screen
2.
3.    [imports...]
4.
5.    class HomeScreen {
6.        private val ipAddressLabel = hasText(IP_ADDRESS)
7.        private val ipAddressSubtitleLabel = hasText("This is the "...)
8.        private val cityLabel = hasText("Brentwood")
9.        private val regionLabel = hasText("England")
10.       private val countryLabel = hasText("United Kingdom")
11.       private val geolocationLabel = hasText("51.6213, 0.3056")
12.       private val postCodeLabel = hasText("CM14")
13.       private val timeZoneLabel = hasText("Europe/London")
14.       private val internetServiceProviderLabel = hasText("Talk"...)
15.       private val openSourceNoticesButton = hasText("Open Source"...)
```

Each screen class represents a **screen**. Every Activity, every Fragment, every Dialog, or composable can have its own screen. The interface of a screen class describes the available interactions with that screen for our imaginary robot.

Screens are stored under the **screen** subpackage (*line 1*) in the **androidTest** folder of the **app** module. As our app scales, we can create feature sub-packages to keep everything tidy. The name of the class is the screen name suffixed with **Screen** (*line 5*).

The actual implementation details of each screen are encapsulated in that screen's screen class. Tests that are using the **HomeScreen** screen class do not need to know the actual text presented on the labels or button (*lines 6 to 15*). In a screen that describes a composable, we find components to interact with using **SemanticsMatcher** objects. These objects are constructed with a lambda that, given a **SemanticsNode** instance, returns true if it matches certain criteria and false otherwise. Compose ships with a few ready-made matchers, such as the **hasText** function. If none of the existing matchers fit our usecase, we can create our own.

In general, we prefer to describe *what an element is expected to contain* rather than *its type, an ID, or the ID of a resource*. Types and IDs are implementation details that we should not have to worry about. Finding views by their type, ID, or by their place in the hierarchy should be a last resort. Such implementations are highly fragile and would require greater maintenance efforts. We want our screen classes to interact with a screen as a user would, not as a developer.

Let us continue exploring the file:

HomeScreen.kt (continued)

```
17.      fun ComposeContentTestRule.seeIpAddressLabel() {
18.          assertIsDisplayed(ipAddressLabel)
19.      }
20.
21.      fun ComposeContentTestRule.seeIpAddressSubtitleLabel() {
22.          assertIsDisplayed(ipAddressSubtitleLabel)
23.      }
24.
25.      ...
26.
27.      fun ComposeContentTestRule.tapOpenSourceNotices() {
28.          onNode(openSourceNoticesButton).performTouchInput { click() }
29.      }
30.
31.      private fun ComposeContentTestRule
32.          .assertIsDisplayed(matcher: SemanticsMatcher) {
33.              waitUntilExactlyOneExists(matcher, timeoutMillis = 5_000L)
34.          }
35.  }
```

On *line 17*, we see an example of an interaction function. Functions whose names are prefixed with **see** are *assertion* functions. As mentioned earlier, we prefer to avoid such functions in favor of assuming that the screen is in an expected state. However, in some cases, there is no valid action to be taken on a screen, leaving us with assertions as the only sensible mechanism of validation. The **seeIpAddressLabel** function (*lines 17* to *19*) serves us in such a case.

The function takes no arguments. Within the function body, we use the **SemanticsMatcher** instance we kept a reference to in the **ipAddressLabel** field. (*line 18*), to verify that the IP address label is displayed. Our verification is done by calling the **assertIsDisplayed** extension function of the **ComposeContentTestRule** class. We will discuss it shortly. Most of the interaction functions in the home screen class are assertion functions, so I omitted a few to allow us to focus on different types of interaction functions.

On *line 27*, we can see the **tapOpenSourcesNotices** function. It represents another type of interaction function. This function's name is prefixed with **tap**, which tells us that it is an *action* function. Unlike *assertion* functions, action ones *interact* with an element on the screen, as a user would. In this case, the function taps the composable that matches using the **SemanticsMatcher** that we assigned to **openSourceNoticesButton** field (*line 28*).

Before we wrap up the home screen test class, I promised that we would discuss the **assertIsDisplayed** extension function. On *lines 31 to 34*, you can see its implementation. This function is there to improve the stability of our test. Sometimes, because of background operations, the UI can take a bit longer to update to the right state. This function takes a **SemanticsMatcher** object and gives the UI five seconds (5,000 milliseconds) to provide a composable that matches it. In our case, if the component has not appeared by that time, it is reasonable to assume that it will not appear, and the matching should fail.

This concludes our home screen test. We have now covered the most common types of tests we would encounter as developers. However, we ignored an important element of many apps: network calls. What happens when our app relies on an online API to provide it with data? This will be the topic of the next chapter.

Conclusion

When developing production apps, we want confidence that our app works. Manual testing is slow and prone to human error. End-to-end automated testing is a valuable tool to have in our toolbox. Good tests follow similar principles to those of Clean Architecture, concerns are separated, and implementation details are abstracted away. Using the Robot or Page Object Pattern, this abstraction becomes easy.

Expect most of your efforts to go into the initial setup of the testing framework. Once that is done, most of your efforts could go into coding descriptive tests.

In the next chapter, we will explore upgrading our tests with support for fake network calls. We will see how stubbing external dependencies makes our tests much more powerful.

Points to remember

When implementing your end-to-end tests, remember:

- Break your app down into screens.

- Define an interface for each screen that reflects how a user (or a robot) would interact with it.

- Implement the end-to-end testing framework early. This will make writing tests later less scary and less time-consuming.

CHAPTER 10
Mocking the Server

The system was full of bugs. And the bugs were on strike.

- Terry Pratchett, Going Postal

Introduction

Many apps rely on a network connection to work. They use an API to log in and establish a session, query an API for data, or update data on a system in the cloud.

If we ignore these dependencies entirely when writing our tests, our tests could still pass. However, a new risk factor was introduced. Our tests may now be flaky because of external factors, such as connectivity issues and the current state of the server. They are also likely to run slower, often considerably so.

Structure

In this chapter, we will cover the following topics:

- Reasons to mock the server
- Mocking the server
- Using MockWebServer
- Stubbing a Ktor client

Objectives

In the previous chapter, we learned how to write end-to-end tests. However, our tests were limited to either running locally or relying on remote servers.

In this chapter, we will learn that relying on remote servers is impractical and how we can work around this limitation. After reading this chapter, you should be able to write end-to-end tests that run against a fake local server instead of making real network calls.

Reasons to mock the server

Running an app that requires a network connection or Bluetooth devices in a test environment is problematic. Allowing such external dependencies introduces a risk factor.

Tests may now fail because of connection drops, because of high latency, or because of API downtime. None of these reasons justify our tests failing. Our code has not changed, nor has it stopped performing as expected. These failures would not be reliably reproducible.

Another aspect of the risk introduced is performance. Making API calls is slow. We rely on the network capabilities of the device running the tests, the environment in which the tests are run, as well as the responsiveness of the endpoint we hit. This will slow us down as developers and may be expensive in resource costs. The same is true for Bluetooth devices; pairing and communication can be quite slow.

Lastly, we will not always have a dedicated endpoint for testing. This means that we will not have full control of the state of the system. *What if we want to test how an Italian dish behaves in our restaurant app, but no Italian dishes exist on our system right now? What if there was a dish in the remote database that we relied on, and just got deleted?*

Due to these factors that could lead to tests being flaky and slow, I strongly suggest that we mock our APIs. Instead of testing our app against real data, we will test it against local stubbed data that mimics the real data.

Does this mean that we will no longer test the back end? Absolutely not. It is extremely important to test our APIs. However, the frequency at which we test our APIs, the order in which we make API calls, neither of these should be coupled to the frequency in which we run our end-to-end tests or the order in which our app makes these calls.

We should be able to run our API tests several times a day, maybe every hour or even every minute. Furthermore, we should not have to wait for our app tests to run and interact with the app UI to fire off our test calls. Waiting for the app tests will be both slow and incredibly confining.

How to test our APIs is a separate discussion that is outside of the scope of this book. We will therefore not explore this topic further. Suffice to say, it should be done, but it should be done separately from our app testing efforts.

We have covered *why* we want to stub our remote APIs. In the next section, we will discuss the *how*. Just a quick side note before we do: the server is not the only thing that we may want to mock. For example, Bluetooth devices present a similar challenge and should also be mocked.

Mocking the server

Our app makes network calls. We do not want to rely on these calls, so we are going to mock the server. Our goal is to use as much of our production code as possible. This means that we will make every effort to only stub the *outside world*, i.e., resources that are external to our app. We want our app to think that it is still talking to a real API. This increases our test coverage and ensures that we catch any issues within our external resource handling code.

Let us start by discussing network requests and responses. Specifically, let us discuss HTTP/S requests and responses.

In its simplest form, a request can be identified by a URL:

MockRequest.kt

```
1.    package com.mitteloupe.whoami.test.server
2.
3.    data class MockRequest(val url: String)
```

This and all other server mocking classes live in the **test.server** subpackage (*line 1*). We can expand the **MockRequest** to include other details about the request, such as HTTP headers, the request body, or its query string. We can even replace the **url** string variable with a matcher to allow for pattern matching. For our example, we will leave it at having a field for the request URL.

Every request that we intercept should produce a response of sorts. This is why we have a **MockResponse** class:

MockResponse.kt

```
1.    package com.mitteloupe.whoami.test.server
2.
3.    data class MockResponse(
4.        val code: Int = 200,
5.        val headers: List<Pair<String, String>> = emptyList(),
6.        val body: String = ""
7.    )
```

The class that represents server responses is a data class with three constructor arguments, all of which are optional:

- An HTTP response code (*line 4*), which defaults to **200**, which translates to **OK**, and is the normal HTTP success response code.

- A list of HTTP headers (*line 5*). These are pairs of key and value strings. The default is an empty list.

- The body of the response as a string (*line 6*).

On its own, the **MockResponse** class does not offer any easy way of constructing the different types of responses that we need in our tests. To make it easier for us to construct different types of responses, we introduce response factories. Response factories implement the **MockResponseFactory** interface:

MockResponseFactory.kt

```
1.    package com.mitteloupe.whoami.test.server.response
2.
3.    [imports...]
4.
5.    interface MockResponseFactory {
6.        fun mockResponse(): MockResponse
7.    }
```

MockResponseFactory is an interface for constructing **MockResponse** instances. Different classes that implement this interface represent different server behaviors. We will go over three of the most common response types next: a **simple** response, an **error** response, and a **sequence** one. Other response type factories can be added depending on the app requirements. In the past, I have added a **WebSocketResponseFactory** to initiate web socket connections. Implement the interface as you see fit.

Each implementation of **MockResponseFactory** needs to implement the **mockResponse()** function (*line 6*). This function returns a **MockResponse** object. Our first response type factory is **SimpleResponseFactory**:

SimpleResponseFactory.kt

```
1.    package com.mitteloupe.whoami.test.server.response
2.
3.    [imports...]
4.
5.    data class SimpleResponseFactory(
6.        private val code: Int = 200,
7.        private val headers: List<Pair<String, String>> = emptyList(),
8.        private val bodyFileName: String? = null
9.    ) : MockResponseFactory {
10.       private val body by lazy {
11.           if (bodyFileName == null) {
12.               ""
```

```
13.                } else {
14.                    getAssetAsString(bodyFileName)
15.                }
16.            }
17.
18.        override fun mockResponse() =
19.            MockResponse(code = code, headers = headers, body = body)
20.    }
```

The **SimpleResponseFactory** data class constructs **MockResponse** instances with the body property obtained from a resource file. It has three optional constructor arguments, mirroring those of the **MockResponse** class. Note that the factory has a nullable **bodyFileName** parameter instead of the **body** string that **MockResponse** has.

The body of the mock response is evaluated in the **body** lazy field (*lines 10 to 16*), which returns an empty **String** if no file name was provided (*line 12*) or the contents of the file if a name was provided (*line 14*). The **getAssetAsString** function is static, and we will look at it later.

Providing none of the arguments to the constructor would lead to the factory producing **MockResponse** instances that represent empty **200 OK** HTTP responses.

The **mockResponse** function's implementation of the **SimpleResponseFactory** class returns a **ServerResponse** object with the constructor-provided response code and headers (*lines 18 and 19*). We named this response implementation **SimpleResponseFactory** because it is almost pass-through. Let us move on to the next response type that we have.

Our second response type factory is **ErrorResponseFactory**:

ErrorResponseFactory.kt

```
1.    package com.mitteloupe.whoami.test.server.response
2.
3.    import com.mitteloupe.whoami.test.server.MockResponse
4.
5.    sealed class ErrorResponseFactory {
6.        object NotFound : MockResponseFactory {
7.            override fun mockResponse() = MockResponse(code = 404)
8.        }
9.    }
```

ErrorResponseFactory is a sealed class, allowing us to easily extend it to support different error types. The one provided in this example is **NotFound** (*lines 6 to 8*), which returns a **MockResponse** object with a **404** code (the HTTP response code for **Not found**) upon calls to **mockResponse** (*line 7*).

Before moving on to see how we use the requests and responses that we just discussed, I have one outstanding debt to you. In the **SimpleResponseFactory** class, we came across the static **AssetReader** reference. **AssetReader** is an object for, you guessed it, reading assets:

AssetReader.kt

```
1.    package com.mitteloupe.whoami.test.asset
2.
3.    [imports...]
4.
5.    fun getAssetAsString(name: String): String =
6.        processAssetStream(name) { stream ->
7.            stream.bufferedReader().readText()
8.    }
9.
10.   fun <OUTPUT> processAssetStream(
11.       filename: String,
12.       performOnStream: (inputStream: InputStream) -> OUTPUT
13.   ): OUTPUT = InstrumentationRegistry.getInstrumentation()
14.       .context.assets.open(filename)
15.       .use { stream -> performOnStream(stream) }
```

The **AssetReader.kt** file is part of the **architecture:instrumentation-test** Gradle module. Instead of hardcoding data into our code, we can extract it into files that are bundled with our tests. To do that, we create an **assets** folder under **androidTest**. Any file saved under **assets** will be deployed to the test device and will be accessible via code.

The **getAssetAsString** function (*lines 5* to *8*) is a convenience static function that returns the contents of such a deployed file as a **String**. It relies on the **processAssetStream** function that is introduced on *lines 10* to *15*. We will get to this second function next, but for now, note that as arguments we pass in the name of the asset (the **name** parameter) and a lambda. The lambda takes the **InputStream** instance that is passed in, wraps it with an **InputStreamReader** instance, and then a **BufferedReader** one (this is done for us when we call **bufferdReader** function). Finally, it reads the stream as text.

We mentioned the **processAssetStream** function just now, let us inspect it. This is another static function. It looks for the file specified via the **filename** argument in the **assets** folder and opens it as a stream (*lines 13* and *14*). Note that we use the instrumentation-provided context. Finally, in a **use** block, guaranteeing that the stream is closed when we are done, it executes the **performOnStream** lambda argument on the stream and returns the result (*line 15*).

Now that our requests and responses are sorted, it is time that we combine them into a request-to-response mapper. We will start by pairing requests and response factories together:

MockRequestResponseFactory.kt

```
1.    package com.mitteloupe.whoami.test.server
2.
3.    import com.mitteloupe.whoami.test.server.response.MockResponseFactory
4.
5.    data class MockRequestResponseFactory(
6.        val request: MockRequest,
7.        val responseFactory: MockResponseFactory
8.    )
```

The **MockRequestResponseFactory** data class is saved in **architecture:instrumentation-test** Gradle module and describes a roundtrip interaction with an API: from a request fired off by the app (*line 6*) to a mocked response to be returned for that request (*line 7*).

We now need a store to hold all our possible interactions with APIs. We will call it a **ResponseStore**:

ResponseStore.kt

```
1.    package com.mitteloupe.whoami.test.server
2.
3.    private typealias MockRequestResponsePairList =
4.        List<Pair<String, MockRequestResponseFactory>>
5.    private typealias MockRequestResponseMap =
6.        Map<String, MockRequestResponseFactory>
7.
8.    abstract class ResponseStore {
9.        val responseFactories by lazy {
10.            internalResponseFactories.toValidatedMap()
11.        }
12.
13.        protected abstract val internalResponseFactories:
14.            MockRequestResponsePairList
15.
16.        private fun MockRequestResponsePairList
17.            .toValidatedMap(): MockRequestResponseMap {
18.                val responses = toMap()
19.                check(responses.size == size) {
20.                    "Duplicate Request/Response key declared. " +
21.                        "Make sure all Request/Response keys are unique."
22.                }
23.                return responses
```

```
24.                }
25.    }
```

The **ResponseStore** class is an abstract one and is saved in our **architecture:instrumen-tation-test** Gradle module. It is implementation agnostic in that it does not specify any concrete request/response factory pairs. Instead, it provides a framework for implementing a class that does. Starting from the top of the file, we can see that, like all other server-related classes in our test implementation, **ResponseStore** lives under the **server** subpackage.

The next lines (*3* to *6*) contain **typealias** statements. We use the declared type aliases to make our code a little more readable.

After the type aliases, we get to the class itself. The first declaration in the class is of the **responseFactories** map. It is a map of a unique identifier string to a **MockRequestResponseFactory** instance. The content of the map is evaluated lazily on first access by processing the **internalResponseFactories** list of pairs of (hopefully unique) identifier strings and **MockRequestResponseFactory** instances. *Why hopefully?* Well, because the identifiers are used in annotations, and so cannot be an enum, a sealed class, or a sealed interface. We have no way of making sure that the same string is not used twice by accident to represent two different **MockRequestResponseFactory** instances.

This is where the **toValidatedMap** extension function (*lines 16* to *24*) comes into play. This function converts our list of pairs to a map and then makes sure that we did not lose any data in the conversion (*lines 19* to *22*). This gives us run-time safety. While it is not as great as having compile-time safety, it is the best that we can do given the annotation constraints.

The abstract **ResponseStore** class is extended to a concrete class in our **app** Gradle module:

AppResponseStore.kt

```
1.    package com.mitteloupe.whoami.server
2.
3.    [imports...]
4.
5.    const val IPIFY_ENDPOINT = "/ipify/"
6.    const val IPINFO_ENDPOINT = "/ipinfo/"
7.
8.    const val REQUEST_RESPONSE_GET_IP = "Get IP"
9.    const val REQUEST_RESPONSE_GET_IP_DETAILS = "Get IP Details"
10.
11.   class AppResponseStore : ResponseStore() {
12.       override val internalResponseFactories = listOf(
13.           REQUEST_RESPONSE_GET_IP to MockRequestResponseFactory(
14.               request = MockRequest(IPIFY_ENDPOINT),
15.               responseFactory = SimpleResponseFactory(
```

```
16.                      code = 200,
17.                      bodyFileName = "api/get_ip.json"
18.                  )
19.              ),
20.          REQUEST_RESPONSE_GET_IP_DETAILS to MockRequestResponseFactory(
21.              request = MockRequest("${IPINFO_ENDPOINT}$IP_ADDRESS/geo"),
22.              responseFactory = SimpleResponseFactory(
23.                  code = 200,
24.                  bodyFileName = "api/get_ip_details.json"
25.              )
26.          )
27.      )
28.  }
```

We start implementing our **AppResponseStore** by declaring constants for the endpoints that we intend to respond to in our tests (*lines 5 to 6*). These are relative paths.

Next, we declare the IDs identifying the interactions that we need for our tests (*lines 8 and 9*). Each interaction has a unique identifier. At this point, you must be thinking that we should be using an enum or a sealed class to declare these identifiers. Unfortunately, as I mentioned earlier, we intend to use these IDs as annotation arguments. Annotations do not support enums or sealed classes as arguments. Therefore, using any such structure would only lead to a false notion of uniqueness. It is up to us to maintain uniqueness, either manually or in code. In the preceding **ResponseStore** example, we solved this in code.

As the number of interactions that we have grows, we may want to create a nested structure within a **RequestResponseId** object to maintain some order.

We continue to declare our **AppResponseStore** class (*lines 11 to 28*). This class is a container for a list of **Pair** objects, where each contains an interaction identifier and a **MockRequestResponseFactory** object (*lines 12 to 27*). Each ID constant that we declared earlier (*lines 8 and 9*) appears once (and only once) and is paired with an appropriate **MockRequestResponseFactory** object that represents the request and the expected response for when we make that request.

We can see that our first interaction identifier, **REQUEST_RESPONSE_GET_IP**, maps to a **MockRequestResponseFactory** instance. The instance is constructed with two arguments:

- A **MockRequest** object that is instantiated with the **IPIFY_ENDPOINT** path (*line 14*).

- A response factory of the type **SimpleResponseFactory**, instantiated with a code of 200 (**HTTP OK**) and the path of a JSON asset: **api/get_ip.json** (*lines 15 to 18*). This file will be a simple JSON text file containing an IP address in the same format as the real server's. We will store it in the **assets** folder for it to be bundled with our tests.

Our second interaction identifier, **REQUEST_RESPONSE_GET_IP_DETAILS**, maps to a similar structure (*lines 20 to 26*). The **IP_ADDRESS** constant that is used on *line 21* is a global constant that is saved in the **Constants.kt** file and lives in the **com.mitteloupe.whoami.constant** package.

I mentioned that we were going to use the interaction IDs in an annotation. Now would be a good time to check out that annotation:

ServerRequestResponse.kt

```
1.    package com.mitteloupe.whoami.test.annotation
2.
3.    @Target(AnnotationTarget.FUNCTION)
4.    annotation class ServerRequestResponse(
5.        val requestResponseIds: Array<String>
6.    )
```

With the **ServerRequestResponse** annotation file, we are back in the **architecture:instrumentation-test** Gradle module.

The first thing that is worth noting is that this is the first file in this section to be kept under the **annotation** subpackage rather than **server** (*line 1*). This will allow us to continue expanding our test solution with other annotations.

Our annotation is designed to target test functions, hence, on *line 3*, we specify that our annotation targets functions.

The **ServerRequestResponse** annotation accepts an array of interaction ID strings via the **requestResponseIds** field (*line 5*). This is where we see why our interaction IDs are constrained to being **String** primitives, as I mentioned earlier.

Before we see how the new annotation is processed, we should explore one last interface, the **ResponseBinder**:

ResponseBinder.kt

```
1.    package com.mitteloupe.whoami.test.server
2.
3.    interface ResponseBinder {
4.        var testName: String
5.
6.        fun bindResponse(
7.            requestResponseFactory: MockRequestResponseFactory
8.        )
9.
10.       val usedEndpoints: Set<MockRequest>
```

```
11.
12.         fun reset()
13.    }
```

Imagine that you had two instances of **MockRequestResponseFactory**. Imagine that both instances responded to the same **MockRequest** object, but each used a different **MockResponseFactory** instance. In every one of your tests, you would only need one of the two (or neither), but never both. So, while both are necessary for the test suite, only one may be required for a specific test. That is where the **ResponseBinder** interface comes in. It is designed to register, or bind, a **MockRequestResponseFactory** object to a test (see **bindResponse(MockRequestResponseFactory)** on *lines 6 to 8*).

The **ResponseBinder** interface has a second responsibility: it exposes the set of requests that were made during the test (**usedEndpoints**, *line 10*). Having this information at the end of a test helps us identify unused stubs. If we expect these unused stubs to be used, we can fix the app to make sure that this happens. If not, we can confidently remove these stubs and keep our tests clean. To help us identify the tests in question, we have a variable named **testName** that we can update per test (*line 4*). We will see how its value is set later.

After a test is completed, we should unbind all request-response pairs and reset the set of used requests. Otherwise, we will be carrying these values from test to test. Resetting both the bound pairs and the used requests is done by calling the **reset()** function (*line 12*).

With the **ResponseBinder** interface covered, it is time we moved on to the implementation of this interface. The next part is a bit tricky. It is also entirely outside of the context of this book. However, because I found it so challenging to gather all the information needed to make this solution work, I am sharing it with you.

Using MockWebServer

To test our app like it would work in a production environment, we want it to make real HTTP requests and process real HTTP responses. The good news is that there is a solution. If you are using Retrofit or OkHTTP3, **MockWebServer**[1] comes to the rescue. If you are using Ktor, you can use **MockEngine**[2]. For other networking libraries, you would have to find a similar solution.

Up until now, our solution was applicable to any networking library we chose to use. In this section, we will focus on the MockWebServer solution. Towards the end of this chapter, we will demonstrate a Ktor alternative. We will then introduce the **WebServerRule**, which is networking library agnostic, like the code that we explored so far.

Up until Android Pie (API 28), life was easy. We could serve HTTP responses and not worry about encryption. Since Android Pie, however, the rules have changed. With heightened

---

1 **https://github.com/square/okhttp/tree/master/mockwebserver**
2 **https://ktor.io/docs/http-client-testing.html**

security, we now need to use secure connections (HTTPS). Workarounds exist, but most require tags that were only introduced in Android Nougat (API 24). If we want to support older API versions, using secure connections is the easiest solution.

With that in mind, **MockWebServerProvider**, shown as follows, is the simplest implementation I could come up with:

MockWebServerProvider.kt

```kotlin
1.    package com.mitteloupe.whoami.test.server
2.
3.    [imports...]
4.
5.    class MockWebServerProvider {
6.        private val algorithm by lazy {
7.            KeyManagerFactory.getDefaultAlgorithm()
8.        }
9.
10.       private val server by lazy {
11.           val mockWebServer = MockWebServer()
12.           val thread = thread(priority = MAX_PRIORITY) {
13.               mockWebServer.start()
14.           }
15.           thread.join()
16.           Logger.getLogger(MockWebServer::class.java.name).level = ALL
17.
18.           val keyStorePassword = "123456".toCharArray()
19.           val serverKeyStore = KeyStore.getInstance("BKS")
20.           processAssetStream(
21.               "teststore_keystore.bks"
22.           ) { keyStoreStream ->
23.               serverKeyStore.load(keyStoreStream, keyStorePassword)
24.           }
25.
26.           val keyManagerFactory = KeyManagerFactory
27.               .getInstance(algorithm)
28.               .apply { init(serverKeyStore, keyStorePassword) }
29.
30.           val trustManagerFactory = TrustManagerFactory
31.               .getInstance(algorithm)
32.               .apply { init(serverKeyStore) }
33.
```

```
34.              val sslContext = SSLContext.getInstance("TLSv1.2")
35.              sslContext.init(
36.                  keyManagerFactory.keyManagers,
37.                  trustManagerFactory.trustManagers,
38.                  null
39.              )
40.              val socketFactory = sslContext.socketFactory
41.
42.              mockWebServer.useHttps(socketFactory, false)
43.
44.              mockWebServer
45.          }
46.
47.      val serverUrl: String
48.          get() {
49.              var result = ""
50.              val thread = thread(priority = MAX_PRIORITY) {
51.                  result = server.hostName + ":" + server.port
52.              }
53.              thread.join()
54.              return result
55.          }
56.
57.      fun mockWebServer(dispatcher: Dispatcher): MockWebServer {
58.          server.dispatcher = dispatcher
59.
60.          return server
61.      }
62.  }
```

I will leave investigating what this code does to you; I encourage you to spend the time to understand it. What I do want to highlight is the public-facing interface of **MockWebServerProvider**.

First, we have the **serverUrl** field on *lines 47* to *55*. This field provides us with an address that we can use to send requests to the **MockWebServer** instance in the form of **host:port**. We can use that address to replace our production domain address before making requests.

Next, we have the **mockWebServer** function (*lines 57* to *61*). This function takes a MockWebServer **Dispatcher** object argument and returns a reference to the **MockWebServer** instance with the dispatcher assigned to it. We will discuss **MockDispatcher**, which is a concrete implementation of the **Dispatcher** abstract class, momentarily.

For **MockWebServerProvider** to work, there is one more thing that we need to take care of. We need to generate the **teststore_keystore.bks** file (see *line 21*) and save it under the **assets** folder. Generating this file is a two-step process:

1. Download **BouncyCastle[3]**, which is a cryptography API. I am assuming that you downloaded it to **~/Downloads/bcprov-jdk15on-169.jar**.

2. Run the following command from your terminal:

   keytool -genkey -v -alias localhost -ext SAN=dns:localhost -keypass fake_ password -storepass fake_password -keyalg RSA -keysize 2048 -validity 10000 -storetype BKS -keystore teststore_keystore.bks -provider org. bouncycastle.jce.provider.BouncyCastleProvider -providerpath ~/Downloads/ bcprov-jdk15on-1.69.jar

Following these steps should lead to the creation of a **teststore_keystore.bks** file in your current directory. Once generated, simply copy or move the file to your **androidTest/assets** folder.

Now, let us look at the **MockDispatcher** class, our MockWebServer's **Dispatcher** abstract class implementation:

MockDispatcher.kt

```
1.    package com.mitteloupe.whoami.test.server
2.
3.    [imports...]
4.
5.    class MockDispatcher :
6.        Dispatcher(),
7.        ResponseBinder {
8.        override var testName: String = ""
9.
10.       override val usedEndpoints: Set<MockRequest>
11.           field = mutableSetOf()
12.
13.       private val responses =
14.           mutableMapOf<MockRequest, MockResponseFactory>()
15.
16.       override fun bindResponse(
17.           requestResponseFactory: MockRequestResponseFactory
18.       ) {
19.           responses[requestResponseFactory.request] =
20.               requestResponseFactory.responseFactory
21.       }
```

---

3 https://repo1.maven.org/maven2/org/bouncycastle/bcprov-jdk15on/1.69/

```
22.
23.        override fun reset() {
24.            responses.clear()
25.            usedEndpoints.clear()
26.        }
27.
28.        override fun dispatch(request: RecordedRequest): MockResponse {
29.            val endPoint = request.path!!.substringBefore("?")
30.            val matchingRequest = responses.entries
31.                .firstOrNull { requestResponse ->
32.                    requestResponse.key.url == endPoint
33.                }?.also { requestResponse ->
34.                    usedEndpoints.add(requestResponse.key)
35.                }
36.            val response = matchingRequest?.value?.mockResponse() ?:
37.                MockResponse(code = 404).also {
38.                    Log.w(
39.                        "MockDispatcher",
40.                        "$testName: ${request.path} not stubbed!"
41.                    )
42.                }
43.            return MockResponse().apply {
44.                headers = Headers
45.                    .headersOf(*response.headers.toArray())
46.            }.setResponseCode(response.code)
47.                .setBody(response.body)
48.        }
49.
50.        private fun Collection<Pair<String, String>>
51.            .toArray(): Array<String> =
52.            flatMap { listOf(it.first, it.second) }.toTypedArray()
53.    }
```

A **Dispatcher** (*line 6*) is a MockWebServer abstract class for handling stubbed server requests.

The **dispatch** function (*lines 28 to 48*) is called whenever the server needs to process a request and return a response.

On *lines 29 to 35*, we convert the **request** argument to a corresponding **MockRequestResponseFactory** instance. We do so by first taking the URL of the request and stripping any query string (*line 29*). We then match that URL against those of the request keys until we find a match (*lines 31 to 33*). If we find a match, we set the **matchingRequest** variable to the request and response entry and record the request in the **usedEndpoints** field (*lines 33* to *35*). If we do not find a match, we set the **matchingRequest** variable to **null**. This is the simplest way to identify requests. In your implementation, you may want to introduce a more thorough translation of requests to **MockRequestResponseFactory** instances. You may have noticed that I use the not-null assertion operator (**!!**). While I strongly advise against using it in production code, tests should be more forgiving. If I expect the value to not be **null**, I am happy for my test to fail if the value is indeed **null**. This offers me an opportunity to investigate why my assumption was wrong.

Given an entry with a **MockResponseFactory** instance value, we now obtain a **MockResponse** instance by calling its **mockResponse()** function (*line 36*). On *lines 37* to *42*, we handle missing responses by instantiating a generic **404** server response object.

Now that we have the data for our response, we can instantiate a MockWebServer **MockResponse** instance (*line 43*). We proceed to set its headers (*lines 44* and *45*), a response code (*line 46*), and the response body (*line 47*).

The headers are assigned by converting a **List** of key and value **String Pair** objects to a flat **String Array** (*lines 45, lines 50* to *52*). On *line 45*, we use the spread operator (*****) to convert the **String Array** to a **String vararg**.

This concludes our coverage of the MockWebServer solution. Next, we will take a quick look at a Ktor implementation.

Stubbing a Ktor client

In order to mock server responses, Ktor provides us with the **MockEngine** class. Using the **MockEngine** class, we can introduce a solution like that proposed for OkHttp previously (see **MockDispatcher**):

MockResponseEngine.kt

```
1.    package com.mitteloupe.whoami.test.server
2.
3.    [imports...]
4.
5.    class MockResponseEngine : ResponseBinder {
6.        override var testName: String = ""
7.
8.        override val usedEndpoints: Set<MockRequest>
9.            field = mutableSetOf()
10.
11.       val mockEngine = MockEngine { request ->
12.           val endPoint = request.url.toString()
13.               .substringBefore("?")
14.           val matchingRequest = responses.entries
15.               .firstOrNull { requestResponse ->
```

```
16.                         requestResponse.key.url == endPoint
17.               }?.also { requestResponse ->
18.                   usedEndpoints.add(requestResponse.key)
19.               }
20.           val response = matchingRequest?.value?.mockResponse() ?:
21.               MockResponse(code = 404).also {
22.                   Log.w(
23.                       "MockResponseEngine",
24.                       "$testName: ${request.url} not stubbed!"
25.                   )
26.               }
27.
28.           respond(
29.               status = HttpStatusCode(
30.                   response.code,
31.                   "Mocked ${matchingRequest != null}"
32.               ),
33.               headers = headersOf(*response.headers.toArray()),
34.               content = ByteReadChannel(response.body)
35.           )
36.       }
37.
38.       private val responses =
39.           mutableMapOf<MockRequest, MockResponseFactory>()
40.
41.       override fun bindResponse(
42.           requestResponseFactory: MockRequestResponseFactory
43.       ) {
44.           responses[requestResponseFactory.request] =
45.               requestResponseFactory.responseFactory
46.       }
47.
48.       override fun reset() {
49.           responses.clear()
50.           usedEndpoints.clear()
51.       }
52.
53.       private fun Collection<Pair<String, String>>.toArray() =
54.           map { header -> Pair(header.first, listOf(header.second)) }
55.               .toTypedArray()
56.   }
```

Just like the **MockDispatcher** class, **MockResponseEngine** implements the **ResponseBinder** interface (*line 5*). It therefore has a **usedEndpoints** field (*lines 8* and *9*), the **bindResponse** (*lines 41 to 46*), and **reset** (*lines 48 to 51*) function implementations. It also has a private **responses** map (*lines 38* and *39*) to store bound responses.

To create a Ktor client, we need an **engine**. Ktor provides a test library that contains a **MockEngine** class for this purpose. The Ktor test library also provides a static function that takes a lambda request handler as an argument and returns a **MockEngine** instance (*lines 11 to 36*).

To process the request, we first extract its URL, stripping out the query string, just like we did in **MockDispatcher** (*lines 12* and *13*). We then obtain a response, again just like we did in the **MockDispatcher** class.

Finally, we respond with the data from our response variable (*lines 28 to 35*). The headers need to be converted to a typed **Array** and applied the spread operator (*****) so they can be used as a vararg argument (*line 33, lines 53 to 55*). Note that we add an optional debugging string to the response status (*line 31*). This is useful if you are seeing **404** responses and want to make sure that the result is caught and stubbed as a **404** rather than simply missing.

Conclusion

If you followed this chapter, you should be sorted out with a working mocked HTTP testing solution. This concludes our end-to-end testing discussion. The principles laid out in this chapter will serve you regardless of the nature of the external dependency. They provide a solid foundation for extension: web sockets and external devices can be faked in a similar fashion or by adding more functionality to the code presented in this chapter.

In the next chapter, we will explore failures and exceptions. We will discuss the differences between the two terms, when to use which, and how to handle them.

Points to remember

When implementing your end-to-end tests, remember:

- Ask yourself: *Do I need to test my app with a real server?* (Hint: It is highly likely the answer is no.)

- Similarly, ask yourself whether you need to rely on external devices such as a Bluetooth device (you guessed it, you probably do not).

- Interaction with devices can usually be abstracted to requests and responses. Use this to define your communication language with the device.

- Remember that each test may require different responses for the same requests.

- It does not matter what libraries you use for external communication, there is always a way to introduce a fake alternative.

CHAPTER 11
Failures and Exceptions

Only those who dare to fail greatly can ever achieve greatly.

- Robert F. Kennedy

Introduction

When developing applications or discussing feature specifications, we tend to focus on the successful scenario, or the happy path.

As developers, it is our responsibility to challenge assumptions. *Will saving the user's details always succeed? Can we always obtain a fresh copy of the terms and conditions to present to the user? What happens if the connection drops? What if the user is trying to create an account with an email address that is already taken?*

Many things can go wrong when a user uses our app. In this chapter, we will discuss how to classify these things and how to handle them in a Clean Architecture fashion.

Structure

In this chapter, we will cover the following topics:

- Failures or exceptions

- Handling failures

- Handling exceptions

Objectives

After reading this chapter, you should be able to classify unsuccessful scenarios as failures or as exceptions. You should also be able to handle them according to that classification. For us to handle the unhappy paths of our app, we need to understand what could go wrong and how to handle the situations when it does.

Failures or exceptions

How do we know if we are dealing with a failure or an exception? Maybe more importantly: why does it matter?

Both failures and exceptions represent unsuccessful operations. However:

- **Failures** are recoverable and *expected*.

- **Exceptions** are extraordinary, *unexpected* occurrences with no clear recovery path.

Consider the aspect of *expectation*. A good example of a **failure** would be the user providing incorrect login credentials. We know that, given incorrect credentials, login will fail. This is an *expected* failure, and therefore it is a *failure* and not an exception. An **exception**, on the other hand, would be us trying to access an array using an index that is out of bounds. We *do not expect* this scenario to happen, or we would have changed our code to avoid it happening.

Another way to differentiate between failures and exceptions is *our ability to handle them*. With incorrect credentials, we could inform the user that they have provided invalid credentials. An index out of bounds exception is harder to explain to a user and is generally more challenging to address. Did we mean to access an item that was no longer there? Did we calculate the index incorrectly? Us having reached this situation warrants an **Exception** being thrown.

There is an important distinction here. The moment that *we know a scenario can happen*, and know *how to handle it*, it stops being an exception scenario and becomes a failure one. The distinction between failures and exceptions matters because they should be handled differently.

Exceptions are red flags. Something happened that we were not expecting. It is possible that our code has a bug in it. It is also possible that what happened is catastrophic, and we cannot resume the app at all due to its (now unknown) state. Exceptions should be logged and monitored. Our long-term goal is to have as few of them occurring in the app as possible.

Failures are a natural part of the app operation. A user could try to withdraw more money than is currently in their account. They could mistype their credentials. These events should be handled by the app in a graceful manner for the user to have a reasonably good experience.

Handling failures

In the previous section, we discussed what qualifies as a failure event. Now that we know what a failure event is, how do we handle a failure event?

Failures are treated as normal values. In its simplest form, this could be a Boolean. If we take the login example, a **true** value could tell us that the credentials were correct, and a **false** one could tell us that they were not. While this approach could work, I would advise against it for two main reasons, which are outlined as follows:

- It is not *explicitly clear*. What does **true** mean? Did we let the user log in? Did we just validate the credentials? What does **false** mean? Did we fail to get a response from the server? Did the server tell us that the credentials were incorrect? Even with good names, we may find ourselves having to dig into the code to figure it out.

- It is not *easily scalable*. What if we wanted to distinguish between incorrect credentials, the connection dropping before we could get a response from the server, and the server experiencing a temporary problem? With only two values, it is impossible to express that level of detail.

A Boolean is not the best option for handling failures. The next obvious candidates are enum classes and sealed classes or interfaces. All of these options would address the two concerns that we had when we considered a Boolean type: we can name the values to explicitly describe the state that they represent, and we can easily scale either of them to support more states.

It is a good idea to opt for a sealed class or a sealed interface in most cases. Sealed classes are enums on steroids. They allow us to attach different behaviors to each state. In my experience, I ended up refactoring most of my enum classes to sealed classes so that I could invert controls. This refactoring is potentially messy because the naming convention for enums is often **SCREAMING_SNAKE_CASE**, while sealed classes and sealed interfaces are traditionally named using **PascalCase**.

To demonstrate how a failure could be handled, let us imagine a banking app where the user can, amongst other things, close their account. Closing the account can fail if there is unsettled debt, if the account is already closed, or if there is a technical problem.

Following our Clean Architecture methodology, we will start with the Domain layer:

CloseAccountResultDomainModel.kt

```
1.  package com.bestbank.bankingapp.closeaccount.domain.model
2.
3.  sealed class CloseAccountResultDomainModel(
4.      val isSuccessful: Boolean = false
5.  ) {
6.      data object Success : CloseAccountResultDomainModel(isSuccessful = true)
```

```
 7.        data object UnsettledDebt : CloseAccountResultDomainModel()
 8.        data object AlreadyClosed : CloseAccountResultDomainModel()
 9.        data object TechnicalIssue : CloseAccountResultDomainModel()
10.   }
```

CloseAccountResultDomainModel, as its name implies, is a Domain model. As such, it meets all our expectations for Domain models covered in *Chapter 3, The Domain Layer*. Its individual subclasses (*lines 6 to 9*) are stripped off in the **DomainModel** suffix for brevity.

We have a single successful scenario value (*line 6*). Every failure we want to be able to report to the user is represented by its own value (*lines 7-9*).

The Domain model has an **isSuccessful** Boolean property (*line 4*). The reason for having this property is that from a feature perspective, our journey forks out into two main paths: the happy (successful) path and the unhappy (failed) path. If the account was closed successfully, we want to show the user a success screen. Failure would probably lead to us notifying the user of the failure, explaining what went wrong. Being able to determine success or failure by reading a property instead of inspecting the class type reads better, is more efficient, and is more scalable. We can now add other success states (imagine a **DeletionPending** state, for example) without having to update our check for success.

As we are likely to have more failure states than success state in this case, we opted for defaulting the **isSuccessful** property to **false**, allowing us to only specify a **true** value in the one case (**Success**, *line 6*) that is indeed successful. This leads to less repetition. There is a counterargument for this choice. An alternative approach could have been to require specifying a value for **isSuccessful** in every state. It would have led to some repetition, but it would have guaranteed that we would not forget to assign the appropriate value when introducing a new state. Both approaches are valid.

Names for the different state values are designed to reflect the states that they represent in a clear way. The idea is to allow any reader, even without domain knowledge, to be able to understand what each value represents. This is not always possible, of course, but we always aim for this level of simplicity. A reader should have no problem guessing what an **UnsettledDebt** result means when the user is trying to close an account. The same is true for **AlreadyClosed** and **TechnicalIssue**.

We can now expect the **CloseAccountUseCase** class to return a **CloseAccountResultDomainModel** object. We can also expect the repository interface to contain a **closeAccount** function that returns a **CloseAccountResultDomainModel** object.

Let us consider the Presentation layer next. Here is the Presentation model:

CloseAccountResultPresentationModel.kt

```
1.    package com.bestbank.bankingapp.closeaccount.presentation.model
2.
```

```
3.   sealed interface CloseAccountFailurePresentationModel {
4.       data object UnsettledDebt : CloseAccountFailurePresentationModel
5.       data object AlreadyClosed : CloseAccountFailurePresentationModel
6.       data object TechnicalIssue : CloseAccountFailurePresentationModel
7.   }
```

When comparing the Presentation model to the Domain one, we can see some interesting differences. Aside from the obvious different subpackage (**presentation** rather than **domain**) and the suffix (**PresentationModel** instead of **DomainModel**), we replaced **Result** with **Failure**.

Having the **isSuccessful** property in the Domain model allowed us to easily treat failures differently from success. We can now have a dedicated sealed interface that focuses solely on the type of failure that we encountered. A mapper can map every Domain failure state to a presentation failure state. The mapper can safely throw an exception for every successful state argument because it does not expect to get called with successful states.

This is how the viewmodel check would look:

CloseAccountViewModel.kt (snippet)

```
1.        private fun processClosingAccountResult(
2.            result: CloseAccountResultDomainModel
3.        ) {
4.            if (result.isSuccessful) {
5.                emitNavigationEvent(AccountClosed)
6.            } else {
7.                val failureResult = resultDomainToFailurePresentationMapper
8.                    .toPresentation(result)
9.                notify(failureResult)
10.           }
11.       }
```

The **processClosingAccountResult** function will be called when we obtain a **CloseAccountResultDomainModel** object after executing the account deletion usecase. If the result is successful (*line 4*), we emit an event for navigating onwards (*line 5*). Otherwise, we map the result to a **CloseAccountFailurePresentationModel** object (*lines 7 and 8*) and notify the user (*line 9*). Here is the **ResultDomainToFailurePresentationMapper** class:

ResultDomainToFailurePresentationMapper.kt

```
1.   package com.bestbank.bankingapp.closeaccount.presentation.mapper
2.
3.   class ResultDomainToFailurePresentationMapper {
4.       fun toPresentation(result: CloseAccountResultDomainModel) =
```

```
5.          when (result) {
6.              is Success -> error("Expected a failure state")
7.              is UnsettledDebt -> {
8.                  CloseAccountFailurePresentationModel.UnsettledDebt
9.              }
10.             is AlreadyClosed -> {
11.                 CloseAccountFailurePresentationModel.AlreadyClosed
12.             }
13.             is TechnicalIssue -> {
14.                 CloseAccountFailurePresentationModel.TechnicalIssue
15.             }
16.         }
17. }
```

The mapper takes a **CloseAccountResultDomainModel** object as an input (*line 4*). It then maps it using a **when** statement (*lines 5 to 16*). We start by ruling out having a **Success** state (*line 6*). If we had more than one successful state, we would have listed them all here, separated by commas. Our mapper class expects to only receive a failure state value as input. With the successful state out of the way, we can map every Domain failure to the corresponding Presentation one (*lines 7 to 15*).

Following the Presentation layer, we can proceed to implement the UI layer. For success, we can simply navigate to a success screen. See *Chapter 7, Dependency Injection and Navigation*. For failure, we may want to navigate to an error screen, or we may want to present an informative message. Since we can learn more from the latter, we will present a message:

CloseAccountResultUiModel.kt

```
1.  package com.bestbank.bankingapp.closeaccount.ui.model
2.
3.  [imports...]
4.
5.  sealed class CloseAccountFailureUiModel(
6.      @DrawableRes val iconResourceId: Int,
7.      val message: String
8.  ) {
9.      data class UnsettledDebt(
10.         private val resources: Resources
11.     ) : CloseAccountFailureUiModel(
12.         R.drawable.icon_unsettled_debt,
13.         resources.getString(R.string.error_unsettled_debt)
14.     )
15.
```

```
16.        data class AlreadyClosed(
17.            private val resources: Resources
18.        ) : CloseAccountFailureUiModel(
19.            R.drawable.icon_account_closed,
20.            resources.getString(R.string.error_account_already_closed)
21.        )
22.
23.        data class TechnicalIssue(
24.            private val resources: Resources
25.        ) : CloseAccountFailureUiModel(
26.            R.drawable.icon_technical_issue,
27.            resources.getString(R.string.error_technical_issue)
28.        )
```

The **CloseAccountFailureUiModel** sealed class relies on an icon resource ID (*line 6*) and a message, which is a String. As **CloseAccountFailureUiModel** is a part of the UI layer, it can comfortably have access to Android Resources. The instance of Resources (*lines 10, 17, and 24*) will be provided to the individual states by the Presentation to UI mapper. It is also possible to make the message a composable instead if we are using Jetpack Compose.

Each state provides an appropriate icon resource ID (*lines 12, 19, and 26*) annotated with the **@ DrawableRes** annotation, as well as a string obtained from the **Resources** instance (*lines 13, 20, and 27*). This lets our code query the state for an icon resource ID or a message without worrying about the type of error.

With the UI covered, let us go back to the DataSource layer. How does a failure scenario look from the Datasource perspective? Refer to the following:

CloseAccountResultDataModel.kt

```
1.    package com.bestbank.bankingapp.datasource.account.model
2.
3.    sealed interface CloseAccountResultDataModel {
4.        data object Success : CloseAccountResultDataModel
5.        data object UnsettledDebt : CloseAccountResultDataModel
6.        data object AlreadyClosed : CloseAccountResultDataModel
7.        data object TechnicalIssue : CloseAccountResultDataModel
8.    }
```

Remember, our Data models are a part of our contract with our DataSources. They contain the minimal amount of data needed by the Data layer to determine the state. In this case, the Data model turns out to be very similar to the Domain one. The most notable difference is that we omitted the **isSuccessful** Boolean that is present in the Domain model. Having that field in our Data model would not be helpful.

Our DataSource can now focus on returning to us the appropriate state based on the API response. This conversion is likely to happen in an API to Data mapper.

Finally, our Data layer can tie the Domain and the DataSource layers together. It will contain a Repository implementation of the interface that we introduced in the Domain layer. It will also have a mapper that maps the Data model to the corresponding Domain one.

We now have a complete picture of a failure scenario, from a DataSource, to the Data layer, to the Domain, the Presentation, and finally the UI. Next, we will explore exception scenarios.

Handling exceptions

In the previous section, we discussed the handling of failures. Failures are expected, unsuccessful scenarios. However, what happens when we encounter an unexpected problem? What if we expected a certain field to always exist in the response, but the field is unexpectedly missing? What if an object that should be there simply is not?

These are the types of scenarios that should be handled by throwing exceptions.

In our Clean Architecture implementation, we want to respect the Dependency Rule when it comes to Exceptions, too. We do not want our UI to be tightly coupled to a networking exception, for example.

There are two ways in which we can address this concern.

First, we catch all exceptions in our **UseCaseExecutor** class (see *Chapter 3, The Domain Layer*) and make sure to wrap them in an **UnknownDomainException** object if they are not already instances of subclasses extending the **DomainException** abstract class. This means that every **Exception** that is thrown by code in the DataSource, Data, or Domain layers will almost always end up becoming a **DomainException**.

The reason that we must be careful with this assumption is that if the **Exception** was thrown from a different thread, it would not be caught by the **UseCaseExecutor** object. If you are switching threads, you should make sure that you are handling exceptions thrown from those threads.

The second way of ensuring that we respect the Dependency Rule is to throw Domain exceptions from our Data layer. This would also mean declaring Data exceptions in the DataSource layer. We can then rely on a try…catch mechanism to catch any **Exception** object and rethrow it as a Data exception. The Data exception can, in turn, be caught and rethrown as a Domain exception.

Once an **Exception** is thrown by the **UseCaseExecutor** object, we can handle it using the **onException** lambda argument that is passed to the **UseCaseExecutor** instance when the **execute** function is called.

Let us look at an example. We will use the same scenario described in the failures section: our user is using our banking app to delete their account. Only this time, instead of one of the expected failure scenarios, we are getting an unknown API response that we are not sure how to handle. Let us assume that we decided, as part of our *delete account* feature, to let users know when a server error occurred.

As with our failure scenario and with every feature that we implement, we will start with the Domain layer:

ServerDomainException.kt

```
1.  package com.bestbank.bankingapp.closeaccount.domain.exception
2.
3.  import com.bestbank.bankingapp.architecture.domain.exception.DomainException
4.
5.  data class ServerDomainException(
6.      val throwable: Throwable
7.  ) : DomainException(throwable)
```

Exceptions are stored under the **exception** sub-package of a feature under a layer (**domain**, in this case) sub-package (*line 1*).

We name our exception as descriptively as we can, suffixing it with **DomainException** (see *line 5*).

Our **ServerDomainException** constructor accepts a **Throwable** object as an argument (*line 6*). This lets us pass the cause of the exception to it. Having a reference to the **Throwable** object can help us with debugging later.

All of our Domain layer exceptions extend **DomainException**, and this one is no exception (see *line 7*. Pun intended).

It is now the responsibility of our repository to catch thrown exceptions by the datasource and determine which should lead to throwing a **ServerDomainException** object. This logic can be extracted to an **Exception** mapper to avoid code repetition.

The repository (or rather, the mapper that is used by the repository) will be looking for a particular exception:

ServerDataException.kt

```
1.  package com.bestbank.bankingapp.datasource.account.exception
2.
3.  data class ServerDataException(
4.      val throwable: Throwable
5.  ) : RuntimeException(throwable)
```

The Data exception represents datasource server exceptions in a language that the repository understands. If the datasource object catches a server-related exception that it is not sure how to handle, it can wrap it in a **ServerDataException** object and throw it.

Since it is perfectly fine for the UI to know about Exceptions thrown by either the Presentation or the UI layers, and since UI exceptions are unlikely to find their way into the Presentation layer (at least when following **Model-View-ViewModel** (**MVVM**). With **Model-View-Presenter** (**MVP**), for example, this can still happen), this wraps up the subject of exceptions in Clean Architecture for Android.

Conclusion

Things can go wrong with our apps. When they do, we need to be prepared to handle them. Identifying what could go wrong is the first step. The second step is to determine which scenarios qualify as failures and which warrant throwing an Exception.

In this chapter, we discussed ways to classify unhappy paths. We then covered our approach to handling failures. Lastly, we discussed handling the unexpected, namely exceptions. In the next chapter, we will see how to implement a new feature in our Clean Architecture app.

Points to remember

When approaching the implementation of a feature, there are a few things that we should keep in mind:

- We should always ask ourselves what can go wrong.

- Treat known issues that we know how to handle as failures.

- Consider anything that could go wrong unexpectedly to be an exception.

- Remember that exceptions thrown from different threads must be handled separately.

Join our Discord space

Join our Discord workspace for latest updates, offers, tech happenings around the world, new releases, and sessions with the authors:

https://discord.bpbonline.com

CHAPTER 12

Implementing a New Feature

It's not a bug, it's a feature.

- Anonymous software developer

Introduction

In the last chapter, we discussed exceptions and errors. In this chapter, we will discuss what defines a feature. We will then proceed to implement a complete feature.

Whether you are a single developer or a part of a large team, breaking down the implementation of a feature is helpful in several ways:

- The first advantage is that it helps us structure our change. It is easier to implement a feature when you can start by focusing on the requirement and gradually implement the behavior around it.

- The second advantage is that it is easy to break our change down into small commits that will not affect our codebase until the feature is complete, all the while keeping the test coverage high.

- The third advantage is team-specific: breaking down the work by layers allows your team to work in parallel. The team can start splitting work to implement the Domain and the DataSource layer. Once the Domain and DataSource layers are in place, work on the Presentation and the Data layers can progress in parallel. Finally, work on the UI, dependency injection, and navigation can commence.

Before we dive into the technical bits, let us first understand what a feature *is*.

Structure

In this chapter, we will cover the following topics:

- The definition of a feature
- Starting with the Domain layer
- Implementing the Presentation layer
- Implementing the UI layer
- Implementing the Data and DataSource layers
- Implementing navigation

Objectives

By the end of this chapter, you should know what a feature is. You should also know how to implement a feature in a structured Clean Architecture way. For us to keep scaling our app, we will need to break it down into features. For us to do that, we must first understand what a feature is. With that understanding, we can proceed to the actual implementation of a feature.

The definition of a feature

To define an app, it helps to be able to break it down. This is because the smaller parts have less complexity than the whole. Since the smaller parts are simpler, they are easier to understand. This helps in having a mental picture of the app, making it easier to grasp.

One way of breaking down an app, especially a Clean Architecture app, is by layer. However, although examining the Domain layer could give us a rough idea of its behavior, this kind of separation does not help us much in terms of understanding what the app does.

Breaking the app down by its capabilities is often more helpful if we want to understand what the app does. For example, in a banking app, the user will probably be able to check their balance and make payments to various accounts.

These capabilities are also known as **features**. A feature could be as large as a section of the app. In a social networking app, for example, allowing the user to manage their profile could be such a feature (this could be called the *profile management* feature). A help section is another example. A feature could also be as small as allowing the user to update their contact details. Such a feature may be a sub-feature of the *profile management* feature or a standalone *contact details* feature.

When we discuss a feature, we are not referring to *how* a capability is provided to the user. Instead, we are referring to *what* the user could do by using that feature. The *how* lies in the code implementing the feature.

So, if we look at the delete account feature, we do not care how the deletion occurs. We only care that the user can delete an account. The exception to the rule would be when the *how* differentiates one feature from another. For example, if deleting an account by email is an existing feature, and we want to add the option to delete an account by fax (what year is this?), we will now have two features: *delete account by email* and *delete account by fax*.

Now that we have a better understanding of what a feature is, let us proceed to the implementation of one. In the next sections, we will implement the *add a custom record* feature to our **WhoAmI** app.

The requirement

The *add a custom record* feature will allow the user to manually add a new record to the connection history. Before we start implementing it, we have the following set of requirements:

- The feature will consist of a single screen.

- The screen will have an input field and a button that is labeled **Save**.

- By default, the text field will be populated with the current user's IP address as presented on the home screen, if it is known.

- This feature will allow the user to type in any value as an IP address into the input field.

- The user can navigate away from the feature by going back.

- The user can also navigate back by saving the new IP address as present in the input field. This is done by tapping the **Save** button.

- If the user saved the IP address, it will be added to their connection history.

- Navigation to the feature will be done by tapping a button on the home screen that is labeled **Add manually**.

With these requirements in mind, let us get down to business.

Starting with the Domain layer

In this section, we will start the implementation of the *add a custom record* feature. As the name suggests, this feature will allow a user to add a custom record to their connection history.

You will notice that the title of this section is different from all the following titles in this chapter. It is the only one that does not start with *Implementing* and instead uses *Starting with*. This is because I cannot emphasize enough how important it is to follow this order of implementation.

When starting to implement the feature, we immediately have a rough idea of what we want the user to be able to do: we want them to be able to manually provide connection details and save them to the connection history.

We know that our request model would need to contain the connection details. We know that the minimal amount of information that a connection record has is an IP address. This gives us our **NewRecordDomainModel** class:

NewRecordDomainModel.kt

```
1.    package com.mitteloupe.whoami.addrecord.domain.model
2.
3.    data class NewRecordDomainModel(
4.        val ipAddress: String
5.    )
```

We started by creating the **addrecord** package and the **domain** sub-package under it. Then, under the **model** sub-package, we implement the **NewRecordDomainModel** request model. We name the model by the data that it stores, hence the **NewRecord** prefix (*line 3*). The **DomainModel** suffix (still on *line 3*) reflects the layer in which this model exists.

The model holds one field: the IP address (*line 4*). If we wanted to add more initial details about the connection, they would go in this class.

Next, we declare a repository interface with a function that takes the model that we just created as an input and has no return value. We expect all requests to add a new record to succeed:

AddNewRecordRepository.kt

```
1.    package com.mitteloupe.whoami.addrecord.domain.repository
2.
3.    import com.mitteloupe.whoami.addrecord.domain.model.NewRecordDomainModel
4.
5.    interface AddNewRecordRepository {
6.        fun addNewRecord(newRecord: NewRecordDomainModel)
7.    }
```

We introduce the **repository** sub-package for our repository interface (*line 1*). We name our repository by the functionality it exposes for our usecase (**AddNewRecord**) and suffix its name with **Repository** (*line 5*).

The repository interface exposes only one function (*line 6*), to be used by our usecase. This follows the interface segregation[1] SOLID principle. The interface segregation principle states

---

1 https://www.baeldung.com/java-interface-segregation

that we should not expose methods that we do not need. The **addNewRecord** function receives an instance of the **NewRecordDomainModel** class that we covered earlier and has no return value.

We now have enough information for us to implement our usecase:

AddNewRecordUseCase.kt

```
1.  package com.mitteloupe.whoami.addrecord.domain.usecase
2.
3.  [imports...]
4.
5.  class AddNewRecordUseCase(
6.      private val addNewRecordRepository: AddNewRecordRepository,
7.      coroutineContextProvider: CoroutineContextProvider
8.  ) : BackgroundExecutingUseCase<NewRecordDomainModel, Unit>(
9.      coroutineContextProvider
10. ) {
11.     override fun executeInBackground(
12.         request: NewRecordDomainModel
13.     ) { addNewRecordRepository.addNewRecord(request) }
14. }
```

We save the new usecase under a newly created **usecase** sub-package. We choose a descriptive name for our usecase, starting with a verb in the imperative form, followed by an adverb and a noun: **AddNewRecord**. We suffix the name with **UseCase** (*line 5*).

AddNewRecordUseCase relies on an instance of **AddNewRecordRepository**, which we created earlier and is provided on *line 6*. It extends **BackgroundExecutingUseCase** with the input generic type of **NewRecordDomainModel**, and the output type of **Unit** (*line 8*).

The **executeInBackground** function is implemented to call **addNewRecord** on the **AddNewRecordRepository** instance (*line 13*).

Had we known of any valid exception scenarios, we could have also declared relevant Domain exceptions. The same is true for failures: had we known of any valid failure scenarios, we could have replaced the **Unit** return value with a sealed class or a sealed interface (see *Chapter 11, Failures and exceptions*).

We could also implement a stub repository now, allowing us to plug in the usecase into a viewmodel straight away.

I know that you must be tired of me mentioning this by now, but do not forget to unit-test your usecase. In this case, making sure that **addNewRecord** is called with the right request should suffice.

This completes the Domain layer. Next, we will implement the Presentation layer.

Implementing the Presentation layer

With the Domain layer done, we can proceed with the Presentation layer.

We know that the usecase expects a **NewRecordDomainModel** object. The details for constructing that Domain model should be provided by the user via the UI layer. This requirement will take the form of a Presentation model:

NewRecordPresentationModel.kt

```
1.    package com.mitteloupe.whoami.addrecord.presentation.model
2.
3.    data class NewRecordPresentationModel(
4.        val ipAddress: String
5.    )
```

Under the **addrecord** feature package, we add the **Presentation** layer package and then introduce a **model** sub-package under it (*line 1*).

The field of the Presentation model in this case is identical to that of the Domain model. We expect the UI layer to provide us with the IP address of the new record to be added to the connection history (*line 4*).

To map the Presentation model to a Domain model, we need a Presentation to Domain mapper:

NewRecordDomainMapper.kt

```
1.    package com.mitteloupe.whoami.addrecord.presentation.mapper
2.
3.    [imports...]
4.
5.    class NewRecordDomainMapper {
6.        fun toDomain(newRecord: NewRecordPresentationModel) =
7.            NewRecordDomainModel(ipAddress = newRecord.ipAddress)
8.    }
```

We create the Presentation to Domain mapper under the **mapper** sub-package (*line 1*).

In *line 5*, we declare our mapper. The mapper is named by taking both the names of the input and output models into account. In this case, both models (**NewRecordPresentationModel** and **NewRecordDomainModel**) share the same prefix, so repeating the **NewRecord** part of their name twice would be redundant. We also omit the obvious **Model** suffix. Since the mapper lives in the Presentation layer, we also omit the Presentation part from the name. This leaves us with the **NewRecordDomain** prefix. Our suffix is **Mapper**, leading to the complete name of **NewRecordDomainMapper**.

As is the case with all our Clean Architecture mappers, **NewRecordDomainMapper** exposes a single function, with a name prefixed with **to** and suffixed with the name of the output layer, **Domain** (*line 6*). The function takes a new record Presentation model as its input and returns a new record Domain model with the same IP address (*line 7*).

The last requirement that our viewmodel has is for us to specify its state models, namely a view state, a notification class, and a success event model:

AddRecordViewState.kt

```
1.    package com.mitteloupe.whoami.addrecord.presentation.model
2.
3.    sealed interface AddRecordViewState {
4.        data object Loading : AddRecordViewState
5.        data object Idle : AddRecordViewState
6.    }
```

View states are kept under the **model** sub-package of their feature's layer package (*line 1*). Our view state is a sealed interface, and it has two states: **Loading** and **Idle** (*lines 4 and 5*, respectively). Note that **AddRecordViewState** does not hold the new record details at all. This is because we aim for one source of truth for our data, and the viewmodel is *never* it. Data is either owned by the UI (as the user is providing it prior to submission) or by the Data layer (to be accessed via the Domain layer). We will provide the viewmodel with the new record details when they are needed, and it will pass them on to the Domain layer.

Let us take a look at the notification model next:

AddRecordPresentationNotification.kt

```
1.    package com.favedish.presentation.addnewdish.model
2.
3.    import com.mitteloupe.whoami.architecture.presentation.notification.
      PresentationNotification
4.
5.    class AddDishPresentationNotification : PresentationNotification
```

Our notification class is empty for now. We could use it later to inform the user of any issues occurring while trying to add a new record. This class can be skipped altogether by introducing an empty **NoNotification** object that can be used by any viewmodel that is not concerned with notifications.

We covered the view state and the notification models, all that is left is the navigation event model:

AddRecordPresentationDestination.kt

```
1.    package com.mitteloupe.whoami.addrecord.presentation.navigation
2.
3.    import com.mitteloupe.whoami.architecture.presentation.navigation.
      PresentationNavigationEvent
4.
5.    sealed interface AddRecordPresentationNavigationEvent :
6.        PresentationNavigationEvent {
7.        data class OnNewRecordAdded(
8.            val savedIpAddress: String
9.        ) : AddRecordPresentationNavigationEvent
10.   }
```

Our initial implementation of the *add a new record* feature assumes a single exit point from the feature: that of successfully adding the new record. Note that we describe what leads to navigation, or *why* we navigate, not *where* we navigate. That is because the *where* is a broader app concern, managed in the app itself.

The **PresentationNavigationEvent** sealed interface implementation is useful for grouping all the feature-specific exit points of the *add a new record* feature. Its sole subclass is the **OnNewRecordAdded** data class (*lines 7 to 9*), which takes the newly added IP address as an argument (*line 7*).

With a usecase, all Presentation models and a mapper for the new record models done, we are ready to implement our viewmodel:

AddRecordViewModel.kt

```
1.    package com.mitteloupe.whoami.addrecord.presentation.viewmodel
2.
3.    [imports...]
4.
5.    class AddRecordViewModel(
6.        private val addNewRecordUseCase: AddNewRecordUseCase,
7.        private val newRecordDomainMapper: NewRecordDomainMapper,
8.        useCaseExecutor: UseCaseExecutor
9.    ) : BaseViewModel<AddRecordViewState, AddRecordPresentationNotification>(
10.       useCaseExecutor
11.   ) {
```

The viewmodel is declared under the **viewmodel** sub-package (*line 1*).

On *line 5*, we can see that the name of our viewmodel matches that of the screen that it represents (**AddRecord**), with the **ViewModel** suffix added to it. The viewmodel depends on an

AddNewRecordUseCase instance (*line 6*) and a **NewRecordDomainMapper** instance (*lines 8 and 7*). It also requires a **UseCaseExecutorProvider** object (*line 8*) to satisfy the **BaseViewModel** superclass requirement.

The generic types that we provide for **BaseViewModel** are **AddRecordViewState** and **AddRecordPresentationNotification** (*line 9*), both of which we declared earlier. Let us continue to the body of the viewmodel:

AddRecordViewModel.kt (continued)

```
12.        fun onAddNewRecordAction(record: NewRecordPresentationModel) {
13.            updateViewState(Loading)
14.            addNewRecord(record)
15.        }
16.
17.        private fun addNewRecord(record: NewRecordPresentationModel) {
18.            val domainRecord = newRecordDomainMapper.toDomain(record)
19.            addNewRecordUseCase(
20.                value = domainRecord,
21.                onResult = { updateRecordSaved(record.ipAddress) }
22.            )
23.        }
24.
25.        private fun updateRecordSaved(ipAddress: String) {
26.            updateViewState(Idle)
27.            emitNavigationEvent(OnNewRecordAdded(savedIpAddrss = ipAddress))
28.        }
29.    }
```

The only action that we expect to have in our *create a new record* feature is that of adding a new record, which is represented by the **onAddNewRecordAction(NewRecordPresentationModel)** function on *lines 12* to *15*. When this function is called, we start by updating the view state to the **Loading** state (*line 13*), followed by adding the new record on *line 14*.

The actual adding of a new record happens on *lines 17* to *23* in the **addNewRecord(NewRecordPresentationModel)** function. We start by mapping the new record Presentation model to a Domain model using the Presentation to Domain mapper (*line 18*). We continue to execute the appropriate usecase, passing in the Domain new record instance as an input (*line 20*). On the next line, we provide a lambda that executes the **updateRecordSaved(String)** function, passing in the IP address provided via the **record** argument of the **addNewRecord** function. This lambda will be executed when the usecase completes its job successfully.

The **updateRecordSaved(String)** function (*lines* 25 to 28) starts by updating the view state to the **Idle** state (*line 26*). It then tells the UI layer that a navigation event occurred, providing an **OnNewRecordAdded** Presentation navigation event object (*line 29*). The navigation event instance contains the IP address that was added in case we wanted to highlight the new IP on the next screen.

With unit tests in place to cover the mapper and the viewmodel, we have high confidence that our Presentation layer is now complete and working. We can now proceed to implement the UI layer.

Implementing the UI layer

Having the Presentation layer code in place makes implementing the UI layer much easier. There is no need for stubs, and our feature should be ready to test drive as soon as the UI is done. So, without further ado, let us start implementing our UI layer.

For this feature, we will create a composable form that lets the user fill in an IP address in an input field and save the new record by tapping a button labeled **Save**. We will also pre-populate the input field with an existing IP address, if one is provided.

A good starting point would be to implement a UI to Presentation mapper to produce **NewRecordPresentationModel** instances from IP address strings. It has no requirements other than the Presentation model, which we already have:

NewRecordPresentationMapper.kt

```
1.    package com.mitteloupe.whoami.addrecord.ui.mapper
2.
3.    [imports...]
4.
5.    class NewRecordPresentationMapper {
6.        fun toPresentation(ipAddress: String) =
7.            NewRecordPresentationModel(ipAddress = ipAddress)
8.    }
```

Following our established convention, the mapper is stored under the **mapper** sub-package of the **ui** feature package (*line 1*).

The **NewRecordPresentationMapper** class is a simple one with a single function. Its role is to take the user's input and convert it to a model that our viewmodel understands. The single function, **toPresentation(String)**, takes an IP address as a string (remember that layers can use primitives or models to represent data, in this case, the UI model is of type **String**) and returns a corresponding **NewRecordPresentationModel** object (see *lines 6* and *7*).

We now have everything that we need to create our **AddRecordDependencies** class. Our screen composable will rely on this class. Refer to the following code:

AddRecordDependencies.kt

```
1.    package com.mitteloupe.whoami.addrecord.ui.di
2.
3.    [imports...]
4.
5.    data class AddRecordDependencies(
6.        val viewModel: AddRecordViewModel,
7.        private val addRecordNavigationMapper:
8.            NavigationEventDestinationMapper<
9.                AddRecordPresentationNavigationEvent>,
10.       private val addRecordNotificationMapper:
11.           NotificationUiMapper<AddRecordPresentationNotification>,
12.       val newRecordPresentationMapper: NewRecordPresentationMapper
13.   ) : BaseComposeHolder<AddRecordViewState,
14.       AddRecordPresentationNotification>(
15.       viewModel,
16.       addRecordNavigationMapper,
17.       addRecordNotificationMapper
18.   )
```

The **AddRecordDependencies** class is responsible for providing our composable with all the dependencies that it requires. We create it under the **di** sub-package of the **ui** layer package.

We start with the viewmodel and its associated mappers (*lines 6 to 11*). Note that we do not need to have concrete navigation or notification mappers at this point. We will still need to introduce them, but doing so later will not prevent our code from compiling.

Next, we add the new record mapper that we just created. Finally, we make sure that **AddRecordDependencies** extends the **BaseComposeHolder** abstract class, specify the generic types for it, and pass in all the required arguments (*lines 13 to 18*).

Having implemented the **AddRecordDependencies** class, we can proceed to create our composable:

AddRecordDependencies.kt

```
1.    package com.mitteloupe.whoami.home.ui.view
2.
3.    [imports...]
4.
5.    @Composable
6.    fun AddRecordDependencies.AddRecordScreen(
7.        navController: NavController,
```

```
 8.            initialIpAddress: String?,
 9.            modifier: Modifier = Modifier
10.    ) {
11.        ViewModelObserver(navController)
12.
13.        AddRecordContents(
14.            modifier = modifier,
15.            initialIpAddress = initialIpAddress,
16.            onRecordAddedClick = { ipAddress ->
17.                val newRecord = newRecordPresentationMapper
18.                    .toPresentation(ipAddress)
19.                viewModel.onAddNewRecordAction(newRecord)
20.            }
21.        )
22.    }
23.
```

The preceding **AddRecordScreen** composable function is the container for our screen. It binds the screen to the viewmodel, but does not deal with the actual user interface, as we will see.

On the first line of the file, we can see that the composable is saved under the **view** sub-package of the **ui** layer one. We proceed to annotate our composable function with the **Composable** annotation (*line 5*).

On *line 6,* you can see that our composable extends the **AddRecordDependencies** class. This gives the composable access to the viewmodel, the new record UI to presentation mapper and the **ViewModelObserver** composable. Our composable requires a **NavController** instance, an initial IP address string, and by convention, an optional **Modifier** instance (*lines 7 to 9*). The **NavController** instance allows us to navigate away from this screen. The initial IP address argument can be used to pre-populate our input field. Finally, the **Modifier** argument dictates how we present the screen.

To bind the composable to the notifications and navigation event states of the viewmodel, we start our function by calling the **ViewModelObserver** composable function, passing in the **NavController** instance that **AddRecordScreen** received as an argument (*line 11*).

As mentioned previously, our composable does not deal with the nitty-gritty of the UI. We encapsulate this detail in the **AddRecordContents** composable, which I leave to you to fill in. For our purpose, it is enough to know that we pass on the **modifier** and **initialIpAddress** arguments to it and handle the event of the user clicking the **Add record** button. When the event triggers, we take the IP address that was typed by the user, map it to a Presentation model (*lines 17 and 18*), and pass it to the **onAddNewRecordAction** function of the viewmodel (*line 19*). Note how we moved from a *click* event (*line 16*) to a more generic *action* (*line 19*) when moving from the UI to the Presentation layer.

Once the composable is ready, we can take a step back and implement an outstanding dependency that we have only mentioned by interface so far: the notification mapper. Some views, like our new feature one, may support no notifications, so we can introduce a reusable **NoNotificationUiMapper** implementation of the **NotificationUiMapper** interface. It could look a lot like the concrete implementation shown as follows:

NewDishNotificationPresentationToUiMapper.kt

```
1.    package com.mitteloupe.whoami.architecture.ui.notification.mapper
2.
3.    [imports...]
4.
5.    class NoNotificationUiMapper :
6.        NotificationUiMapper<PresentationNotification> {
7.        override fun toUi(notification: PresentationNotification): Nothing =
8.            error("Notifications not supported")
9.    }
```

On *line 1*, we can see that the **NoNotificationUiMapper** class is placed under the **mapper** sub-package of the **architecture.ui.notification** package.

Skipping to *line 6*, we see that **NoNotificationUiMapper** implements the **NotificationUiMapper** interface with the **PresentationNotification** interface as its generic type. This means that we also need to implement the **toUi** function (*lines 7* and *8*). We set it to throw an **IllegalStateException** whenever it is called (*line 8*): we do not expect the **toUi** function to be called at all until the first notification is implemented. A more defensive approach could be to have it map all notifications to a global notification that logs every call or does nothing at all.

This completes our UI implementation. Next, we will look at implementing the Data layer.

Implementing the Data and DataSource layers

We just completed implementing the UI layer part of our feature. In a real-life scenario, the Data layer implementation could proceed while the Presentation and UI layers were being implemented. All the Data layer requires is a DataSource implementation. Due to the linear nature of this book (like most books), we will proceed to discuss the DataSource layer now.

Adding a manual record to our address history is no different from adding an automatic one that reflects the current user's connection. This means that our **save(NewIpAddressHistoryRecordDataModel)** function of the **IpAddressHistoryDataSource** interface is all we need. We do not have to make any changes to the DataSource layer. Had our new feature required a new mechanism, this is where we would have been implementing it.

Since we do not need to update our DataSource layer, we can continue to implement the Data layer. As I mentioned before, the repository is a bridge between the feature-aware Domain layer and feature-agnostic datasources.

Before we can implement our repository, we have one debt to pay: we need a Domain to Data mapper for the history record model:

NewDishDomainToDishRequestDataMapper.kt

```
1.    package com.mitteloupe.whoami.addrecord.data.mapper
2.
3.    [imports...]
4.
5.    class NewRecordDataMapper {
6.        fun toData(newRecord: NewRecordDomainModel) =
7.            NewIpAddressHistoryRecordDataModel(
8.                ipAddress = newRecord.ipAddress,
9.                city = null,
10.               region = null,
11.               countryCode = null,
12.               geolocation = null,
13.               internetServiceProviderName = null,
14.               postCode = null,
15.               timeZone = null
16.           )
17.   }
```

The mapper is kept under the **mapper** sub-package of the **Data** layer sub-package belonging to the **addrecord** feature (*line 1*).

Since the input and output model names differ, the mapper name is chosen by taking the input model with its **Model** suffix dropped and suffixed by Mapper (*line 5*). Sometimes a mapper's name is more meaningful if it inherits the name of its output model (or both). Use your judgement. Note that the difference between the model names is not coincidental. It is there because we are switching from feature-aware code to feature-agnostic code.

The name of the **toData** function emphasizes the direction of this mapper. It takes a **NewRecordDomainModel** as an input and returns a corresponding **NewIpAddressHistoryRecordDataModel** object (*lines 6 to 16*). Note that we only read the **ipAddress** field of the input model and assign **null** to all other output fields. Again, this is not coincidental: the datasource is designed to represent the persisted models, and the Data layer holds data that the feature cares about. The mapper bridges this gap.

With the mapper out of the way, let us implement the repository for our feature:

AddNewRecordRepositoryImpl.kt

```
1.    package com.mitteloupe.whoami.home.data.repository
2.
3.    [imports...]
4.
5.    class AddNewRecordRepositoryImpl(
6.        private val ipAddressHistoryDataSource: IpAddressHistoryDataSource,
7.        private val newRecordDataMapper: NewRecordDataMapper
8.    ) : AddNewRecordRepository {
9.        override fun addNewRecord(newRecord: NewRecordDomainModel) {
10.           val dataRecord = newRecordDataMapper.toData(newRecord)
11.           ipAddressHistoryDataSource.save(dataRecord)
12.       }
13.   }
```

On the first line, we see that being a repository class, **AddNewRecordRepositoryImpl** is saved under the **repository** sub-package of the **data** sub-package of our feature (**home**) sub-package.

You will notice that the class name is identical to the interface name, with **Impl** suffixed to it (so we end up with **AddNewRecordRepositoryImpl** on *line 5*). I do not usually go for this suffix, but it is a reasonable tradeoff in this case: we do not, nor do we expect to have any other implementations of this interface in production, so it is hard to give the implementation a meaningful, distinctive name. It is also only going to appear once more in our code, in our dependency injection solution.

The **AddNewRecordRepositoryImpl** class relies on an **IpAddressHistoryDataSource** instance and a **NewRecordDataMapper** one, as can be seen on *lines 6* and *7*. The first provides us with the mechanism to save new records, and the latter maps Domain new record models to Data history record ones.

On *line 8*, we declare that this class is implementing the **AddNewRecordRepository** interface that we created in our Domain layer. On *lines 9* to *12*, we implement the **addNewRecord** function of that interface.

We start by mapping the **NewRecordDomainModel** instance we received on *line 9* to a Data model (*line 10*). On *line 11*, we call the **save** function of the datasource, passing in the newly created Data model.

This is our Data layer (and DataSource one) done. Two quick reminders, and we will proceed to discuss navigation to and from our new feature. The first reminder, as I am sure you have guessed, is not to forget your unit tests. Test every class that is sensible to test. Test mappers, test the repository implementation, and test any new code in a datasource. The second reminder is that the Data layer work can be broken down. We could start with a stubbed datasource, considerably reducing our initial effort. The concrete datasource could come later. Alright, that is all we had to note about the Data layer. Navigation comes next, let us proceed.

Implementing navigation

In the last sections, we covered the implementation of a feature. Once the feature is complete, we want our app to be able to access it. This requires two updates: we need to include its modules in our app **build.gradle** (or **build.gradle.kts**) file, and we need to provide instances of its different classes. In this section, I assume that you updated the **.gradle** file of the **app** module and provided all the required instances using your preferred dependency injection solution.

With this plumbing sorted, all that is left is to expose the feature to the user. This is done by implementing navigation to the feature. The feature would not be truly complete unless navigation out of it was handled, too. In this section, we will see how to plug the feature into the existing app.

Depending on your app-wide navigation solution and the nature of the feature, the way to enter newly introduced screens will vary. For example, navigation in Jetpack Compose is different to navigation via a fragment manager or Android Intents. However, all of these can be implemented using the same pattern, with some changes to the implementation details. We will see what this means shortly.

We will implement navigation to the new add record feature on the home screen. Since our project uses the Jetpack Compose Navigation component, we will start by adding a new route. This is how the **Routes.kt** file will look after our change:

Routes.kt

```
1.    package com.mitteloupe.whoami.ui.main.route
2.
3.    import kotlinx.serialization.Serializable
4.
5.    @Serializable
6.    object Home
7.
8.    @Serializable
9.    data class History(val highlightedIpAddress: String?)
10.
11.   @Serializable
12.   data class AddNewRecord(val ipAddress: String?)
```

The **Routes.kt** file is part of the **app** Gradle module and our navigation solution. We added the new route on *lines 11* and *12*. The **AddNewRecord** class is a data class with a single field, allowing the origin of navigation to specify the initial IP address to use.

At this point, the app will still build and run, but the new route will simply not be used. The next step is to handle the new destination in our **AppNavHost** function:

AppNavHost.kt

```
1.   package com.mitteloupe.whoami.ui.main
2.
3.   [imports...]
4.
5.   @Composable
6.   fun AppNavHostDependencies.AppNavHost(...) {
7.       NavHost(
8.           modifier = modifier,
9.           navController = navController,
10.          startDestination = startDestination
11.      ) {
12.          composable<Home> {
13.              homeDependencies.Home(navController)
14.          }
15.          composable<History> { ... }
16.          composable<AddNewRecord> { backStackEntry ->
17.              val addNewRecord: AddNewRecord = backStackEntry.toRoute()
18.              addRecordDependencies.AddRecordScreen(
19.                  navController,
20.                  initialIpAddress = addNewRecord.ipAddress
21.              )
22.          }
23.      }
24.  }
```

The **AppNavHost** function belongs in the **app** module. It is trimmed to fit in this book. The important thing worth noting is that it is an extension function on the **AppNavHostDependencies** class. As mentioned earlier in the book, this is how we approach dependency injection in Jetpack Compose. This class holds an object containing dependencies for every screen, up until our current change, which included a **HomeDependencies** object (see *line 13*). Now, it also includes an instance of the **AddRecordDependencies** class.

As you can see on *lines 16* to *22*, our code now handles the new **AddNewRecord** destination by showing the **AddRecordScreen** composable, passing in the **NavController** instance and the **ipAddress** value that was passed in when navigating.

To implement navigation to our new feature, we start by introducing a **PresentationNavigationEvent** object in our home feature's Presentation module:

HomePresentationNavigationEvent.kt

```
1.   package com.mitteloupe.whoami.home.presentation.navigation
2.
3.   [imports...]
4.
5.   sealed interface HomePresentationNavigationEvent :
6.       PresentationNavigationEvent {
7.       data object OnViewHistory : HomePresentationNavigationEvent
8.
9.       data class OnSavedDetails(val savedIpAddress: String) :
10.          HomePresentationNavigationEvent
11.
12.      data class OnAddNewRecord(val initialIpAddress: String?) :
13.          HomePresentationNavigationEvent
14.  }
```

In the **HomePresentationNavigationEvent.kt** file, our addition can be seen on *lines 12* and *13*. Like the **OnSaveDetails** class (see *lines 9* and *10*), the **OnAddNewRecord** destination data class has an IP address navigation argument. Unlike the **OnSaveDetails** class, however, its argument is nullable, since we may not have an initial IP address to provide. After the addition, our app would not build. By avoiding the use of the **else** branch, we made sure that the compiler would remind us to handle the new destination in the **HomeNavigationEventDestinationMapper** class. For navigation to work, we must tell our app how to handle the **OnAddRecord** Presentation navigation event, shown as follows:

HomeNavigationEventDestinationMapper.kt

```
1.   package com.mitteloupe.whoami.navigation.mapper
2.
3.   [imports...]
4.
5.   class HomeNavigationEventDestinationMapper() :
6.       NavigationEventDestinationMapper<HomePresentationNavigationEvent>(
7.           HomePresentationNavigationEvent::class
8.       ) {
9.       override fun mapTypedEvent(
10.          navigationEvent: HomePresentationNavigationEvent
11.      ): UiDestination = when (navigationEvent) {
12.          OnViewHistory -> history(null)
13.          is OnSavedDetails -> history(navigationEvent.savedIpAddress)
14.          is OnAddNewRecord -> addNewRecord(navigationEvent.
     initialIpAddress)
```

```
15.        }
16.
17.        private fun history(highlightedIpAddress: String?): UiDestination =
18.            UiDestination { navController ->
19.                navController.navigate(History(highlightedIpAddress))
20.            }
21.
22.        private fun addNewRecord(initialIpAddress: String?): UiDestination =
23.            UiDestination { navController ->
24.                navController.navigate(AddNewRecord(initialIpAddress))
25.            }
26.    }
```

We start by adding a function to handle the new destination (*lines 22 to 25*). You may recall that we discussed different ways of navigating. The **UiDestination** implementation returned by **addNewRecord** is where we implement the navigation behavior that fits our choice. In this case, we use the **NavController** instance. We make sure to take a nullable **initialIpAddress** string argument from the caller and use it to construct the **AddNewRecord** object.

We wrap the change up by adding a branch for a **navigationEvent** argument of type **OnAddNewRecord** (*line 14*). When matched, we map it to the output of the **addNewRecord** function. With this last change, our app can navigate to the new feature.

Now, when we trigger a navigation event for adding a new record, it will be handled correctly. We can now update the **HomeViewModel** class to expect an add new dish action:

HomeViewModel.kt
```
1.    package com.mitteloupe.whoami.home.presentation.viewmodel
2.
3.    [imports...]
4.
5.    class HomeViewModel(...) : BaseViewModel<...>(useCaseExecutor) {
6.        fun onEnter() { ... }
7.
8.        fun onSaveDetailsAction(...) { ... }
9.
10.       fun onViewHistoryAction() { ... }
11.
12.       fun onAddNewRecordAction(initialIpAddress: String?) {
13.           emitNavigationEvent(OnAddNewRecord(initialIpAddress))
14.       }
15.
```

```
16.        ...
17.    }
```

The aforementioned **HomeViewModel** was heavily trimmed to focus on our change. The addition is only three lines long, see *lines 12 to 14*. We can see that the new **onAddNewRecordAction** function has a nullable **initialIpAddress** string parameter.

When the user triggers the add new record action, we want to emit a navigation event for adding a new record screen, and indeed, this is what we do on *line 13*.

At this point, our change is testable, and the app can be compiled and run. Of course, it will not do anything productive yet. For that to happen, we need to update our UI to call the new function.

Let us see what this update to the UI means. Here is an updated **HomeScreen** composable:

HomeScreen.kt

```kotlin
1.     package com.mitteloupe.whoami.home.ui.view
2.
3.     [imports...]
4.
5.     @Composable
6.     fun HomeDependencies.Home(
7.         navController: NavController,
8.         modifier: Modifier = Modifier
9.     ) {
10.        fun relaySavingToViewModel(connectionDetails: HomeViewState) { ... }
11.
12.        fun relayAddingRecordToViewModel(connectionDetails: HomeViewState) {
13.            val initialIpAddress =
14.                (connectionDetails as? HomeViewState.Connected)?.ipAddress
15.            homeViewModel.onAddNewRecordAction(initialIpAddress)
16.        }
17.
18.     ...
19.
20.        HomeContents(
21.            viewState = uiState,
22.            connectionDetails = connectionDetails,
23.            errorMessage = errorMessage,
24.            onSaveDetailsClick = { relaySavingToViewModel(viewState) },
25.            onAddNewRecordClick = { relayAddingRecordToViewModel(viewState) },
26.            onViewHistoryClick = { homeViewModel.onViewHistoryAction() },
```

```
27.                 modifier = modifier
28.         )
29.    }
```

Once again, the file is truncated to help us focus on the changes. The first change we make is adding the **relayAddingRecordToViewModel** function (*lines 12* to *16*). Like **relaySavingToViewModel** before it, this function encapsulates obtaining the presented IP address from the current view state (*lines 13* and *14*) and passing it on to the viewmodel. It does so by calling the **onAddNewRecordAction** function of the viewmodel (*line 15*).

We then complete the implementation by calling the **relayAddingRecordToViewModel** function when **addAddNewRecordClick** is triggered by the **HomeContents** composable (*line 25*).

This wraps up the navigation *to* the feature. What about navigation *from* the feature? We will look into this next. This is the **NavigationEventDestinationMapper** implementation for outgoing destinations from our new feature:

NewRecordNavigationEventDestinationMapper.kt

```
1.    package com.mitteloupe.whoami.navigation.mapper
2.
3.    [imports...]
4.
5.    class NewRecordNavigationEventDestinationMapper :
6.        NavigationEventDestinationMapper<AddRecordPresentationNaviga-
      tionEvent>(
7.            AddRecordPresentationNavigationEvent::class
8.        ) {
9.        override fun mapTypedEvent(
10.            navigationEvent: AddRecordPresentationNavigationEvent
11.        ): UiDestination = when (navigationEvent) {
12.            is OnNewRecordAdded -> upThenHistory(navigationEvent.
      savedIpAddress)
13.        }
14.
15.        private fun upThenHistory(highlightedIpAddress: String?) =
16.            UiDestination { navController ->
17.                navController.popBackStack(route = Home, inclusive = false)
18.                navController.navigate(History(highlightedIpAddress))
19.            }
20.    }
```

The navigation mapper pattern should be familiar to you by now. Since we only have a single navigation event (**OnNewRecordAdded**, *line 12*) to handle, this mapper is quite straightforward. When the event is reported, we translate it to a **UiDestination** implementation that navigates up and then to the **History** route using the **NavController** instance (*lines 15 to 19*). We make sure to pass in the saved IP address to be highlighted.

With this mapper, we now have a fully working navigation solution for our new feature, and the feature is complete.

Conclusion

In this chapter, we covered the implementation of a new, end-to-end feature in Clean Architecture. We discussed the order in which the different layer implementations should be performed, and navigation to and from the feature screen. Implementing your own features should look very similar to the example presented in this chapter.

In the next chapter, we will deal with a requirement to make a change to an existing Clean Architecture feature.

Points to remember

When approaching the implementation of a new feature, there are some things that are worth remembering:

- Do not rush it. Implement features in a structured way. Start with the Domain, proceed to the Presentation and the Data layer, and finally implement the UI and the datasources. Do not take shortcuts. Shortcuts are false promises: you will end up spending longer implementing your feature.

- Test, test, test. Make sure to have good test coverage before introducing any changes to your app. Ensure that all tests are updated to reflect the new requirements and that all tests pass after your changes.

- Clean Architecture is designed to allow you to make decisions as late as possible, if ever. Do not worry if you are not sure which storage mechanism you intend to use. Do not worry if the UI is not finalized. Implement something that works and revisit it as needed.

CHAPTER 13
Dealing with Changes

The wind of change

Blows straight into the face of time

- Scorpions

Introduction

In the previous chapter, we implemented a new feature. In this chapter, we will challenge ourselves to modify an existing feature.

Change is inevitable. This is the fundamental understanding at the heart of Clean Architecture. We design our apps to handle change gracefully. With the help of the Dependency Rule and the different layers, this makes some changes incredibly isolated and therefore easy. Other changes reach for the core of the system, or the Domain layer, and therefore have a more significant, rippling effect.

This chapter is all about introducing change. Let us not waste words and dive right in.

Structure

In this chapter, we will cover the following topics:

- Dealing with changes

- Changing a datasource
- Changing the user interface

Objectives

By the end of this chapter, you should have a vivid idea of what change looks like in a Clean Architecture app. You should be able to take a change requirement, translate it into a plan of action, and implement it, modifying only the relevant code in the applicable layers.

Dealing with changes

Features rarely remain unchanged. Most frequently, the changes we face are external to the business logic, or the Domain layer. Changes tend to be needed for the user interface or the DataSource layer to support API changes or alternative storage solutions.

This happens to be one of the cases in which Clean Architecture shines.

Changes to the UI often remain within the UI layer, and do not concern the Presentation layer, and certainly not the Domain, Data, or DataSource layers. Examples include different texts, colors, views, composables, and even different UI technologies (think switching from XML to Compose).

Changes to navigation often affect no more than the Presentation layer and the UI one. The Domain, Data, and DataSource layers only need to be modified if the business logic changes and new data needs to be obtained to support the navigation. This is quite uncommon, but it happens.

API changes are entirely contained in the DataSource layer. Not even the Data layer is concerned with them. The same is true for decisions around storage solutions. Replacing the memory storage with SharedPreferences? A DataSource concern. Replacing it with a database? Still a DataSource concern. Introducing a cloud API where none existed before? You guessed it, still a DataSource concern. The same is true for implementing a caching solution.

This is important. Even in the most careful of environments, with pair programming in place (and code reviews in addition to or instead of pair programming), great test coverage, and a stellar quality assurance team, change is risky. The fewer the changes that we can introduce to a working system and the smaller their scope, the more likely it is that we can maintain the stability of that system.

The Dependency Rule gives us a lot of code that is resistant to change, in a good sense. It is not that it cannot change or that it resists change. Rather, it is that we have reduced the number of reasons for the code to change. Unless the business logic changes, our usecases (and their tests) as well as our Domain models and interfaces remain stable. Unless the Presentation logic changes, our viewmodels, Domain/Presentation mappers, Presentation models (and their tests, too) remain stable. So do our UI models, Presentation/UI mappers, views, and composables. Unless our storage requirements change, our DataSource layer is stable.

Thanks to our architecture, when change does have to be introduced, it tends to be small and contained in scope. Small changes are better than large changes, for obvious reasons: they are easier to review and validate, and if something terrible happened, they are easy to roll back.

Let us take a look at a couple of examples.

Changing a datasource

First, let us say that we want to replace our local connection history store with a cloud API using Retrofit and Gson. Of course, we could use any library for this, and the choice here was arbitrary. We immediately identify this as a DataSource layer change.

First, let us assume that our API endpoint for saving connection history records receives a JSON in the following format:

```
1.    {
2.          "ip": String,
3.          "ct": String?,
4.          "rgn": String?,
5.          "ctry": String?,
6.          "geo": String?,
7.          "isp": String?,
8.          "postcode": String?,
9.          "timezone": String?
10.   }
```

Let us also see what our local model file looks like:

SavedIpAddressHistoryRecordLocalModel.kt

```
1. package com.mitteloupe.whoami.datasource.history.model
2.
3. data class SavedIpAddressHistoryRecordLocalModel(
4.     val ipAddress: String,
5.     val city: String?,
6.     val region: String?,
7.     val countryCode: String?,
8.     val geolocation: String?,
9.     val internetServiceProviderName: String?,
10.    val postCode: String?,
11.    val timeZone: String?,
12.    val savedAtTimestampMilliseconds: Long
13. )
```

The **SavedIpAddressHistoryRecordLocalModel** class is the model that we currently use to store the local connection history in local persistence. Note that the request includes all the fields that our Local model does, except for the **savedAtTimestampMilliseconds** field. This field is currently set locally and will supposedly be set by the server. Also note how the field names do not quite match those that we chose for our models. This is often the case with APIs that we have to interact with.

We will start by defining a request model in our **datasource:source** Gradle module:

IpAddressHistoryRecordRequestApiModel.kt

```
1.    package com.mitteloupe.whoami.datasource.history.model
2.
3.    import com.google.gson.annotations.SerializedName
4.
5.    data class IpAddressHistoryRecordRequestApiModel(
6.        @SerializedName("ip")
7.        val ipAddress: String,
8.        @SerializedName("ct")
9.        val city: String?,
10.        @SerializedName("rgn")
11.        val region: String?,
12.        @SerializedName("ctry")
13.        val countryCode: String?,
14.        @SerializedName("geo")
15.        val geolocation: String?,
16.        @SerializedName("isp")
17.        val internetServiceProviderName: String?,
18.        @SerializedName("postcode")
19.        val postCode: String?,
20.        @SerializedName("timezone")
21.        val timeZone: String?
22.    )
```

The request model is saved under the **model** sub-package of the **datasource.history** package (*line 1*).

We use the **@SerializedName** annotation (*lines 6, 8, 10, 12, 14, 16, 18,* and *20*) to decouple our model and code from any API naming. The annotation tells the Gson serializer and de-serializer that the field is named differently in JSON than in the Kotlin model. For example, the JSON **ip** field (*line 6*) will be mapped to the **ipAddress** Kotlin field (*line 7*). This is especially valuable when API naming is not clear enough or is not consistent with our app naming of models and fields. Using this annotation also provides further decoupling from the API: field name changes would lead to isolated updates where we only need to update the annotation arguments in our model and nothing else. As an added bonus, using the **@SerializedName** annotation helps with obfuscation, renaming the Kotlin fields would not break functionality.

Next, let us assume that this is the format of the JSON returned by the server when we request the currently saved history records:

```
 1.   [
 2.       {
 3.           "ip": String,
 4.           "ct": String?,
 5.           "rgn": String?,
 6.           "ctry": String?,
 7.           "geo": String?,
 8.           "isp": String?,
 9.           "postcode": String?,
10.           "timezone": String?,
11.           "timestamp": Long
12.       },
13.       ...
14.   ]
```

As we can see, the response is an array of objects similar to those sent in our request, but this time, there is also a timestamp of the time at which the record was saved.

Knowing the response format, we can replace the **SavedIpAddressHistoryRecordLocalModel** class with an **IpAddressHistoryRecordResponseApiModel** class:

IpAddressHistoryRecordResponseApiModel.kt

```
 1.   package com.mitteloupe.whoami.datasource.history.model
 2.
 3.   import com.google.gson.annotations.SerializedName
 4.
 5.   data class IpAddressHistoryRecordResponseApiModel(
 6.       @SerializedName("ip")
 7.       val ipAddress: String,
 8.       @SerializedName("ct")
 9.       val city: String? = null,
10.       @SerializedName("rgn")
11.       val region: String? = null,
12.       @SerializedName("ctry")
13.       val countryCode: String? = null,
```

```
14.         @SerializedName("geo")
15.         val geolocation: String? = null,
16.         @SerializedName("isp")
17.         val internetServiceProviderName: String? = null,
18.         @SerializedName("postcode")
19.         val postCode: String? = null,
20.         @SerializedName("timezone")
21.         val timeZone: String? = null,
22.         @SerializedName("timestamp")
23.         val savedAtTimestampMilliseconds: Long
24.     )
```

The new **IpAddressHistoryRecordResponseApiModel** class represents a single item in the API response array. It resembles the request model. However, there are two important differences: first, it has an additional field for the save-time timestamp (*lines* 22 and 23). Second, its nullable fields are all optional. If the server omits these fields, Gson will know what value to assign to them (**null** in our example).

Moving on to the **datasource:implementation** Gradle module, we no longer need our original Data to Local and Local to Data mappers. Instead, we introduce mappers that transform a **NewIpAddressHistoryRecordDataModel** instance into a corresponding **IpAddressHistoryRecordRequestApiModel** instance and an **IpAddressHistoryRecordResponseApiModel** one to a **NewIpAddressHistoryRecordDataModel** instance. This is the first mapper:

NewIpAddressRecordApiMapper.kt

```
1.     package com.mitteloupe.whoami.datasource.history.mapper
2.
3.     [imports...]
4.
5.     class NewIpAddressRecordApiMapper {
6.         fun toApi(historyRecord: NewIpAddressHistoryRecordDataModel) =
7.             IpAddressHistoryRecordRequestApiModel(
8.                 ipAddress = historyRecord.ipAddress,
9.                 city = historyRecord.city,
10.                region = historyRecord.region,
11.                countryCode = historyRecord.countryCode,
12.                geolocation = historyRecord.geolocation,
13.                internetServiceProviderName =
14.                    historyRecord.internetServiceProviderName,
15.                postCode = historyRecord.postCode,
16.                timeZone = historyRecord.timeZone
```

```
17.            )
18.    }
```

This is the second one:

SavedIpAddressRecordDataMapper.kt

```
1.     package com.mitteloupe.whoami.datasource.history.mapper
2.
3.     [imports...]
4.
5.     class SavedIpAddressRecordDataMapper {
6.         fun toData(historyRecord: IpAddressHistoryRecordResponseApiModel) =
7.             SavedIpAddressHistoryRecordDataModel(
8.                 ipAddress = historyRecord.ipAddress,
9.                 city = historyRecord.city,
10.                region = historyRecord.region,
11.                countryCode = historyRecord.countryCode,
12.                geolocation = historyRecord.geolocation,
13.                internetServiceProviderName =
14.                    historyRecord.internetServiceProviderName,
15.                postCode = historyRecord.postCode,
16.                timeZone = historyRecord.timeZone,
17.                savedAtTimestampMilliseconds =
18.                    historyRecord.savedAtTimestampMilliseconds
19.            )
20.    }
```

We can also introduce the Retrofit service, shown as follows:

AddressHistoryService.kt

```
1.     package com.mitteloupe.whoami.datasource.history.service
2.
3.     [imports...]
4.
5.     interface AddressHistoryService {
6.         @PUT("history")
7.         fun save(request: IpAddressHistoryRecordRequestApiMel): Call<String>
8.     }
```

We introduce the **AddressHistoryService** service under the **history.service** sub-package (*line 1*).

For demonstration purposes, we only implement one endpoint: the one to which we post our request for saving a new IP address record (*lines 6* and *7*). We configure it to return a string, although in real life it is more common for the endpoint to return a JSON, which we could parse using our preferred mechanism.

To complete the change, we need to update our datasource:

IpAddressHistoryDataSourceImpl.kt

```
1.     package com.mitteloupe.whoami.datasource.history.datasource
2.
3.     [imports...]
4.
5.     class IpAddressHistoryDataSourceImpl(
6.         private val addressHistoryService: AddressHistoryService,
7.         private val newIpAddressRecordApiMapper: NewIpAddressRecordApiMapper,
8.         private val savedIpAddressRecordDataMapper:
9.             SavedIpAddressRecordDataMapper
10.    ) : IpAddressHistoryDataSource {
11.        override fun save(record: NewIpAddressHistoryRecordDataModel) {
12.            val savedRecord = newIpAddressRecordApiMapper.toApi(record)
13.            addressHistoryService.save(savedRecord).execute()
14.        }
15.
16.        override fun delete(
17.            deletionIdentifier: HistoryRecordDeletionIdentifierDataModel
18.        ) { ... }
19.
20.        override fun allRecords() = ...
21.    }
```

This is a trimmed and slightly simplified version of **IpAddressHistoryDataSourceImpl**. Of course, to complete the migration to a Retrofit implementation, we would have to also update the **allRecords** and **delete** functions, as well as the relevant mappers and models. Those changes would follow the same pattern that we are seeing here.

The first change we can see is to the injected dependencies (*lines 6* and *7*). We no longer need a **SharedPreferences** instance or a JSON encoder and decoder. These were all part of our local persistence solution. Instead, we now have an **AddressHistoryService** object. The **NewIpAddressRecordLocalMapper** instance was replaced by an instance of **NewIpAddressRecordApiMapper**. Our **SavedIpAddressRecordDataMapper** class has new functionality, but its interface has not changed.

The second change is to the **save** function (*lines 12* and *13*). We start by obtaining an API model from the Data model using the mapper object stored in **newIpAddressRecordApiMapper** (*line 12*). We continue to save the record using the service (*line 13*). We ignore the response for simplicity.

We have not looked at the Gradle changes or the dependency injection work that is required to make this change work, because those are outside of the scope of discussing the DataSource layer code change. However, in this section, we have demonstrated the complexity of changing our storage solution. Hopefully, you agree that this is not a large change.

Changing the user interface

For our second example, let us imagine that we want to replace our home screen footer composable with an Android view. If our architecture serves its purpose well, we should not have to modify any code outside of the UI layer and indeed, this is the case. Let us see how this change looks.

First, let me share with you the existing composable for the home screen footer:

HomeFooter.kt

```
1.    package com.mitteloupe.whoami.home.ui.view.widget
2.
3.    [imports...]
4.
5.    @Composable
6.    fun HomeFooter(
7.        connected: Boolean,
8.        onSaveDetailsClick: () -> Unit,
9.        onViewHistoryClick: () -> Unit,
10.       modifier: Modifier = Modifier
11.   ) {
12.       Column(
13.           modifier = modifier
14.               .fillMaxWidth()
15.               .padding(...)
16.       ) {
17.           Row(
18.               modifier = modifier
19.                   .padding(top = 24.dp, bottom = 24.dp)
20.                   .fillMaxWidth()
21.           ) {
22.               NavigationButton(
```

```
23.                        iconResourceId = R.drawable.icon_save,
24.                        label = stringResource(R.string.home_..._label),
25.                        onClick = {
26.                            if (connected) {
27.                                onSaveDetailsClick()
28.                            }
29.                        },
30.                        modifier = Modifier.weight(1f)
31.                    )
32.                    Spacer(modifier = Modifier.width(16.dp))
33.                    NavigationButton(
34.                        iconResourceId = R.drawable.icon_history,
35.                        label = stringResource(R.string.home_..._label),
36.                        onClick = { onViewHistoryClick() },
37.                        modifier = Modifier.weight(1f)
38.                    )
39.                }
40.            }
41.    }
```

The current **HomeFooter** composable does not require much explanation. The version presented in the book is slightly simplified to fit. It includes two buttons, each one having an icon and a text label. The buttons are arranged in a row across the width of the composable's container. Both buttons execute lambdas when clicked, with the save button having a condition based on the **connected** flag (*line 26*).

Now, let us suppose that we were asked to replace the implementation of the **HomeFooter** composable with an Android View one.

We start by introducing an XML layout for our new footer:

CallToActionButton.kt

```
1.    <?xml version="1.0" encoding="utf-8"?>
2.    <LinearLayout xmlns:android="http://schemas.android.com/apk/res/android"
3.        android:layout_width="match_parent"
4.        android:layout_height="wrap_content"
5.        android:orientation="horizontal">
6.
7.        <Button
8.            android:id="@+id/home_footer_save_button"
9.            android:layout_width="0dp"
10.           android:layout_height="wrap_content"
```

```
11.            android:layout_weight="1"
12.            android:drawableStart="@drawable/icon_save"
13.            android:text="@string/home_save_details_button_label" />
14.
15.        <Button
16.            android:id="@+id/home_footer_history_button"
17.            android:layout_width="0dp"
18.            android:layout_height="wrap_content"
19.            android:layout_weight="1"
20.            android:drawableStart="@drawable/icon_history"
21.            android:text="@string/home_history_button_label" />
22.
23.    </LinearLayout>
```

The XML version of the layout replaces the original **Column** composable with a **LinearLayout** tag. The custom **NavigationButton** composables are replaced with **Button** tags.

Next, we can remove the **Column** composable from **HomeFooter** and use a **LayoutInflater** instance to inflate the XML that we introduced:

HomeFooter.kt

```
1.    package com.mitteloupe.whoami.home.ui.view.widget
2.
3.    [imports...]
4.
5.    @Composable
6.    fun HomeFooter(
7.        connected: Boolean,
8.        onSaveDetailsClick: () -> Unit,
9.        onViewHistoryClick: () -> Unit,
10.        modifier: Modifier = Modifier
11.    ) {
12.        Column(
13.            modifier = modifier
14.                .fillMaxWidth()
15.                .padding(...)
16.        ) {
17.            AndroidView(
18.                factory = { context ->
19.                    LayoutInflater
20.                        .from(context)
21.                        .inflate(R.layout.home_footer, null)
```

```
22.                            .apply {
23.                                findViewById<View>(R.id.home_footer_save_button)
24.                                    .setOnClickListener {
25.                                        if (connected) {
26.                                            onSaveDetailsClick()
27.                                        }
28.                                    }
29.                                findViewById<View>(R.id.home_footer_history_
        button)
30.                                    .setOnClickListener {
31.                                        onViewHistoryClick()
32.                                    }
33.                            }
34.                    },
35.                    modifier = Modifier.fillMaxWidth()
36.                )
37.        }
38.    }
```

As we can see, our change is contained to a single file. The viewmodel will not be affected by the change. The usecases will not be affected, nor the repositories, and certainly not the datasources. All we did was inflate an XML instead of having a composable and added click listeners that trigger the click callbacks.

This completes the migration of the feature from Compose to layout inflation.

The example shown here demonstrates a very small change. Changes can be significantly more complex. We may be changing entire screens from one technology to another. We may want to change component types. We may even choose to replace the entire interface with voice control. As long as the actions available to the user remain the same, the change will be contained to the UI layer.

One could argue that this migration would have been just as easy with any other MVVM implementation and they would be right. MVVM is designed around a similar principle to that of Clean Architecture. Some of the benefits that we see with Clean Architecture exist in any project that implements MVVM correctly. This is not a bad thing. If you used MVVM successfully before, it will only be that much easier for you to see the values Clean Architecture brings to the table by applying the same principles of directional dependencies to the Data layer.

Conclusion

In this chapter, we also discussed how changes to a feature look once the feature is up and running. When facing a changed requirement, you should now be able to recognize the layer to be affected and update that layer in isolation.

In the next chapter, we will discuss the migration of an existing project to Clean Architecture.

Points to remember

When approaching the implementation of a new feature, there are some things that are worth remembering:

- When given a change request, identify the layer or layers that should be affected by the change.

- Plan out your change so that it does not break the project at any time, if possible.

- Most changes can be contained to one or two layers. This is a clear benefit of Clean Architecture.

- Support any change with new or updated tests.

Join our Discord space

Join our Discord workspace for latest updates, offers, tech happenings around the world, new releases, and sessions with the authors:

https://discord.bpbonline.com

CHAPTER 14
Migrating an Existing Project

The first step towards getting somewhere is to decide that you are not going to stay where you are.

- JP Morgan

Introduction

The previous chapter covered updating an existing feature, leveraging the Clean Architecture Dependency Rule. This chapter will cover the migration of an entire existing feature to Clean Architecture.

Migrating an existing architecture does not have to mean a full rewrite of the entire code base. Instead, migration can be broken down into smaller steps.

We will explore several different popular architectures. We will then dig deeper into a couple of the most popular ones and see how to migrate them to Clean Architecture. Finally, we will discuss shifting responsibilities within an existing Clean Architecture solution to move it closer to the implementation that is suggested in this book.

Structure

In this chapter, we will cover the following topics:

- Existing architectures

- Gradual migration from MVP

- Gradual migration from MVVM

- Revisiting existing implementations

Objectives

In this chapter, we will lay out a strategy for migrating existing projects to the Clean Architecture solution presented in this book. By the end of this chapter, you should have the tools to migrate your existing project in a structured way.

Existing architectures

Since the early days of Android, it became apparent that to develop scalable, maintainable applications, we needed to structure our code using some architecture. We needed separation of concerns, because quite often we would end up with god activities or fragments. For a long time, the industry adopted **Model-View-Presenter** (**MVP**) as the go-to architecture to solve this problem.

In MVP, the business logic lives in the **presenter**, which is a standard class. It gets informed of UI events via its public functions. It also instructs the view (usually an Activity or a Fragment) what to present by calling functions on a view interface that is implemented by the activity or fragment. The presenter determines what to present to the user based on the user's input and data exposed to it via repository interfaces representing the model part of the system. The repository interfaces abstracted away API calls, caching, and so forth.

Another common challenge of Android development has always been persistence of state: in some circumstances, such as upon configuration changes or when low on resources, the operating system destroys our Activity and Fragment instances. We get the opportunity to persist their state for later restoration, but forgetting to implement this persistence is a common error.

Google tried to address this problem with the Architecture Components. At the same time, Google officially adopted **Model-View-ViewModel** (**MVVM**) as the recommended architecture[1]. In MVVM, the view observes the **viewmodel** for presentation changes rather than getting instructed directly by the presentation code, as was the case with MVP. Everything else within the architecture remains pretty much the same as it was in MVP: the viewmodel gets notified of UI events via public functions and obtains data via repositories.

There is another architecture that is explored in the Android world: **Model-View-Intent** (**MVI**). It is not as common as MVP and MVVM are, but it is common enough to warrant mentioning. MVI is a unidirectional and cyclical architecture inspired by the Cycle.js JavaScript framework. It is unidirectional in that data flows in one direction: from the View to the Presenter to the

---

1 https://developer.android.com/jetpack/guide

Model (which also holds the business logic). It is cyclical because the Model data flows back to the View.

MVI has its fair share of problems. Above all else, it is very challenging to follow, even for seasoned developers. This is a very serious problem, since reading code takes a considerably larger portion of a developer's day than writing code[2]. It is always good to familiarize yourself with new architectures, because the more tools you have, the more likely you are to have a suitable tool for the problem at hand. Having said that, you can probably manage just fine as an Android developer without ever working with MVI. As mentioned earlier, it is not as popular as MVP or MVVM.

One of the biggest problems with both MVP and MVVM turned out to be that they would not scale well. Instead of having god Activity or Fragment classes, we started having god presenters and god viewmodels. The presenters and viewmodels were simply doing too much.

Another significant problem with many implementations of both architectures is how closely coupled the models are to outside influence. Having repositories in your presenter or viewmodel moves the presentation too close to the data.

In the following sections, we will discuss ways of migrating MVP and MVVM code to Clean Architecture to address these problems.

Gradual migration from MVP

So, you have implemented MVP across your app. You are considering migrating to Clean Architecture but are not sure where to begin.

In this section, we will make a few assumptions.

First, we will assume that you are happy to keep using MVP. If you intend to migrate from MVP to MVVM, you can either start with the migration described in this section and then migrate to MVVM, or you could migrate to MVVM first and jump straight to the next section, where we will migrate from MVVM to Clean Architecture.

Second, we will assume that your presenter interacts directly with repositories. If your presenter communicates with datasources, network services, or any other data-specific entities, a good first step would be to abstract those away behind repository interfaces.

The third assumption is that you have implemented all the Clean Architecture boilerplate mentioned in this book, such as the **UseCaseExecutor**, prior to starting migration.

MVP already provides three of our Clean Architecture layers:

- The UI layer (Fragment classes implementing View interfaces), which we can leave untouched.

---

2 https://bayrhammer-klaus.medium.com/you-spend-much-more-time-reading-code-than-writing-code-bc953376fe19

- The Presentation layer (the Presenter), which we will need to modify slightly.

- The Data layer in the form of repositories. The repositories will likely require heavier modifications.

Before we make any changes, it is a good idea to make sure that we have good test coverage for the Presenter. This will give us confidence that our changes are not breaking the existing logic.

You may want to take another look at the MVP figure (*Figure 14.1*, this is the same figure shown in *Chapter 1, Introduction*):

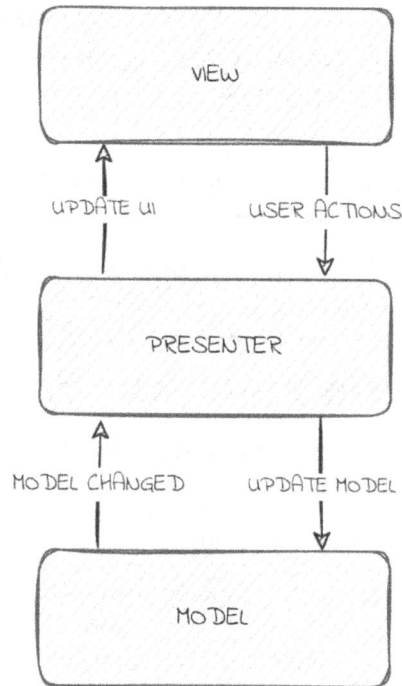

Figure 14.1: *Model-View-Presenter*

With tests in place, we need to identify where usecases would go in the Presenter. These would be where UI events or lifecycle events are reported (look for telling function names such as **onSaveDetailsAction**, **onRefreshContactsAction**, or **onViewReady** in your Presenter, see *Figure 14.2*). In the absence of consistent naming, consider all public functions.

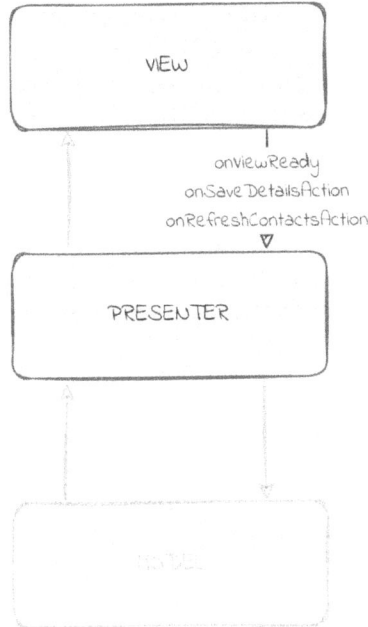

Figure 14.2: The View calls Presenter event functions

Next, we need to note the data that the Presentation layer relies on for each such usecase. These will become our Domain models. In *Figure 14.3*, we see two such models: **FormDetails** and **Contact**. These will become **FormDetailsDomainModel** and **ContactDomainModel**, respectively.

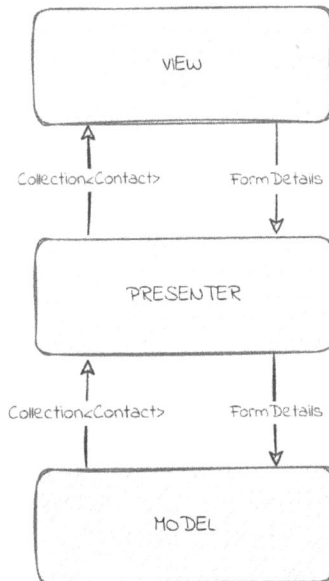

Figure 14.3: Models sent to and from the Presenter

It may be the case that a few repository calls are aggregated. If that is the case, define a model that contains the combination of required data from all calls. This is a good opportunity to drop any field that we do not need from our new model. Let us try to also keep our model structure as flat as possible, avoid nested models unless the nesting is justified. A clue could be the nested model being a data class. It is likely that you can just move the fields from the nested model out into the parent model.

We also need to take note of any inputs required by any of the repository calls. *Is the requirement a Data layer design choice or a sensible Presentation dependency?* For example, a session ID is probably a Data layer concern and should not be considered a part of our usecase input. Form fields and navigation arguments that come from the view, however, are owned by the UI and so should be communicated to the usecase.

Depending on how well the existing repositories represent our requirements, the next step may be to declare new repository interfaces. If we already have a 1:1 mapping of repository function call to usecase, we can skip this step for now. If our usecases were forced to make multiple calls, it may be a good idea to hide this detail in the repository implementation and expose a single repository function for the usecase to call.

We should now have enough information to construct our usecases. For **onSaveDetailsAction**, we probably want to create a **SaveContactDetailsUseCase** class. For **onRefreshAction**, we probably need a **GetContactsUseCase** class. We can use the input and output Domain models that we designed earlier to set the usecase inputs and outputs, respectively. We will inject the existing or new repository interfaces into the usecases via their usecase constructors.

Remember that repositories abstract datasources. Datasources should be providing Data models. If they provide raw API, database, or any external model type, these should be mapped to Data models. Before introducing new datasources, check if any of your existing datasources are fit for purpose, potentially with small tweaks if necessary.

To bridge the different Domain models and their corresponding Data models provided to the repositories, we should implement appropriate mappers. Once we made sure that all previous repository calls correspond to the new repository interfaces, using mappers where needed, our Data and Domain layers are complete.

Before we can plug the usecases into the presenter, we need to implement Domain to Presentation and Presentation to Domain mappers. These are responsible for taking the Domain data provided to and by the usecases to Presentation models that we can pass back to the UI.

The last step in migrating the implementation is to inject a usecase executor, the new usecases, and all Domain to Presentation and Presentation to Domain mappers to the presenter. We can remove all injected repository instances, too. We can then replace all repository calls with usecase executions. We map data going into the usecase and data coming back from the usecase and going back to the View as required.

With this last step, our migration is complete. You can see an example of the final flow of data in *Figure 14.4*. Since we kept our tests up to date throughout the process, we can refactor our implementation with confidence. This process can be repeated until all screens are migrated. Make sure not to abandon the process mid-migration, a mixed architecture project is a major source of confusion.

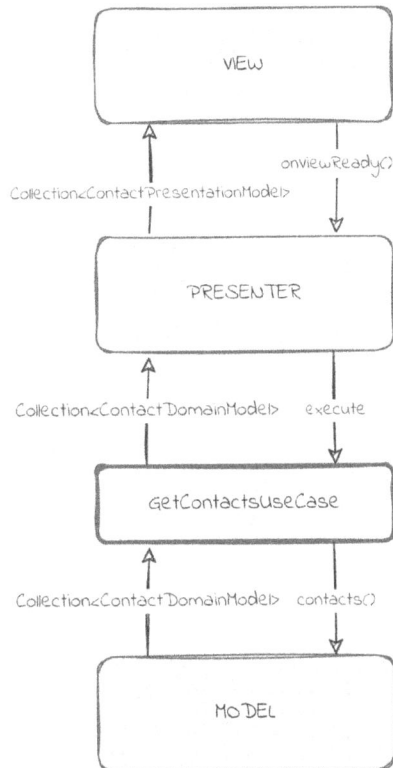

Figure 14.4: MVP migrated to Clean Architecture

We have seen how to migrate a feature in an app that has an MVP architecture. If your app architecture follows MVVM rather than MVP, the next section is for you.

Gradual migration from MVVM

In the previous section, we saw how an MVP screen could be migrated to Clean Architecture. In this section, we will follow a similar process for MVVM. If you read the previous section, you will find a lot of similarities. That is because to migrate either an MVP or an MVVM solution to Clean Architecture, we essentially inflate the Model, which usually represents repositories (the Clean Architecture Data layer) and datasources (just like in Clean Architecture) to become a Domain layer, a Data layer, and eventually the DataSource layer as well. So, reading both the MVP and MVVM sections is a good way to instill the ideas driving the migration to Clean Architecture.

At the risk of sounding redundant, before making any changes, make sure that you have good test coverage. Having tests means that we can comfortably make changes with the confidence of not breaking the existing functionality.

Figure 14.5 is a quick reminder of what MVVM looks like (this is the same figure that we have seen in *Chapter 1, Introduction*):

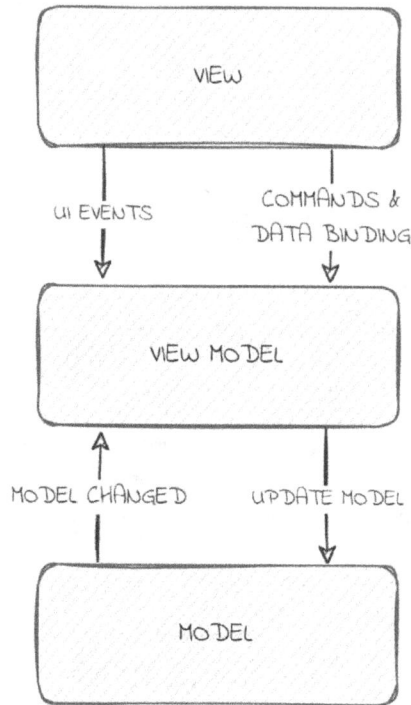

Figure 14.5: *Model-View-ViewModel*

Our first step is to find the usecases that are driving the screen that we are migrating to Clean Architecture. These would usually be the answers to these two questions: *what can the user see*, and *what can the user do on this screen*? If your app manages the user's Pokémon card game collection, and we are migrating the card collection screen, the users can probably see their list of cards as soon as the screen loads. This would be addressed by a **GetAllCardsUseCase** class. Can the users remove cards from their collection from this screen? If so, we would need a **RemoveCardFromCollectionUseCase** class.

We will assume that the current implementation of the card game collection app is the one that is presented in *Figure 14.6*:

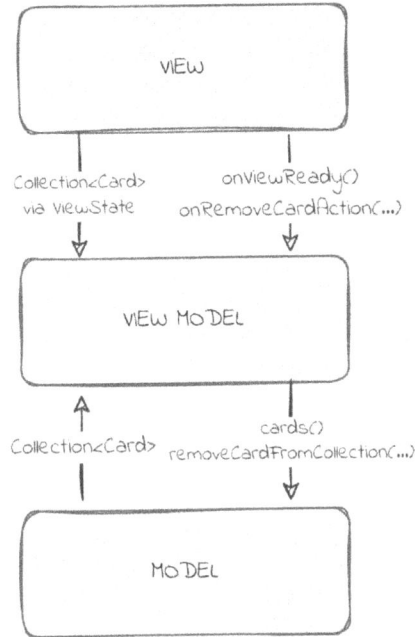

Figure 14.6: MVVM card collection app implementation

To create the two usecases that we identified, we need to establish their repository interfaces. For **GetAllCardsUseCase**, we would need a **GetAllCardsRepository** interface with a single function, **getAllCards()** (or simply **cards()**) that requires no arguments and returns a **Collection** of type **CardDomainModel**. The model should only contain fields that are required for presenting a card to the user. An identifier is often required too, so that we can reference a specific card, for example, when removing a card from the collection.

The **RemoveCardFromCollectionUseCase** class would require a **RemoveCardFromCollectionRepository** interface with a **removeCardFromCollection()** function. This function will require an identifier for the card to be removed. It may not need to return a value; its execution completion could be enough to indicate success.

The input and output of our usecases would be identical to those of the repository interfaces that we declared. So, the execution function of the **GetAllCardsUseCase** class will have a **Unit** input and a **Collection<CardDomainModel>** output. The execution function of the **RemoveCardFromCollectionUseCase** class will have a **String** input (assuming that the card identifier is a **String**) and a **Unit** output.

We now need mappers. We want to map the **CardDomainModel** instances provided by **GetAllCardsUseCase** from Domain to Presentation, so that we could emit it to the UI. We also want to categorize any models that were previously returned by the repository to the viewmodel as Data models. This means that we need to map these Data models to Domain models, then return those from the repository. This way, we can make the existing repository conform to the new repository interfaces.

We may have chained the execution of two repository function calls before; let us say that one call was made to get the IDs of all cards and another to get the details for all cards. If so, we will now move that logic into the repository implementation. This tidies up our viewmodel and abstracts the Data layer details away from the Presentation layer and the Domain layer.

Finally, we can add the **UseCaseExecutor** and the new usecases to the viewmodel. We will also need to add the Domain to Presentation mapper (likely named **CardPresentationMapper**) to the viewmodel. Remove all repositories and leverage usecases to communicate with the Data layer via the Domain layer instead.

With all the changes mentioned previously done, we should have a working Clean Architecture feature, similar to the one shown in *Figure 14.7*. As we migrate more features, we should have greater confidence in our understanding of the architecture. This should make progress speed up over time.

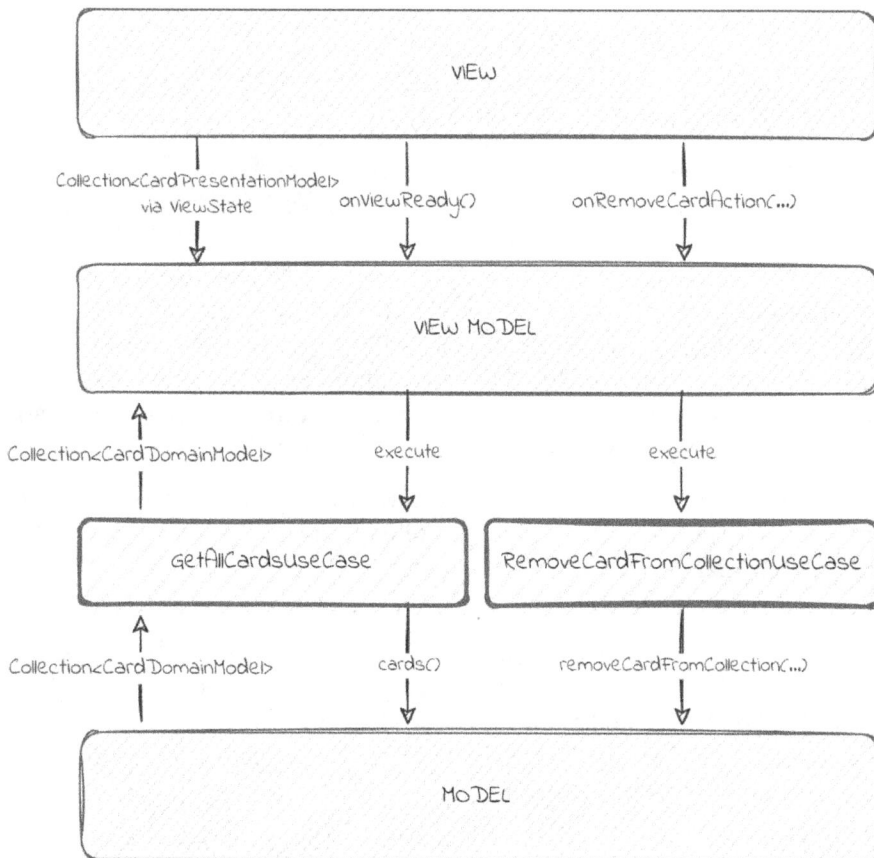

Figure 14.7: *MVVM migrated to Clean Architecture*

In the next section, we will discuss scenarios where Clean Architecture was implemented differently from how this book suggests and how to tackle these scenarios.

Revisiting existing implementations

It is quite common for first attempts at Clean Architecture to not go quite as planned. Unless the boundaries and responsibilities of all participants in the solution are clear, it is easy to end up with code that does not achieve the goal that we set out to achieve: consistent, scalable, and maintainable code.

Let us look at some common mistakes and ways to correct them:

- **Usecases depending on concrete repositories**: If we follow Google's architecture, we are going to make this mistake. By making usecases depend on concrete repositories, we are tightly coupling them to the Data layer.

  One of the key advantages of Clean Architecture is its Dependency Rule. The Dependency Rule is designed to protect the Domain layer from external changes. Tightly coupling our Domain layer to the Data layer implementation details defeats this purpose.

  > Note: **To fix this problem, introduce a repository interface, and make sure that it returns Domain models. You may have to use mappers in the concrete repository to bridge the model gap.**

- **Usecases doing too much**: A common mistake to find is that usecases are doing too much. This is a problem because usually it means that the usecases are tightly coupled to the Data implementation details (or, less commonly, to the Presentation implementation details).

  To determine if a usecase is overstepping its boundaries and doing too much, ask yourself this question: *if my Data implementation changed, would the usecase have to be updated?* For example, if the usecase is obtaining data from one source and it uses that data to make a second request, it is likely that it is doing too much. If it obtains data and then filters it, it is probably doing too much, too. It is sensible to imagine a scenario where the Data layer could provide us with just the data that we need at some point, making us update our usecase.

  > Note: **To fix the problem, move the logic to the Data layer. Then, ask yourself whether the logic belongs in the Data layer (whether it is in a repository or a Domain to Data or Data to Domain mapper) or in a datasource, close to the source.**

- **Presentation involved in UI work**: It is not always easy to draw the line between Presentation and UI. This is true for MVP, MVVM, and other architectures, too. Our UI already has some built-in logic and state: it handles user input, checkbox behavior, focus, and scrolling, to name a few. So, where do we draw the line?

  A good question to ask yourself is this: *is the logic specific to this UI? If I had a much bigger screen, would I have to worry about scrolling? If I swapped this item-selection mechanism for another, should the Presentation care?*

> Note: **If you realize that your Presentation is too tightly coupled to your UI choices, you could simplify your code and improve the layer separation by moving UI logic out of the Presentation layer and into the UI. The benefit of making this change is that if you decide to change your UI later, the Presentation (and its associated tests) can remain unaffected. Its logic has not changed.**

- **UI ignoring the Presentation**: This is the opposite of the previous problem. Most commonly, this manifests itself as buttons that trigger navigation when clicked. Let your Presentation layer drive navigation. This has several benefits: decisions are made in just one place, making them easier to understand and follow, and we end up with testable logic. That latter benefit also means that we have live documentation of our expectations. Another benefit is consistency. A new developer (or future us) approaching the implementation has expectations of where to find navigation decisions. Those expectations should be proven justified.

> Note: **To fix the problem, move the navigation logic from the UI layer to the Presentation one. Have the UI layer inform the Presentation layer of the event that took place.**

- **UI code instructing the Presentation code**: This is true for both MVVM and MVP. Depending on the architecture that you choose, it may apply to your project too. The UI layer should not tell the Presentation layer what to do. Instead, it should inform the Presentation layer of events that took place, and let the Presentation decide what to do with those events. This is a generalized form of the UI, ignoring the presentation problem that we just covered.

> Note: **To fix this problem, a good start is to name your Presentation functions that are exposed to the UI in the form of events. So, for example, do not have a `save()` function. Instead, have an `onSaveAction()` function. Remember, naming is important. It helps us be consistent and visualize the solution better. Then, make sure that you call the right function from the right place.**

- **Presentation that is tightly coupled to the UI**: This happens when we use UI terms in our Presentation layer, or leak Android code or resources into our Presentation layer.

> Note: **The fix to this problem involves avoiding the use of UI terminology in your Presentation layer. Remember that the UI could change. What happens to be a button now could be a different mechanism in the future. Let the UI make the decision by abstracting your event function names. Instead of naming your function `onResetClick()`, name it `onResetAction()` or `onResetIntent()`. That way, the mechanism chosen by the UI never clashes with our naming, and we will not need to rename our Presentation method name when the UI changes.**

- **Reusing functions incorrectly**: It is often tempting to call a Presentation layer function that we know would do what we expect, although its named intention is different.

For example, imagine that we have an **onItemSelected** function in our viewmodel. Imagine that we know that this function navigates to the next screen. We now have a new requirement: a save button that also navigates to the next screen. It is tempting to call **onItemSelected** when the button is tapped. After all, this will achieve our goal. However, this is the wrong thing to do.

The first reason is that it is misleading. If we had a breakpoint on **onItemSelected**, we would reach it when tapping the new button. Why? It is confusing. The second reason is that we may, later, decide that item selection behaves differently. Approaching the code, we will find that the **onItemSelected** function is called when an item is selected. So, we would go and update that function. In doing so, we will introduce a regression, because the save button behavior should not have changed.

> Note: **What do we do, then? The easiest solution is to introduce a new function in our viewmodel, called onSaveAction. Then, extract the common behavior from onItemSelected to a private function. Maybe call it navigateForward. Now both onItemSelected and onSaveAction can call navigateForward. Our intention is clear now, and revising the behavior of the button and the item selection becomes easier and less error-prone.**

- **Mappers doing too much**: Quite often, mappers grow out of control. There are two indications of this: one is too many permutations in our unit tests. The other indication is nested when statements. It should be very rare for us to have more than one **when** statement in a mapper. This is because every **when** statement increases the complexity of our mapper drastically, growing the number of permutations exponentially.

> Note: **Luckily, the solution is simple: extract the nested when statements to separate mappers and inject those mappers into our mappers. Now, we can mock or stub those mappers when testing our mappers. Of course, we should test the new mappers as well, but that would be quite straightforward since they have a simple when statement implementation.**

Conclusion

Implementing Clean Architecture in an existing project does not mean that we need to rewrite the whole project. It does not mean that we have to migrate the entire project in one go, either. In this chapter, we saw how we could go about migrating an existing MVP or MVVM project. We also discussed adjusting existing Clean Architecture implementations to better align with the Clean Architecture solution proposed in this book by going over some common mistakes and ways to address them.

The next chapter will cover all the different bits and pieces that did not quite fit anywhere else in this book but are still worth mentioning.

Points to remember

To migrate your existing project to Clean Architecture, remember that:

- There should always be tests in place before we start making changes.

- Before migrating any of the code, try to understand the feature. What usecases do we have? What is their input and output?

- You do not need to migrate your whole project at once. In fact, it is better to tackle the problem one screen at a time. This approach better mitigates risk by introducing smaller, isolated changes.

- There are common mistakes that could cost us time and effort. Many are listed in this chapter. Avoiding them can save you a lot of time and effort.

Join our Discord space

Join our Discord workspace for latest updates, offers, tech happenings around the world, new releases, and sessions with the authors:

https://discord.bpbonline.com

CHAPTER 15

Other Bits and Bobs

A place for everything and everything in its place.

- My grandfather (and apparently a few others)

Introduction

In the last chapters, we discussed what Clean Architecture was, what its strengths were, how to implement it in an Android project, and how to migrate existing projects to it. We also discussed testing our app. A few chapters were dedicated to each one of these topics. However, after covering all these topics, there are still some points left. These do not fit in any of the previous chapters, but are important enough to go over, which is why we have this chapter.

Structure

In this chapter, we will cover the following topics:

- Incidental and accidental duplication
- Long-running operations
- Sharing models across layers
- Flattening and sanitizing data structures
- Handling permissions

- Cross-platform insights
- Software engineering best practices

Objectives

This chapter should give you a deeper understanding of some Clean Architecture choices and why they are made. You will learn when to duplicate code (and when not to), why we do not reuse models across layers, and how we approach API response structures. You will have a more informed opinion on cross-platform code sharing. We will also explore long-running operations in a Clean Architecture project and handling permissions.

Incidental and accidental duplication

Any software engineer with an interest in best practices is bound to come across the DRY principle. **Don't Repeat Yourself** (**DRY**) is an important principle. The rationale behind the DRY principle is that logic written just once can be maintained in just that one place. Once we start copying and pasting code around, we risk forgetting to update any one of these copies when we introduce a change. This quickly leads to bugs that we could have avoided by not repeating ourselves to begin with.

To avoid repeating ourselves, we try to reuse code and make code reusable. This principle applies to all parts of our code. Instead of copying and pasting code, we extract it to a function that we can reuse. Models that fit more than one requirement are often moved out of their original package into a common package to allow reuse.

Developers often confuse the avoidance of repetition of *ideas* or *logic* with the avoidance of repeating *code*. This is a dangerous mistake to make. If we abstract away code that is identical but would change for *different reasons*, we create incorrect coupling. The next step is often to complicate the abstracted code further by introducing more logic to it to handle the different cases it covers. This is a red flag that tells us that DRY should not have been applied in the first place.

We call this an incidental duplication. The same code may look the same right now, but that may simply be a coincidence. For example, two screens presenting a car model may present the same details for that car right now. However, over time, it is possible that those presentation requirements will diverge. We do not want changes to one screen to affect the other. This duplication is incidental. Removing this duplication will lead to tightly coupling two unrelated requirements.

What this means is that before we copy and paste code, we need to ask ourselves whether the duplication is *accidental* or *incidental*. Before applying DRY and refactoring code that seems duplicated, we need to ask ourselves the same question. If the duplication is *accidental*, and we expect changes to *always* apply to both instances (or as many duplicated instances as we have), by all means, extract a reusable component and use it. Leaving the code as is would be asking for trouble. However, remember that if the duplication is *incidental*, you will be tightly coupling code that should not be related.

Long-running operations

Android offers us two main mechanisms for handling long-running operations. One is the **WorkManager** and the other is Android **Service** classes (not to be confused with Retrofit services). Both solutions are handled by datasources in our Clean Architecture solution.

The responsibility of a datasource in the context of long-running operations is twofold:

- Launch the operation.
- Observe the progress of that operation and report back to the usecase (via a repository).

You probably already know how to launch a **Service** or run a **Worker**. What is important to note is that since datasources exist in the outermost circle of our Clean Architecture implementation, they have access to the Android SDK, and so to **Context** instances and to the **WorkManager** framework. Launching the long-running operation can take place as early as the datasource is instantiated or when a request for data is made (by calling a function on the datasource). Which option to choose depends on your app requirements.

Once launched, our long-running operations can asynchronously return data. For us to return that data to the repository, we need to keep an open communication channel with it. We have many options here: we could use a Kotlin **Flow** (this is the approach that I would recommend), **LiveData** objects, or we could implement the Observable pattern, to name a few.

Figure 15.1 demonstrates the flow of data from the execution of a usecase to the usecase returning the result obtained via a **Service** object. Note that repositories, datasources, and **Service** instances are usually bound to the lifecycle of an Android **Context** instace. We can choose to dismiss them earlier if needed. Of course, their removal from memory would be up to the garbage collection process.

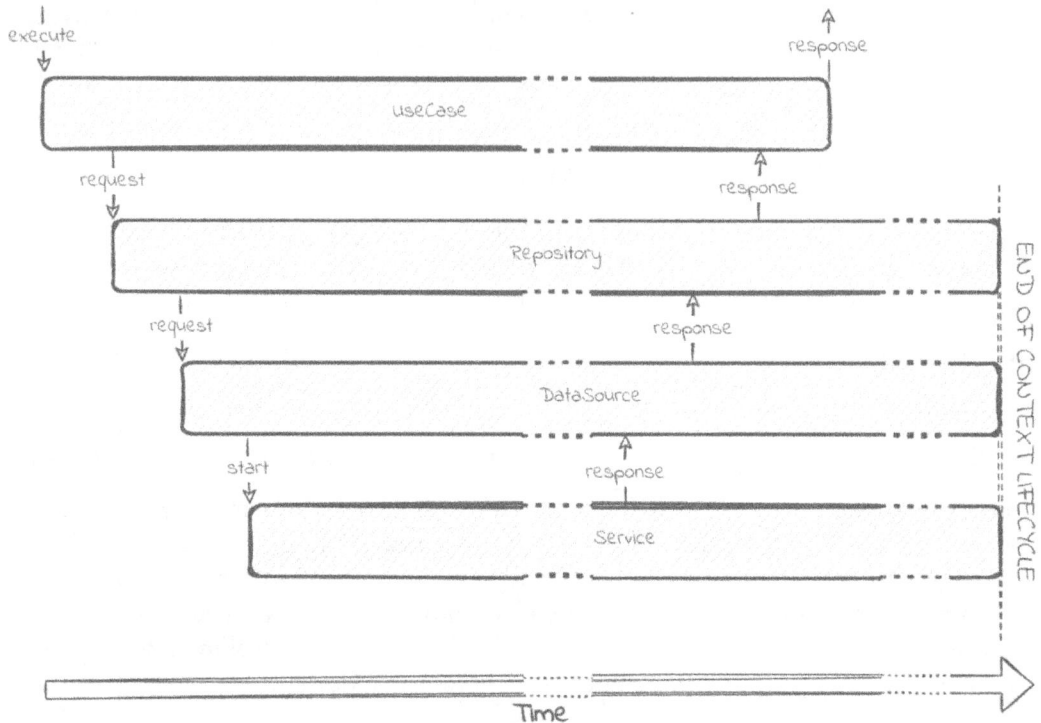

Figure 15.1: A usecase returning data via a service

Sharing models across layers

When implementing Clean Architecture, we are often faced with identical models between two (or more) layers. It may feel redundant. Our DRY principle bells may be going off. That is a good thing. It means that our instincts are sharp.

However, do not be tempted to cut corners and reuse models. The risks far outweigh the benefits of having fewer mappers and models.

For example, let us imagine that we wanted to treat Presentation models as UI models. This may feel like an idea that could save us time. After all, many of our Presentation models are almost identical to UI models. Let us stop and think about the contents of UI models. UI models contain concrete UI values, such as resource IDs (of drawable, color, and string resources, for example). To merge Presentation and UI models, we would have to pollute our Presentation layer with UI details and values. This is bad because now Presentation models have two reasons for change: changes to the Presentation logic and changes to UI implementation details. This adds fragility to our Presentation layer.

Let us take another example. Let us say that we want to omit our API or Database models and only use Data models. The problem here is the same as in the preceding UI and

Presentation example: our Data models may have annotations that are tool-specific. Room models are different to Realm models, for example. Gson has its own annotations (such as the **@SeriazliedName** one), which are different from those of Moshi (which uses the **@Json** annotation instead). Our models will now have more than one reason for change: API changes and local store changes would both require updating the model. Our Data layer will now change more often, and change means risk.

How about if we let the Domain models leak to the UI and omit the Presentation model? Or omit the Data models and let Domain models be used directly by datasources? This is probably the worst possible compromise. This will tightly couple our models to UI (or Data) details. Instead of having the Domain layer as the most stable one, we will now have to update it whenever our UI or datasource requirements change.

Note: **While Clean Architecture does not dictate the number of layers that we should have, the layers suggested in this book all serve a clear purpose. Resist the temptation to skip layer implementations. This advice alone could save you countless hours of refactoring work by keeping your code consistent and robust.**

Flattening and sanitizing data structures

It is quite common for remote APIs to have nested structures. Sometimes these structures are justified and serve our app as well. Sometimes, though, they are structured based on server-side constraints. Mirroring these structures in our app not only ties us to an API implementation but also introduces a level of complexity that we do not need.

Let us imagine an employee entity returned from the server:

```
1.  {
2.      "name": "John Doe",
3.      "hiringDetails": {
4.          "salary": "$100,000",
5.          "lastPromotionDate": "01/01/2021"
6.      }
7.  }
```

John's salary and last promotion date are stored in a nested object assigned to the **hiringDetails** field. Do we need this nesting? It is very likely that we do not. Our data model could look like this:

```
1.  data class EmployeeDataModel(
2.      val name: String,
3.      val salary: FormattedNumber,
4.      val lastPromitionDate: Date
5.  )
```

The flattened structure can save us at least one model and one or two mappers. If we designed our Domain model with the API in mind, we might have ended up creating even more unnecessary models and mappers. This can be avoided by flattening the structure.

Sometimes, we want to use a new model where none existed in the API response. This is often true when multiple fields can be consolidated to one logical type. Take the following example of an API that provides us with the state of a smart lightbulb:

```
1.  {
2.      "isOn": false,
3.      "brightness": 80
4.  }
```

We can replace this model with a sealed class with two states:

```
1.  sealed class LightStateDataModel {
2.      data class On(val brightness: Int) : LightStateDataModel()
3.      object Off : LightStateDataModel()
4.  }
```

The **LightStateDataModel** couples the brightness with whether the light is on or off. It makes sense because the two are closely related. Granted, we lose some data here: we might want to know the light brightness setting even when the light is off. In that case, we can move the brightness field up from **On** to **LightStateDataModel** and add it to the **Off** state as well. Often, one API field depends on the value of another, and coupling them as a single model expresses that coupling best.

Yet another scenario is when two fields can be consolidated into one and do not require a new type to be introduced. Imagine a work calendar API that returns the details of a single event. Imagine that the duration of the event is returned in two fields: **durationUnit** and **durationValue**. We can choose the most precise unit available as the one that we would use, and convert values from all other units to that unit. If the second unit is the most granular that our API can get, we can have a **durationSeconds** field. Our API to Data mapper can handle the unit conversion from hours, minutes, and so forth to seconds. We lose the original specified unit, but that may be an acceptable loss; we can always send the time back to the server after converting it to a unit of our choice.

Lastly, sometimes API expose fields that we do not need at all. Not implementing such fields in our API models at all is the best route forward. This follows the YAGNI principle: you are not gonna need it. Another principle this aligns with is the KISS principle: keep it simple, stupid. In other words, we may never need this field, and by introducing it, we are committing to maintaining it. If the field name or type changes, we have to worry about updating our code accordingly. It is safest not to implement dead code.

Handling permissions

One of the most significant security and privacy features of Android is its permission system. It allows the user to decide what permissions to grant to each app on their device.

In our Clean Architecture implementation, checking whether permission is granted is the responsibility of a datasource. Remember that datasources are a part of the outermost circle of our Architecture and so have access to the Android SDK.

Let us consider an app that allows the user to take a picture using their camera. This operation requires that the app has permission to access the camera (**android.permission. CAMERA**). To check whether the user has granted us this permission, we implement a **GetCameraPermissionStateUseCase** class (see *Figure 15.2*). This usecase will, in turn, call a **CameraPermissionRepository** interface. The repository implementation will rely on a **PermissionDataSource** class.

Once the usecase tells our viewmodel (via its success callback) what the permission state is, the viewmodel can proceed to either navigate to the camera interface or to the native permission request dialog.

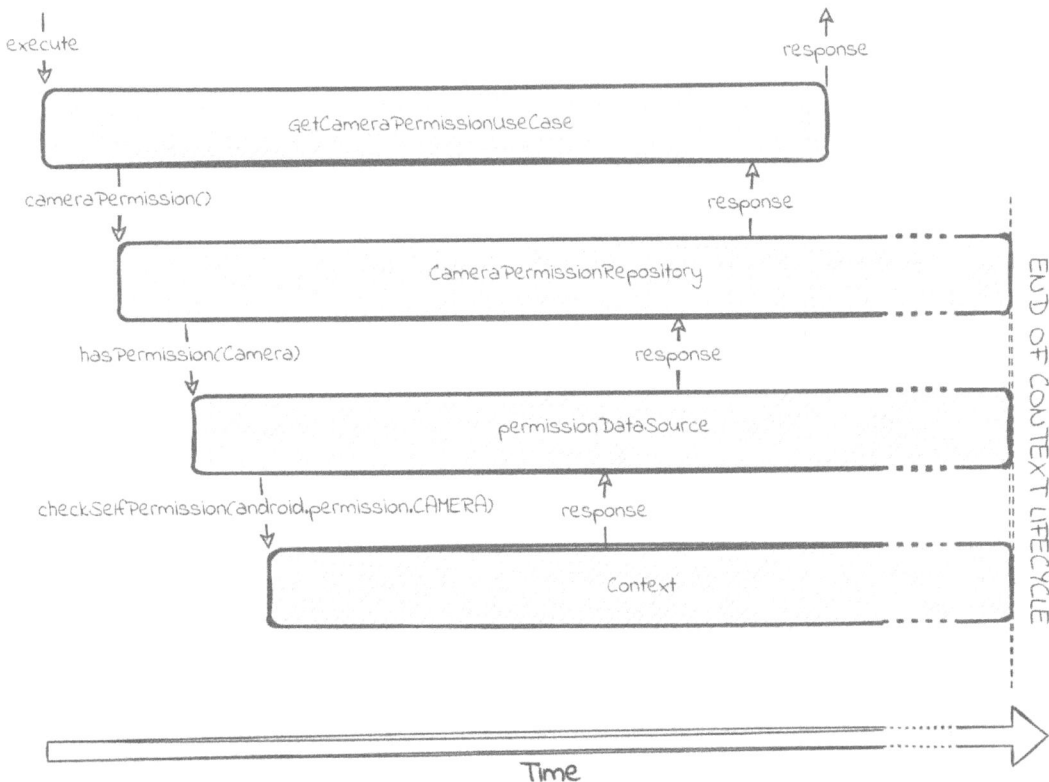

Figure 15.2: A usecase returning the camera permission state

Cross-platform insights

While this book is about Android and native Kotlin implementations, it will not be complete if we ignore the topic of cross-platform systems.

Different projects have implemented cross-platform solutions to varying degrees of success. With Clean Architecture, we have an interesting opportunity to share common layers between platforms using Kotlin Multiplatform (or, with some juggling, other cross-platform solutions).

This is a tempting proposition: maintaining code once can save considerable amounts of time. It is important to remember that there is a tradeoff here. It is very likely that different platforms will have different requirements: permission systems differ, hardware differs. Some differences are the result of each platform offering its own unique features. Polluting common code with logic that only concerns some of the supported platforms is not good practice. It increases the risk of bugs since that risk is proportional to the complexity of the code. The alternative is to aim for the lowest common denominator. This is not the best option either, as it ties our hands when we want to use the latest and greatest features. This will mean punishing our users for our technical choices.

Taking the risk into account, we can implement a hybrid solution. In such a solution, common code exists which is used by both platforms, but each platform can add functionality on top of it to cater for the differences. For example, each platform can have its own usecases in addition to the common ones.

Let us take a simple weather reporting app as an example. Most of our Domain layer is likely to be identical. We are likely to need a common **GetWeatherForDayUseCase** class, and the models and repository interface associated with that usecase are likely to be common, too.

How about the repository implementation? In all likelihood, this can be identical between platforms, too, as can the datasource interfaces.

Datasource implementations may differ. We may want to use different networking libraries. We do not have to, though. There are cross-platform libraries that we could use, since we know that all platforms we intend to support will hit the same API with the same data and expect the same response.

What about the Presentation layer? This is where we are likely to start seeing differences: one platform may require permission to access the user's location. Another platform may be able to access that information without any such permission or may have asked for that permission in a different way. Not only does this affect the public interface of our viewmodel, but it may affect our view state model, because we may want to communicate the permission state to the user. For this reason, it may be a good idea to implement the Presentation layer per platform.

How about the UI? This is where platforms tend to differ the most: different widgets, different layouts, and so forth. Even if every other aspect of our app is shared between platforms, it is probably best to keep the UI implementation platform-specific. Many cross-platform solutions cut corners when it comes to their UI, to the detriment of their users.

Another obvious option that we have is to share no code at all. The architecture, while having some overhead in the form of many classes, is designed to be quite light. Classes should be reasonably small; boundaries should be clear. Having the freedom to move in isolation, in the native language of each platform, may benefit all platforms. It also enables each platform to choose its own architecture.

It is worth noting that all cross-platform solutions add significant complexity to any continuous integration and deployment solution that you may have.

Software engineering best practices

One of the concerns that some developers have is that Clean Architecture takes all the thinking and problem-solving away from them. If everything is already solved by the architecture, where is the developer's creative freedom? The answer is simple. Clean Architecture does not solve the unique, hard problems that each project introduces. It solves all the boring and repetitive problems. These are not challenging or fun to solve. They have been solved countless times, and spending time solving them again is a pure waste.

Another similar concern is raised around common software engineering best practices. Whether it is object-oriented principles, functional programming principles, SOLID, DRY, or KISS, do we abandon them? The answer to this question is *absolutely not*. We should keep all of these principles in mind when designing our mappers, our datasources, viewmodels, and views. Our code should still be readable, easy to maintain, and well tested. We should leverage design patterns to write code that is easily understood by new developers (and our future selves).

Threading can still be a challenge, and so immutability would benefit us greatly. Every other good habit that we picked up along the way is still valid. This is still Android, and everything that we know about Android still holds. Clean architecture does not tie our hands. It provides us with a template into which we can pour our knowledge and experience.

The tools of our trade are still applicable, too: Android Studio benefits greatly from the existing features of IntelliJ and offers us extremely powerful refactoring tools. Is your mapping function growing too complex to follow, but still not enough to justify extracting code to another class? Consider refactoring by extracting some of the logic to a well-named private function. Is your viewmodel logic repeated for different events? Apply DRY and move it to a common function.

If you come across a problem that you cannot fit into a sensible Clean Architecture solution, do not give up. Ask a colleague, involve the community. If time is of the essence, solve it using your familiar tools. However, if a Clean Architecture solution presents itself, you would be wise to prioritize revisiting your implementation. Leaving rogue patterns in the code can have an ever-growing cost: before you know it, the same solution is copied over to another part of the code, and your solution becomes inconsistent and unpredictable.

Conclusion

This chapter touched on some common Clean Architecture debates, such as trimming down the number of models in our app, handling external resources, and sharing code between platforms. It also wrapped up our review of Clean Architecture for Android. You should now be able to comfortably start your own Clean Architecture project, join a team working on an existing Clean Architecture project, or migrate your existing project to Clean Architecture.

If you are not converted, you should at least have a clear understanding of the proposition of Clean Architecture. Maybe it will inspire you to come up with a better architecture. As developers, we should never settle for the tools that we currently have. So, by all means, not only do you not have to follow the advice in this book, but you are encouraged to challenge the ideas put forward in it. This will help in making the next edition better.

Points to remember

When implementing, there are tempting shortcuts that we could take. It is worth keeping in mind that:

- Each layer in our architecture serves a purpose. Removing layers will come at a cost.

- Clean Architecture is designed to decouple business logic from external influences such as remote APIs. Do not let APIs (or the UI) drive your design.

- If you are considering adopting a cross-platform solution, be sure to weigh the pros and cons. It is not an easy choice to make either way.

Join our Discord space

Join our Discord workspace for latest updates, offers, tech happenings around the world, new releases, and sessions with the authors:

https://discord.bpbonline.com

Appendix
XML and Views

The first edition of this book focused on XML and Activity, Fragment, and View classes. In this edition, the focus shifted to Jetpack Compose. When developing native Android apps, Activity classes, at the very least, are still relevant. Since a lot of existing projects still use XMLs, Activity, Fragment, and View classes, I decided to add the relevant sections from the first edition in this appendix.

As the code presented here was extracted from its respective chapters and condensed into a single appendix, I must apologize for it not being as well-structured. I hope that you will still find it useful.

It is also worth noting that there were some changes to the code that were introduced in this edition of the book:

- In the first edition, the code was packaged by layer and only then by feature. This edition changes this recommendation and packages code by feature first and only then by layer.

- The first edition used LiveData instead of Kotlin Flows.

- The app in the first edition was FaveDish, not WhoAmI.

With this in mind, let us explore the code.

Base classes

When the viewmodel class updates the view state, we need to bind that state to the views managed by a Fragment, Activity, or View class. This is done via a class that implements the **ViewStateBinder** interface:

ViewStateBinder.kt

```
1.  package com.favedish.ui.architecture.binder
2.
3.  import com.favedish.ui.architecture.view.ViewsProvider
4.
5.  interface ViewStateBinder<in VIEW_STATE : Any,
6.      in VIEWS_PROVIDER : ViewsProvider> {
7.      fun VIEWS_PROVIDER.bindState(viewState: VIEW_STATE)
8.  }
```

ViewStateBinder is a part of our architecture, and as such, resides in the **com.favedish. ui.architecture.binder** package (*line 1*). This interface relies on two generic types: a **VIEW_STATE** (which can be any class and is expected to be the input to the **bindState** function) and a **VIEWS_PROVIDER**, which would need to be a subtype of **ViewsProvider** (*lines 5* and *6*). **ViewsProvider** is an empty interface defined under **com.favedish.ui.architecture. view**. Both generic types are annotated with an **in** variance, as both are only read.

The **VIEWS_PROVIDER.bindState(VIEW_STATE)** extension function (*line 7*) makes accessing the views provided by the **ViewsProvider** easier. As the name suggests, implementations of **bindState** will bind the data provided in the **VIEW_STATE** to the views provided by the **VIEW_STATE**.

Next, we will cover the **BaseFragment** class:

BaseFragment.kt

```
1.  package com.favedish.ui.architecture.view
2.
3.  [imports...]
4.
5.  abstract class BaseFragment<VIEW_STATE : Any, NOTIFICATION : Any> :
6.      Fragment(), ViewsProvider {
7.      internal abstract val viewModel:
8.          BaseViewModel<VIEW_STATE, NOTIFICATION>
9.
10.     abstract val layoutResourceId: Int
11.
```

BaseFragment is an abstract class with two generic types: **VIEW_STATE** and **NOTIFICATION**. Both are constrained to **Any**, requiring non-nullable type arguments. These generic types map directly to the generic types defined in our **BaseViewModel** class. Indeed, the first field defined in **BaseFragment** is the viewmodel instance (see *lines 7* and *8*). This is an abstract field and would be implemented by concrete Fragments providing a specific viewmodel object. **BaseFragment** also implements the **ViewsProvider** interface. This fact will serve us later when binding child **Views** of the inflated layout to our **Fragment**.

Next, on *line 10*, we have the abstract **layoutResourceId** field. This will be overridden with the ID of a Fragment layout resource ID.

Continuing with *line 12*, we have an abstract **DestinationPresentationToUiMapper** field:

BaseFragment.kt (continued)

```
12.    abstract val destinationMapper: DestinationPresentationToUiMapper
```

Concrete Fragment classes override the **destinationMapper** field to provide a mapper responsible for translating **PresentationDestination** objects to **UiDestination** ones. In the UI context, the app navigates *to* a destination. The UI destination interface looks like this:

UIDestination.kt

```
1. package com.favedish.ui.architecture.model
2.
3. interface UiDestination {
4.     fun navigate()
5. }
```

The **UiDestination** interface resides in the **model** package under **architecture** and **ui** (*line 1*). The interface contains a single function: **navigate()**. The concrete implementations of this interface will handle navigation to a specific screen:

BaseFragment.kt (continued)

```
13.    abstract val notificationMapper:
14.        NotificationPresentationToUiMapper<NOTIFICATION>
15.    abstract val viewStateBinder:
16.        ViewStateBinder<VIEW_STATE, ViewsProvider>
17.
```

Following the **destinationMapper**, we have the **notificationMapper** field (*lines 13* and *14*), which serves a similar purpose. When the viewmodel informs us that the user should be notified, this mapper maps the Presentation notification object to a UI one that handles the presentation of the notification to the user.

The **notificationMapper** is followed by the **viewStateBinder** field (*lines 15* and *16*). This field holds a reference to the class responsible for binding the view state to the **View** classes that are managed by the current concrete **Fragment** object:

BaseFragment.kt (continued)

```
18.          override fun onCreateView(
19.              inflater: LayoutInflater,
20.              container: ViewGroup?,
21.              savedInstanceState: Bundle?
22.          ): View {
23.              val view = inflater.inflate(layoutResourceId, container,
                 false)
24.              view.bindViews()
25.              observeViewModel()
26.              return view
27.          }
28.
29.          abstract fun View.bindViews()
```

Continuing with our **BaseFragment**, on *lines 18* to *27*, we override the **onCreateView(LayoutInflater, ViewGroup?, Bundle?)** function. We start by inflating the layout we defined earlier (*line 23*, also see *line 10* for the resource ID). We proceed to bind the inflated views (*line 24*, more on this momentarily). On *line 25*, we start observing the viewmodel class. We will expand on this shortly. Finally, on *line 26*, we return the view we inflated on *line 23*.

On *line 29*, we see our view binding extension function, **View.bindViews**. This function allows us to bind views to individual fragments, ideally by calling **findViewById** on the View we inflated on *line 23*. I urge you to follow this path rather than rely on ViewBinding or any other trendy solution. Historically, different solutions took the Android world by storm, such as **Butterknife** (both 1 and the not-backward-compatible 2) and the soon deprecated **synthetics (Kotlin Android Extensions)**. The only solution to outlive them all is **findViewById**. It is simple and reasonably concise, and unless you switch to **Jetpack Compose**, you are not likely to have to change it once implemented.

Next, we will take a look at the implementation of **observeViewModel**:

BaseFragment.kt (continued)

```
30.      private fun observeViewModel() {
31.          viewModel.viewState.
         observe(viewLifecycleOwner, ::applyViewState)
32.          viewModel.notification.observe(
33.              viewLifecycleOwner, ::showNotification
```

```
34.            )
35.              viewModel.destination.observe(
36.                  viewLifecycleOwner, ::navigateToDestination
37.              )
38.          }
39.
```

As you would expect, the role of the **observeViewModel** function (*lines 30 to 38*) is to observe the **LiveData** fields of the viewmodel object. When the **viewState** field emits a new value (*line 31*), the **applyViewState** function will be executed with the new state. When a **notification** object is posted, the **showNotification** function will be executed with the notification data (*lines 32 to 34*). Lastly, when a **destination** object is posted, the **navigateToDestination** function will get executed with the destination data (*lines 35 to 37*).

The implementation of the **applyViewState, showNotification** and **navigateToDestination** functions is simple:

BaseFragment.kt (continued)

```
40.      private fun applyViewState(viewState: VIEW_STATE) {
41.          with(viewStateBinder) {
42.              bindState(viewState)
43.          }
44.      }
45.
46.      private fun showNotification(notification: NOTIFICATION) {
47.          notificationMapper.toUi(notification).show()
48.      }
49.
50.      private fun navigateToDestination(
51.          destination: PresentationDestination
52.      ) {
53.          destinationMapper.toUi(destination).navigate()
54.      }
55. }
```

Starting with **applyViewState** (*lines 40 to 44*), we use **viewStateBinder** (declared on *lines 15 and 16*) to bind the provided **viewState**, which is a **VIEW_STATE**, to the **Views** held by this fragment. This is achievable because **BaseFragment** implements the **ViewsProvider** interface (see *line 6* earlier).

showNotification (*lines 46 to 48*) takes a generic **NOTIFICATION** type as input. It then uses the **notificationMapper** declared on *lines 13 and 14* to map it to a UI notification. Given that UI notification, it calls **show()** to present the notification to the user. Note how the UI notification encapsulates the details of how a notification is shown.

Finally, **navigateToDestination** (*lines 50* to *54*) works in a similar way to **showNotification**. It takes a **PresentationDestination** as an input, maps it to a UI destination using the **destinationMapper** declared on *line 12*, and then executes the **navigate()** function on the UI destination.

End-to-end testing

Some of the code presented in the first edition of this book related to testing apps written using the Android View system. Let us look at some classes that were used to test that environment. You may find some of them useful, even in the context of the updated code shown in this book.

Before each test is run, we want to launch an **Activity** object for the tested UI to live in. This is usually done in the **setUp** function of each test, which is annotated with the **@Before** annotation. Launching the **Activity** object can be done using the **TestLauncher** class as follows:

TestLauncher.kt

```kotlin
1.   internal sealed class TestLauncher<ACTIVITY : Activity> {
2.       abstract fun launch(): ActivityScenario<out ACTIVITY>
3.
4.       data class FromClass<ACTIVITY : Activity>(
5.           private val activityClass: KClass<out ACTIVITY>
6.       ) : TestLauncher<ACTIVITY>() {
7.           override fun launch(): ActivityScenario<out ACTIVITY> =
8.               ActivityScenario.launch(activityClass.java)
9.                   as ActivityScenario<out ACTIVITY>
10.      }
11.
12.      data class WithFragment(
13.          private val fragmentClass: KClass<out Fragment>,
14.          private val fragmentArguments: Bundle = bundleOf()
15.      ) : TestLauncher<HiltTestActivity>() {
16.          override fun launch(): ActivityScenario<HiltTestActivity> =
17.              ActivityScenario.launch(HiltTestActivity::class.java)
18.                  .onActivity { activity ->
19.                      with(activity.supportFragmentManager) {
20.                          val fragment = fragmentFactory.instantiate(
21.                              checkNotNull(fragmentClass.java.classLoader),
22.                              fragmentClass.java.name
23.                          ).apply {
24.                              arguments = fragmentArguments
```

```
25.                                    }
26.                              commitNow {
27.                                  replace(R.id.main_fragment_
        container, fragment)
28.                              }
29.                          }
30.                      }
31.    }
```

This is an extracted version of **TestLauncher**, which originally existed in the **BaseTest** class. **TestLauncher** is a sealed class that provides us with different ways of launching a screen via its subclasses. It has one generic type, **ACTIVITY** (*line 1*), or extends the Android **Activity** class and allows us to specify the type of the **Activity** class that we want to launch.

The **TestLauncher** class exposes a **launch** function (*line 2*), which is implemented by the various subclasses to return an **ActivityScenario** instance. An **ActivityScenario** class is the driving engine behind the **Activity** that is holding the UI that we are testing. It launches the containing **Activity** object and manages its lifecycle for us.

Let us explore the two extensions of the **TestLauncher** class, starting with the **FromClass** implementation (*lines 4 to 10*). This data class has a parameter of the type Kotlin class of **Activity** (*line 5*). The **FromClass** class implements the **launch** function to provide an **ActivityScenario** that launches an instance of the said **Activity** class type (*lines 7 to 9*). To launch an activity, we call the **launch** function of the **ActivityScenario** instance, passing in the Java class of our **Activity** class (*lines 8 and 9*).

The second class extending **TestLauncher** is the **WithFragment** class (*lines 12 to 30*). The constructor of the **WithFragment** class takes two arguments. The first (line 13) is a Kotlin class of type **Fragment**. We use the **out** variance annotation to essentially tell the compiler that we are happy to accept subclasses of **Fragment** as the generic type. The second argument (*line 14*) is optional and can be used to provide a **Bundle** that will be passed to the newly created **Fragment** instance as its **arguments** value.

A key part of our solution for launching **Fragments** directly is a test-only **Activity** subclass named **HiltTestActivity**. It is passed to **TestLauncher** as its generic type (*line 15*) and so becomes the generic type for the returned **ActivityScenario** instance (*line 16*) and the **Activity** instance that we launch (*line 17*).

If your app is a single-activity app, one such **Activity** class should suffice. If you have more than one **Activity** class in your app, you may require more than one such test **Activity**. This solution presented here can be scaled to accommodate such a requirement by adding a generic **Activity** type to the **WithFragment** class.

We will look at the (very short) **HiltTestActivity** class implementation momentarily.

With the **HiltTestActivity** object launched on *line 17*, the lambda provided to the **onActivity** function (*line 18*) is triggered. We grab its **supportFragmentManager** value on *line 19*. This allows us to avoid repeating ourselves when we access its **fragmentFactory** value on *line 20*, as well as when we commit a **replace** transaction (*lines 26* to *28*) with our test **Fragment** instance. On *lines 21* and *22*, we pass the **Fragment** class loader and the class name to the **Fragment** factory. We assign the fragment arguments to the newly created fragment on *lines 23* to *25*. This is it. With this implementation, the **WithFragment** class will launch any **Fragment** for us within a **HiltTestActivity** container.

As promised, let us take a quick look at the **HiltTestActivity** class:

HiltTestActivity.kt

```
1.    package com.favedish.test
2.
3.    [imports...]
4.
5.    @AndroidEntryPoint
6.    class HiltTestActivity : AppCompatActivity(R.layout.activity_main)
```

This is the whole implementation. It is a class extending **AppCompatActivity** and annotated with **@AndroidEntryPoint**. The annotation is used by Hilt to enable members' injection in some Android classes, such as **Activity** and **Fragment**.

HiltTestActivity inflating **R.layout.activity_main** is important. Our navigation solution relies on a **main_fragment_container** container **View**, which would not exist without an appropriate layout. In its absence, navigation would fail. This requirement is therefore specific to our example.

Conclusion

Currently, Google is pushing Jetpack Compose as the default UI implementation. This means that most new Android projects are likely to use Compose. As we learned throughout the book, this is a UI implementation detail. The impact of this change on the architecture as a whole is minimal. If it were not, our architecture would not have delivered on its promise.

Despite this fact, having concrete implementations in our UI layer can make our lives easier. For that reason, I chose to include the legacy View implementation. Projects that have not migrated to Compose should not be left behind.

Index

www.ingramcontent.com/pod-product-compliance
Lightning Source LLC
Chambersburg PA
CBHW061806210326
41599CB00034B/6893